RIDING
THE
RUNAWAY
HORSE

Also by Charles Kenney

D U K A K I S: An American Odyssey
(with Robert L. Turner)

RIDING THE RUNAWAY HORSE

The Rise and Decline of Wang Laboratories

Charles C. Kenney

Little, Brown and Company

Boston   Toronto   London

First Edition

The author is grateful for permission to reprint the following copyrighted material:

Excerpts from *Lessons* by An Wang. Copyright © 1988 by Wang Institute of
Graduate Studies. Reprinted by permission of Addison-Wesley.

"System Errors: Wang, Bogged Down by Debt, Could Face Loss of Independence,"
by William M. Bulkeley, *Wall Street Journal,* July 13, 1989. Reprinted by permission.

Excerpt from the article "Wang's Search for a New Market," by Eric N. Berg, *The
New York Times,* October 14, 1984. Copyright © 1984 by The New York Times
Company. Reprinted by permission.

Excerpt from the article "Move Over, Digital Equipment," by Robert Lenzner, *The
Boston Globe,* December 1979. Courtesy of The Boston Globe.

Library of Congress Cataloging-in-Publication Data

Kenney, Charles C.
    Riding the runaway horse : the rise and decline of Wang
Laboratories / by Charles C. Kenney — 1st ed.
        p.   cm.
    Includes index.
    ISBN 0-316-48919-0
        1. Wang Laboratories, Inc. — History.   2. Computer industry — United
States — History.   3. Electronic industries — United States — History.
4. Wang, An, 1920–   . I. Title.
HD9696.C64W364   1992
338.7'61004'0973 — dc20   91-23454

10   9   8   7   6   5   4   3   2   1

MV NY

*Published simultaneously in Canada
by Little, Brown & Company (Canada) Limited*

Printed in the United States of America

For my father

"[T]he hardest task of all . . . was riding the runaway horse."

Former IBM chairman
Thomas Watson, Jr.,
from *Father, Son & Co.:
My Life at IBM & Beyond*

Contents

RIDING
THE
RUNAWAY
HORSE

ONE

"I'm Sorry"

A N WANG did not look well. Though he was sixty-nine years old, he was normally in robust health, as vibrant and energetic as any thirty-five-year-old. And though he was just five feet, six inches tall, one hundred and thirty pounds, his reputation was enormous, easily large enough to imbue this diminutive man with a formidable presence.

But late on this humid summer afternoon — August 4, 1989 — with the temperature pushing 90 degrees and a toxic-looking haze blanketing greater Boston, An Wang appeared alarmingly slight and shrunken. His voice sounded as feeble as his body looked. Although he was a terse man who spoke in broken English with a thick Chinese accent and sometimes a stutter, his words generally carried a quiet strength. On this sultry day his words came in a croak, a guttural echo of Brando as Don Corleone.

His condition, in view of what he had been through, was not surprising. Just twenty-one days earlier, Wang had endured ten hours of punishing surgery, during which a malignant tumor had been removed from his throat. The diagnosis was esophageal cancer, a deadly disease.

But something worse than that was on An Wang's mind this Friday afternoon, worse at least to a Chinese man steeped, as An Wang was, in the tradition of Confucius, the philosopher whose teachings had guided the lives of billions of Chinese through the ages. Wang's task on this day was as difficult as anything he had ever faced in his extraordinary life. An Wang held dear the Confucian teachings on which he had been raised, teachings that all but sanctified the relationship between father and son.

Now, as he neared the end of his life, An Wang was about to do violence to that most sacred of relationships.

He had little choice. His company, Wang Laboratories, Inc., which only a few years earlier had been one of the great business success stories in the world, verged on utter collapse. With his son Frederick as president, the company had just sustained a stunning $424 million loss for the fiscal year. In only a matter of years, his company's stock had lost more than 90 percent of its value in the greatest boom market in history!

An Wang's dream had long been to pass on his corporate empire and to have it flourish under the guidance of his two sons.

But it was not to be. This dream that had seemed so tantalizingly close had become a nightmare. On this very day An Wang would fire his son.

In the beginning, the son had come first.

Nine months after Fred Wang's birth in September of 1950, An Wang boldly shucked the security of academia and struck out on his own. In founding Wang Laboratories, he would have to overcome not only the formidable odds stacked against any new venture, but he would also have to combat the mistrust of Asians that was so fresh in the minds of Americans during the postwar years.

From the very start, Wang Labs was a reflection of this persistent, unflaggingly optimistic man. His was an unshakable confidence accumulated over time, a belief he could succeed no matter what the odds or the environment. The foundation of his steely certainty had been laid during one of the most chaotic times in one of the most turbulent places in world history. From the early 1920s until the mid-1940s in China, An Wang had survived the savage civil war between the Nationalists and the Communists, the murderous slaughter of the invading Japanese, and the loss of half his family.

Few of Wang's friends in the United States knew anything at all about his life in China. Wang was an intensely private, even secretive man. Rare indeed were the occasions when he spoke about a personal matter to anyone outside his immediate family. Even men who had worked closely with him for half a lifetime had no idea that he had been married in China before coming to the United States.

After making his way to America at the age of twenty-five, Wang had quickly earned a Ph.D. from Harvard. At the prestigious Harvard Computation Laboratory, Wang worked on the cutting edge of the world computer revolution, proving as he did so that he was not at all out of place in a field that had attracted some of the great minds of the age.

Surely there were others with as much sheer brainpower as Wang, but few had his combination of brains *and* determination. From the start, he went at the business with an extraordinary single-mindedness. He would not be deterred. He would churn ahead, moving, pressing forward, always driving.

Physically, he was in fact rather ordinary looking. More often than not, a smile appeared on his full, oval face. He was a formal man, with a rather awkward manner, who walked with a purposeful, stiff-legged gait. He would often bow his head in a quick, jerky motion of greeting.

But, the Doctor, as Wang was almost universally known, was as impressive intellectually as he was unimpressive physically. After Harvard, Wang led his company through a dozen years of moderate success. But the company's plodding days were over when Wang's breakthrough invention in 1964 of a precursor to the modern desktop calculator caught the fancy of the engineering and scientific worlds. Suddenly, Wang calculators were selling by the truckload, and when Wall Street discovered the company, Wang Labs went public as one of the most celebrated stocks of the late 1960s, opening its first *day* of trading at 12½ and closing at 40.

Later, it was the invention of a pioneering new computer — the Wang Word Processing System — that propelled the company through its greatest years. Wang Labs rode the word processing system and two small computers through a period of sustained growth rivaled by few companies ever in the modern industrial world. Revenues doubled every other year for six years, and from just 1977 to 1982, Wang grew nearly tenfold! The work force exploded at an astounding rate — from 4,000 to 24,800 in just five years. In 1976 Wang wasn't even in the top fifty of the country's leading computer companies. By 1981, it had climbed to number eleven.

There was magic in the twelve-story towers that sprouted out of the Merrimack Valley soil thirty miles west of Boston. The people of Wang began to believe that anything was possible, and in the computer industry, anything could only mean one thing: overtaking IBM.

This dream was embraced not by some wild-eyed band of lunatics, but by An Wang himself. So fervently did he believe in this destiny for his company that he kept a secret chart plotting the growth of his company against IBM, and projecting that Wang Laboratories would overtake the international behemoth in the mid-1990s.

Why not believe in such madness? Hadn't the company proved it could do anything? Hadn't it proved to be one of the greatest stocks ever? From 1976 to 1983, the effective price of Wang shares climbed from $6 to $800 per share. In 1976, an investment of slightly less than $8,000 would have appreciated in 1983 to $1 million! An Wang's 59 million shares, worth $2.3 billion, made him one of the wealthiest men in the country.

He had been so right for so many years that there grew around him an aura of invincibility. Otherwise rational men invested him with nearly superhuman powers. He could see the future, it was said, and for years he had. From Shanghai to Lowell, he went from having nothing to ruling one of the fastest growing Fortune 250 companies in history. In the process he became a deity of sorts, a man who could not err. He rose above other men and existed on a separate, higher plane. When the president of the United States presented him, on live network television, with the Presidential Medal of Liberty at the rededication of the Statue of Liberty, An Wang seemed not at all out of place. For he had by then become a certified Great Man — a man of genius, accomplishment, and vast wealth.

But the truth was that he cared little about the wealth or its trappings. His only indulgence was a fondness — a fondness keen enough to cause concern within his family — for the Chivas Regal he enjoyed daily, often at lunch as well as dinner. He didn't care about the chauffeur-driven limousines, the club memberships, or the elaborate security. He owned but two suits at any given moment, identical gray, three-button models from Brooks Brothers. For years this man, whose aversion to flying was so strong that he once traveled from the East Coast to the West Coast on an ocean liner via the Panama Canal, would not permit the company to buy a corporate jet. When he finally relented, his executives purchased a $14 million Gulfstream III outfitted with china bearing the Wang logo and offering not only spacious quarters for executives, but a bedroom, no less, for the Doctor. Aside from his pleasure as his sleek craft cruised ten thousand feet above 747 jumbo jets, accelerating past them as if the monsters were standing still, he cared little for the plane.

He had no real interest in any sort of personal indulgence — not for the homes he came to own, which others persuaded him to buy — a sprawling estate in the elegant San Francisco suburb of Hillsborough, the spacious condominium overlooking the Harbor in Boston, the breathtaking seaside place on the Pacific in Hawaii, the rambling mansion on Cape Cod.

Even after achieving spectacular wealth, he and his wife did not move from the unremarkable suburban home they bought years before. He did not take off on exotic vacations. He rarely spent money on art or any of the luxuries common among the superwealthy, and, in fact, there were years when he gave more money to charity than he earned. His tastes ran to things far more modest, such as the rental, for an hour or two on a winter's night, of an indoor tennis court.

He was happiest with his ever-present pad of graph paper in hand, thinking, jotting notes and ideas. The truth was that An Wang had one pure passion and one pure passion only, and that was his beloved company.

In many respects, An Wang *was* the company. To know his company and its story is to know him. The story of An Wang and his company is far richer than so many business sagas of the eighties in which naked greed and venality, if not outright corruption, were the themes.

An Wang's downfall was rooted not in greed but in his obsessive desire for control of his company. For the Doctor, control meant that he could run the company precisely as he wished, that he could pass his empire on to his two sons, starting with the eldest, Fred. Like his father, Fred was a small man, with a thick mop of salt-and-pepper hair and an engaging smile. He had never worked anywhere except his father's company.

After graduation from St. Paul's and Brown, and summers at Wang Labs, Fred was rotated by his father through a series of assignments designed to expose him to every aspect of the business, all in preparation for his becoming president. Before Fred took over, however, he had to deal with the one non-Asian in whom An Wang had ever vested any substantial clout — John F. Cunningham.

As he worked his way up through the company ranks, starting as a salesman in the field, John Cunningham performed each of his assignments brilliantly. He and the Doctor, working as an unlikely but remarkably simpatico team, together formed the strategies that rocketed the company to such soaring heights. So close and trusting was Cunningham's relationship with the Wangs that Mrs. Wang referred to Cunningham as "our American son."

Cunningham was considered by many the perfect man to lead Wang Laboratories into the twenty-first century. He was smart and charismatic. But he was not what he most needed to be to reach the top and stay there at Wang Labs: He was not An Wang's blood.

Fred Wang was barely two months past his thirty-sixth birthday when his father installed him as president of Wang Laboratories in November 1986. The move was hardly greeted with universal enthusiasm.

For years there had been quiet concern about Fred. Members of the board of directors had worried that Fred did not have the experience, the judgment — the overall heft — to lead the company. Ever since the middle of the 1980s, outside directors had made repeated efforts to persuade the Doctor to bring in a professional manager; to give Fred an impressive title if need be, but to avoid placing the young man in operational control of this sprawling, worldwide corporation in the thick of the most competitive industry on earth. The outside directors had beseeched the Doctor to find the smartest, most experienced person available to run the company.

An Wang would not yield. To the directors he said: "He is my son. He can do it."

Fred was not president long before it was painfully clear that he could not do it. In July 1989, Fred Wang was at the helm of a company that had tumbled from a perch atop the computer world to the edge of disaster. While his father lay ill in the hospital, with the company in the midst of a crisis that threatened its very life, Fred appeared before a meeting of the board of directors — a board under the absolute, unquestioned control of the Wang family — and confirmed their worst fears: He was lost. It was clear that he did not understand the magnitude of the problem. Fred described the company's problems as a "management dysfunction."

The outside directors were aghast, terrified by the prospect of this great company going under and by seeing the man who was supposed to be in charge so out of touch with reality. Peter Brooke, a brilliant venture capitalist whose association with Wang Labs went back over thirty years, back to when Fred was seven years old, was stunned by Fred's presentation. Brooke could not believe what he was hearing. The normally reserved Yankee, a collector of fine art, a man of exquisite manners and dignified bearing, a man who bore no ill will whatsoever toward Fred, fumed. "The company was just a step away from bankruptcy, and Fred was business as usual," says Brooke. "He talked about a management dysfunction. A management dysfunction! The company is falling apart around us, and he's talking about a fucking management dysfunction!"

Privately but urgently, Brooke told An Wang that Fred had to go.

After An Wang's release from the hospital, Fred and two other company officials — Harry H. S. Chou, the company vice-chairman, and Paul Guzzi, a close assistant to both Wangs — visited the Doctor late each afternoon to discuss the day's business. On Friday, August 4, Fred and the two other executives arrived at the Doctor's home in Lincoln at approximately four o'clock. They were waved through to the driveway by Wang's security team, which — with the help of infrared sensors that detected any human presence on the grounds — patrolled the property twenty-four hours a day. They entered a house that had undergone a series of renovations and additions, leaving it an eclectic, utilitarian structure.

The four men settled into easy chairs of black felt bordered by stainless steel, high-tech office chairs that had been brought from company offices to Wang's study. This room, where the Doctor spent much of his time at home, working, was spacious and pleasant. Ample light shone in through the many windows. The floor was covered with a burnt orange carpet, the walls with maple paneling. Though large, the study had a cluttered feel. It was crowded with stacks of papers, files, and pieces of computer equipment. Displayed along the walls was a variety of awards, some of the Doctor's twenty-three honorary degrees. On beautifully crafted bookshelves lay one of Wang's prize possessions — a gorgeously bound, red leather Chinese encyclopedia.

Doctor Wang was dressed, as was his custom away from the office, in dark suit pants and a lighter-toned gray sweater shirt. The other three men were clad in summer-weight business suits.

As the four men started their meeting, it was clear that the company was in grave trouble, that the quarterly results demanded drastic change of some kind.

The old man felt he had no choice.

In the sticky heat of Friday, August 4, An Wang fired his son.

When he said that Fred had to leave the company, Fred was taken aback. It took a moment for him to absorb the enormity of his father's decision. This would mean leaving the only place he had ever worked in his life. But he would not be a normal person being fired from a normal job. Fred's departure would be far more humiliating, for it would be front-page news. He would be damaged goods. He would be known to the world as the man who had presided over the demise of a once great corporation. The company declines, nearly goes under, and the one personnel change that is made — the *only* management change made — is the dismissal of Fred Wang. There would be no question but that the world would think Wang's collapse was Fred's fault. An Wang, by his actions, was saying as much.

There was silence in the room for a long, frozen moment. No one moved. No one spoke.

As quickly as he could, Fred recovered. He had always been a good son, a dutiful son. He had always sought to please the great man who was his father, and he did so now. He accepted his father's decision.

Neither Fred nor his father betrayed even a hint of emotion, but that was their nature. Guzzi was choked with sadness and near tears. My God, here was this brave man, in terrible pain, just out of the hospital, fighting for his life, and he does what for him is the most painful thing he would ever have to do in his life.

Fred returned to his office, where he took a phone call from his wife, Laurie, who was at their summer mansion in an exclusive waterfront community north of Boston. She asked how the meeting had gone.

"Not well," Fred replied.

"What happened?" she asked.

"I have to step down," Fred replied.

Laurie was stunned.

"What do you mean?" she asked.

"Just what I said," Fred replied.

Laurie cried.

And so it was done. Fred had taken the fall, become the symbol for all that was wrong with the company. On the news of his departure, Wang stock gained 20 percent in value. Outsiders felt that the man responsible for the company's downfall had finally been jettisoned.

But those who knew the company well, who knew its history and its markets, who knew its strengths and weaknesses, those whose lives had been intertwined with the company, understood that the story was more complex. They realized that Fred Wang had been a problem, had been in over his head, had obviously lacked the experience, the ability, and the drive that running a company such as Wang demanded. But they also knew that Fred was not the only reason for the company's demise.

When those who knew the company best searched for an explanation, their eyes settled not on Fred Wang, but on the one man who had maintained an iron grip on the company for nearly forty years. These people wondered whether the visionary Doctor Wang might have grown a bit myopic in his later years, whether he had succumbed to the great danger inherent in running a family business — placing the family's role in the company ahead of the health of the business, ahead of tens of thousands of shareholders.

The men and women who knew the company's story were struck by the irony that Wang Labs' success had been so phenomenal that it had actually contained the seeds of the company's undoing, that the by-products of success had led inexorably to failure.

They saw in particular that the once flawless vision of the founder — the intellect and imagination that had brought the company to such great heights — had also resulted in a dangerous and ultimately costly overreliance on An Wang.

They wondered whether success had insulated the Doctor, had created within him the sort of arrogance that allows a man to say of one of the most powerful and successful corporations in world history, "IBM is not that formidable."

A few even wondered whether An Wang wasn't, ultimately, a tragic figure. His story, and that of his company, contained the essential elements demanded of a classical tragedy. Within the story there was conflict between the main character and a superior force in the universe. In Wang's case, the superior force was no less than the weight of thousands of years of Chinese tradition. Most important, An Wang was a heroic character whose story ended disastrously not through happenstance, not because outside forces intervened to rain down upon Wang some terrible fate, but as a direct result of choices he freely made. It was with good reason that those who knew the company best wondered whether the man who shattered the dream of An Wang was none other than An Wang himself.

That night, An Wang did something that, for him, was terribly unusual: He phoned Fred at home to find out how he was doing.

"You okay?" the father asked.

"I'm okay," said the son.

"It was a very difficult decision," the father said.

The son said he understood.

Before he hung up, An Wang said something his son had rarely, if ever, heard from his father's lips.

Said the father to the son: "I'm sorry."

TWO

"He Is Very Genius"

WITH THE REVOLUTION of 1911 came the fall of the Manchu Dynasty, the close of thousands of years of dynastic rule, and the dawning of a new age in China. But that ancient nation's transition to the modern world was so turbulent that during all of An Wang's years there — from his birth in 1920 until his departure for America in 1945 — there was no sustained respite from bloodshed. Though Wang himself survived, by the time he left he had lost both his parents and a sister.

On the heels of the revolution a new and powerful sense of nationalism swept the country as a Chinese republic was set up in 1912 under provisional president Dr. Sun Yat-sen. The revolution of 1911 achieved half its goal — it destroyed the monarchy. But its effort to establish a democratic state in China failed miserably. The revolution, in fact, marked what Harvard's John King Fairbank, one of the world's leading China scholars, describes in *The United States and China* as "the beginning of a prolonged crisis of authority and central power in the world's most ancient state."

President Sun Yat-sen's ineffectual government collapsed after only a year, and, incredibly, this sprawling nation remained without a central leader until 1919. The void was filled by powerful regional warlords, who led the nation by default, and whose reigns were murderously oppressive.

During Wang's childhood in the 1920s, two powerful forces emerged to battle for control of China: the Nationalist Guomindang, led by Chiang Kai-shek, and the Chinese Communists, led by Mao Tse-tung. For twenty years, China was in a state of war. Either the Nationalists and the Communists were fighting each other, or together they were battling warlords or Japanese invaders.

This period was appropriately termed the Age of Confusion. And it was amid this wrenching social upheaval and armed conflict that An Wang was born on February 7, 1920. The incessant fighting "disrupted every aspect of my childhood," Wang wrote in his autobiography, *Lessons,* published in 1986. "It was a time of complete uncertainty, not just for me and my family but for the institutions and ideas that had previously defined China."

For the first six years of An Wang's life, his father lived with his family only on weekends. During the week, Wang's father moved to a community thirty miles outside Shanghai where he worked as a schoolteacher. Though he had completed only the first year of college, that was far more education than most Chinese ever dreamed of receiving. The Wangs were hardly a prominent or wealthy family, but they were by no means at the bottom of the social scale. The elder Wang's education and his practice of ancient Chinese medicine, in fact, gave him a fair degree of status within the community.

When Wang's father was away teaching, the family lived with Wang's maternal grandparents in Shanghai. At the time, Shanghai was a huge metropolis of two million people, a city ruled in sections by a series of warlords who controlled the opium trade. The only truly safe areas of Shanghai were the so-called protectorates, territories established and protected by foreign governments.

When Wang was six years old, his family moved to Kun San, where the elder Wang had been teaching. It was then a small city of about ten thousand people along the Yangtze, thirty miles inland from Shanghai. For a while, Wang's life stabilized in this pleasant community. Since there was no first or second grade in the local school there, Wang began classes in the third grade, and for the rest of his school years he would remain two years younger than his classmates. Yet, from the beginning, Wang was an exceptional student. In the early grades he had some difficulty with subjects demanding rote memorization, but he excelled at math and sciences requiring keen conceptual thought.

The influence of the West upon Chinese education was significant. Wang's course work, in fact, was strikingly similar to what American pupils studied each day, and even included English. Wang was so bright that a teacher once used his work as an example to goad an older pupil, he writes in his autobiography: "Here is a boy who is two years younger than you," the teacher said, referring to Wang, "and yet his exam score is close to 100, and here is your test, whose score could be counted on the fingers of one hand."

While his early classroom work was important in laying the ground-work for his higher education, Wang was educated outside of the class-room in the early years as well, and that informal education may have been as significant as his classroom studies. For when Wang was growing up, there occurred a revival of Confucian principles which would have an important impact on his life.

During reminiscences about his life in 1985, as Wang was preparing to write his autobiography, he talked with his ghostwriter, Eugene Linden, about Confucianism. (This conversation revealed, in addition to his thoughts, Wang's struggle, even late in his life, with spoken English.) "My opinion of Confucianism in China is Confucianism is almost like a religion because the whole country governed by his principle over the last two thousand years," he said during the conversation. "And even the Communists now embrace that back again. My opinion of Confucianism twenty-five hundred years ago that he was born and I feel that he laid down certain principles really a revolutionary idea twenty-five hundred years ago. Lot of Confucianism's teachings, a lot of them are very close to the church preachings and the Bible's principles. Some of things for example that are teachings you don't want to do anything bad to the others things that you don't want them to do to you. That's another one of those principle. Certain ethical principle."

Wang's paternal grandmother took it upon herself to pass along to her grandson the traditions of Confucian thought. Confucianism, he wrote in his autobiography, was "deeply embedded" in his soul.

Students of Confucius, writes Harvard's John Fairbank, were taught to love others "in a graded fashion, beginning with one's own father. . . ."

A crucial if not central function of the Chinese family was, according to Fairbank, "to raise filial sons who would become loyal subjects." The father's position within the family was so dominant that, according to Fairbank, he ruled as a "supreme autocrat." These notions had moved from Confucian teaching into Chinese law, which, in the past, gave such complete authority to a father that he could, if he chose, legally sell his children as slaves. He could even, if their conduct displeased him, kill them.

A pivotal event in Wang's life occurred when he was just nine years old. Since he had started school in the third grade, he had always been two years younger than his classmates, a fact that bothered his parents. When he completed the sixth grade at the age of nine, his parents had to decide whether to send him on to junior high school or to have him repeat the grade. Wang's mother and father favored his repeating the sixth grade. Their belief was that eventually he would be better off if he were only a year younger than his classmates, and they also felt he needed some academic seasoning. He had done poorly in subjects other than science and math and had, in fact, come close to not graduating from grammar school. Wang himself wanted very much to avoid repeating the sixth grade. He found the thought so objectionable that he took the competitive exam for junior high school on his own. He did so, he reveals in *Lessons,* because already he was possessed of a remarkable level of self-confidence and he was certain he could do well on the test.

He not only passed, but among those competing for the fifty to one hundred spaces in the junior high school, he received the highest test score of all.

It was this event, perhaps more than any other during Wang's youth, that established the truly extraordinary level of confidence that An Wang possessed for the remainder of his life. Second only to his brilliant mind, his self-confidence was his greatest asset.

On the basis of another competitive exam three years later, Wang was admitted to a prestigious high school, roughly the Shanghai equivalent of the Bronx High School of Science. Since he could attend only if he boarded, Wang left home at the age of thirteen, never again to live for any protracted period with his family. When he went away to school, Wang left behind an older sister, a younger sister, and a younger brother, and the year after he left, another boy was born. Because of the age disparity, Wang was never close to his younger brothers and sister.

Pursuit of an education took him away from his family, but it also provided Wang with the rigorous intellectual stimulation that permitted his genius to flower. His single-minded drive to learn was not the least bit unusual among middle-class Chinese at the time. Quite the contrary. It is impossible to overstate the value the Chinese placed on education. For centuries, the Chinese system had been based on sheer merit. The most prestigious government positions had long been awarded to eminent scholars who scored well on exacting, blindly graded civil service examinations. For centuries, scholars had commanded the greatest respect, ahead even of farmers, and far ahead of merchants.

In high school Wang was known as a bright, quiet young man who avoided extracurricular activities. Because Wang was two years younger and much smaller than his classmates, he shied away from sports.

Ge Yao Chu, a classmate who would later serve on the board of directors of Wang Laboratories, says high school courses in math, Chinese, English, chemistry, and physics were extremely demanding. Exacerbating the difficulty was the fact that, in later grades, math, chemistry, and physics were all taught using textbooks written in English. The workload required students to attend six or seven hours of class a day, six days a week; most waking hours outside the classroom were spent on homework.

But the hardest work of all did not much challenge Wang. "He was particularly good in mathematics" and in sciences, recalls Stanley Hsu, a classmate of Wang's in both high school and college. Though Wang performed superbly in math and science while in high school, he did poorly in other subjects, Chinese and English included. In fact, he failed a course — Ge Yao Chu believes it was one of those two subjects — his last year of high school. As a result, his teacher in that subject strongly opposed allowing Wang to graduate. Wang's math teacher, convinced of his student's brilliance, so vehemently supported graduation for Wang that the teacher threatened to quit unless Wang matriculated. In fact, he did graduate with his class.

It had been clear since he was a child that An Wang was intellectually gifted. That he was the brightest of the bright became obvious, however, when he took the entrance examination for Chiao Tung University in Shanghai, a school regarded as the MIT of China. Wang received the highest score of any electrical engineering student, and, thus, under the Chiao Tung system, became class president and remained in that position for his four years there.

In the highly competitive atmosphere of Chiao Tung, students worked extremely hard. And yet, a classmate of Wang's, L. S. Tong, recalls that Wang played a good deal of Ping-Pong and "looked like class was not a heavy load for him. He handled it nicely." Wang concedes as much in his autobiography, where he admits to having "found the work easy." He spent more time, he says, playing Ping-Pong than studying engineering, and his constant practice earned him a spot on the university team, where he was quite a good player.

Even though he did not work nearly as hard as other students, in each of his four years at Chiao Tung, Wang won a prestigious national scholarship by scoring among the top ten in an annual test taken by students from throughout China.

In addition to his brilliance, classmates remember Wang as a reserved young man. "He was quiet, very quiet," says Ho-sheng Hu. Recalls Ge Yao Chu: "He talked less and listened more." He was also unemotional, says Ho-sheng Hu. "He always kept his cool. His mind was always very clear."

Wang was well liked by his classmates and greatly respected for his intellect, says classmate Wan-go Weng. "He was a highly disciplined and focused person."

By the standards of the time in China, Wang and his fellow students led a comfortable, sheltered life. During a period of widespread poverty and famine in the land, Chiao Tung students lived in Spartan, but decent quarters, four or five to a dorm room, each with his own bed, desk, and lamp. The food that was served in the dining halls was more than adequate.

For all their privilege, though, the students were hardly unaffected by the turbulence surrounding them. After the Japanese invasion of Shanghai in 1937, matters became so grave that the students were forced to abandon their campus as the university moved its operations to the safety of the French concession, an area whose sovereignty was respected by the Japanese.

The French concession was one of the few safe havens in the city, for when the Japanese assaulted Shanghai with their vastly superior air and sea forces, the result was a vicious massacre of hundreds of thousands of Chinese. The Chinese fought valiantly, spurred by their national pride and by their seething anger at having been humiliated by the demeaning terms of a truce forced upon them in 1933 by the Japanese. The attack was so intense that some students were unable to make it back to school from vacation. Wang and a number of others, fearful that they would be cut off, left home early and returned to school before travel through the war zone became impossible.

Though he was surrounded by war, the bloodshed did not penetrate the nine-square-mile French concession where he spent his remaining years of college. The peace of the concession allowed him to concentrate on his work, which included his classroom studies as well as an additional project he undertook in his spare time — perusing English-language publications such as *Popular Mechanics* and *Popular Science*. He would carefully read and then translate into Chinese any articles that piqued his interest. This not only helped him learn English but also gave him, at a very young age, initial exposure to the electronics marketplace in a country half a world away.

Wang undoubtedly found solace in these intellectual pursuits. His absorption in subjects he found so enjoyable, particularly math and physics, must have diverted his mind from the plight of his family and from whatever anxiety he experienced as a young man separated from them for so long and under such terrible circumstances. The burden of personal sorrow was heavy indeed when he received word during his freshman year that his mother, Z. W. Chien, had died. In his autobiography, Wang is vague about the circumstances surrounding his mother's death. He states that she was not killed in "street violence or Japanese bombings," but was, nonetheless, a "victim of the times."

Only a few years after the death of his mother, Wang received word that his father had been killed. How, Wang was not sure, though he states with assurance that it was "a result of the war." Several years later came even more bad news: his older sister, Hsu, had also been killed.

After the deaths of his father and sister, relatives took in Wang's three remaining siblings, a sister and two brothers, none of whom he would meet again for forty years. Barely twenty years old, Wang was now essentially alone in life. Many young men might have weakened and capitulated under such circumstances, but it seemed to strengthen Wang.

He found that he had become a loner and the fact that he was able, on his own, not only to survive, but to thrive, added to the confidence that had been growing through the years. Ge Yao Chu, who was a year older than Wang but a year behind him in school, said that in spite of his shyness Wang had always had ample self-confidence. "He would have success then gradually build up his confidence and skill," says Chu. "He was more confident in college than in high school."

With good reason. For he graduated in 1940 from arguably China's finest university in the same position in which he had entered: first in his class.

After graduation, Wang spent a year working at Chiao Tung as a teaching assistant before taking a job with the Chinese Central Radio Corporation. In the summer of 1941, Wang and a handful of his college classmates, highly skilled electrical engineers, traveled to the southwest of China and the beautiful interior city of Kueilin. Their assignment was to build radios and transmitters, most of which were to be used by the Chinese in the war against Japan.

Wang was pleased to be able to contribute. His own family had suffered as a result of the conflict and he had heard stories about the starvation and poverty abroad in his land. In the early 1930s the Chinese people were victimized by the combination of a disastrous national economy and catastrophic floods that turned fourteen million Chinese into refugees virtually overnight. Even as the people grew poorer, the voracious appetite of the Nationalist war machine demanded higher taxes. For the Chinese people, "the variations of suffering were endless," observes Yale China scholar Jonathan Spence in his book *The Search for Modern China*. "The eruption of full-scale war with Japan in the summer of 1937 ended any chance that Chiang Kai-shek might have had of creating a strong and centralized nation-state," Spence writes. "Within a year, the Japanese overran east China, depriving the Guomindang of all the major Chinese industrial centers and the most fertile farmland, and virtually severing China's ties to the outside world."

Though it was a wartime effort, the entrepreneur in Wang was evident. Years later, he would fondly recall the "entrepreneurial atmosphere" of the "seat-of-the-pants operation with the spirit of a start-up."

In Kueilin, Wang's group lived three or four to rather cramped dormitory rooms, drank boiled water, and ate meals heavy on hot pepper and bamboo shoots, light on rice and meat. Working in a huge production facility designing equipment that was assembled by a thousand workers in a sprawling factory, Wang and his associates were safely tucked three hundred or so miles away from the fighting. While Kueilin was well within range of Japanese bombers, the city's gorgeous limestone hills provided deep caverns that afforded protection from the bombs.

Though Wang and his colleagues were occasionally required to flee to the safety of the caves, he was able to concentrate well enough on his work to gain a reputation as a top-flight electrical engineer. No matter the complexity of the problem, "he usually came up with a solution," says Ho-sheng Hu.

Another colleague, H. C. Lin, recalls Wang as very clear-minded, with a knack for quickly penetrating the heart of the engineering problem at hand. Wang's talent, says Lin, "was well recognized," and by no less a personage than the president of the Central Radio Corporation himself. Mrs. Thomas T. Eoyang, whose husband worked for the company, vividly recalls an occasion in Kueilin in 1942. At a gathering of engineers at his home there, the president of the corporation motioned toward Wang and confided to the Eoyangs: "Look at Wang. He is very quiet. But he is always thinking. We have to support him all the way up. He is very genius. He will do something one day."

Wang and the other engineers were poor, yet thanks to some of the more socially enterprising young men in their midst, they enjoyed certain amenities. One, of course, was the city of Kueilin itself. For more than a thousand years, Chinese artists have been inspired by the dramatic beauty of the city's sparkling limestone peaks, which drop precipitously to blue-green rivers below.

The engineers also organized their own social events. Stanley Hsu put together what was known as the ABC Club, which was shortened from the ABCDE Club. "A" was for athletics, "B" for bridge, "C" for chorus, "D" for dancing, and "E" for eating. Though Wang was a member of the club, he did not partake of athletics — neither volleyball nor basketball. Nor did he play bridge or join the chorus in singing tunes such as "Home Sweet Home" and other selections from an album received in the mail from Hong Kong called "101 Best Songs." Wang was, however, fond of dancing, says Hsu. He joined in with other club members for waltzes and the fox trot.

It is quite possible that Wang met or at least courted his first wife at club functions. That Wang was married while he was in China is known only to his most intimate friends and those with whom he worked in Kueilin. For whatever reason, Wang apparently wanted his marriage kept secret. Even men with whom he worked at Wang Laboratories for more than twenty years, including trusted senior officials, never knew about his first wife. And his friends from the Kueilin days are extremely reluctant not only to discuss Wang's first wife, but even to acknowledge that she existed. Stanley Hsu, for example, will happily chat about almost any topic from those days gone by, but when Wang's first marriage is raised he flatly refuses to talk further.

Mrs. Eoyang is one of Wang's few friends willing to discuss the subject of his first marriage. She does not recall Wang's first wife's name, but she does remember her as being of "medium size, with very bright eyes, big eyes, very sweet looking." The first Mrs. Wang may have worked at the facility where Wang worked, perhaps as a secretary, says Mrs. Eoyang.

In his autobiography, Wang makes no mention of his first wife. He recalls that shortly before the Japanese overran Kueilin in 1944, Wang's group was evacuated. Soon thereafter, Wang took an examination held to choose a small group of young Chinese engineers who would be sent to work and learn in the United States. Not surprisingly, Wang was selected for the program.

In April 1945, Wang flew over the Himalayas to northeastern India, boarded a train for Calcutta, and caught a ship that sailed across the Indian Ocean, through the Red Sea and the Suez Canal, across the Mediterranean and the Atlantic to Newport News, Virginia.

The Chinese government was paying for the expenses of Wang and his fellow students, and wives were not allowed to accompany their husbands, so Wang's wife remained behind in China. Mrs. Eoyang recalls that when Wang visited her and her husband in New York in 1946, he proudly showed Mrs. Eoyang a winter coat he had bought for his wife for the then precious sum of $70. Sadly for Wang, however, Mrs. Eoyang says that not long after he sent the coat, Wang received a letter from his wife informing him of her plans to seek a divorce.

An Wang was an extraordinarily calm man. He was rarely ruffled. The best indication of Wang's steadiness came when he arrived in the United States in June 1945, and was not in the least bit overwhelmed by or in awe of this modern superpower so radically different from China. In his autobiography, Wang states that when he arrived here the United States seemed to him "a lot like China." In fact, in Wang's immediate world, his life in China and his life in the United States were not very different. In both places, Wang spent his time thinking, studying, and working. His was the world of the intellect, a world easily transported across geographical and cultural borders. The truth was that he lived much of his life within his own mind; a challenging electrical engineering problem is the same whether one confronts it in Shanghai or New York.

Most of the students with whom Wang journeyed to the United States quickly signed on to work at companies such as RCA and Westinghouse, where they could experience the operations and technology of a major American corporation. The Chinese had sponsored the fellowship program so that Chinese scientists could learn U.S. techniques and use that knowledge to help rebuild China after the war. But the thought occurred to Wang that he might very well learn a good deal more at a university than a corporation.

He had heard about Harvard from a professor at Chiao Tung who had done graduate work in Cambridge, and he invoked the professor's name in applying to graduate school. He was promptly admitted, and started at Harvard in September 1945. Wang had not been in a classroom since working at Chiao Tung four years earlier, but he had no trouble getting back into academic life. Of the four courses he took his first semester in Cambridge he received two A's and two A-pluses. He completed the requirements for his master's degree in applied physics in just two semesters.

After receiving his degree, Wang moved to Ottawa, where he went to work for a fellow Chiao Tung graduate who headed the Chinese government's purchasing operation in Canada, but he was soon bored by the work, and in February 1947 he returned to Harvard to pursue his Ph.D. in applied physics. For a time, he lived in a boardinghouse. Then he moved to an apartment just outside Harvard Square at 1640 Cambridge Street, where he roomed with another Chinese student, C. C. Yang, who went on to become a professor in Beijing and play a key role in the Chinese space program. The two students dined together most evenings in an apartment in their building where Ge Yao Chu, Wang's Chiao Tung classmate who would later play a central role at Wang Labs, lived with his wife. Each evening, Mrs. Chu would cook dinner for herself, her husband, and their two friends. The meals were not fancy — rice, vegetables, perhaps some pork, chicken, or fish. They would chat over dinner, but these were not the long, leisurely conversations in which some students have the luxury to indulge. The three men were all doctoral candidates in some of the most demanding areas of science. When dinner was through they promptly retired to an evening of intense study.

Most of their time, in fact, was spent studying or working as teaching assistants. Occasionally, though, Wang would fall into conversation with Chu, Yang, and other Chinese students about events at home. News in American publications suggested that the Nationalists would defeat the Communists, but Wang was hearing from other students, who were getting mail from home, that the Communists were in fact winning. Most of Wang's Chinese friends supported the Nationalists. Wang describes himself at the time as "apolitical," but he says he didn't believe the Nationalists could command enough trust from the Chinese people to win the war.

When it became clear around the middle of 1947 that the Communists would prevail, the question of whether to return to China took on greater urgency for Wang. But what would compel his return? The truth was that the country was in turmoil. There were reports of terrible brutality. With his parents and older sister all dead and his wife having divorced him, he had no urgent emotional ties. Going back made little sense. In America he could pursue his science however and wherever he wished.

He decided to stay and continue work toward his doctorate, which he completed with amazing speed. From the time he selected his topic in May 1947, it was a mere thirteen months before he was awarded his degree. An Wang tucked his doctorate under his arm and headed across the Harvard campus to a laboratory where he joined a handful of pioneers in the new world of computers.

It was not long before Wang settled down personally, as well as professionally. In 1948, at a social gathering for Chinese students in the Boston area, Wang met Lorraine Chiu. She was a charming, sophisticated young woman from a prominent Shanghai family, who was studying English literature at Wellesley College. They courted for less than a year and were married in 1949.

The nature of computing has progressed so far so fast that it is difficult to grasp just how primitive the industry was in the late 1940s. One measure of the uncertainty of the future of computers came from Howard Aiken, the legendary computer pioneer and head of the Harvard Computation Laboratory. After World War II, during which a good deal of early research on computers had been done, Aiken remarked: "There will never be enough problems, enough work for more than one or two of these computers. . . ."

By the standards of the 1990s, early computers were comically slow and clumsy. The first computer built in this country, the ENIAC (Electronic Numerical Integrator and Calculator), completed in June 1944, cost $487,000 and took up 1,800 square feet! Today, a computer that can perform all the functions of which ENIAC was capable and much more can be bought at any shopping mall — in the form of a pocket calculator — for a few dollars. Computing has advanced so spectacularly that, according to computer lore, if car prices and fuel efficiency had improved at a rate comparable to price and performance progress in computers, it would be possible to buy a Rolls-Royce for $2.70, and it would get two million miles to a gallon of gasoline!

Though the early computers seem quaint today, the truth is that the people who performed the pioneering work in the 1940s were brilliant — a select cadre of intellectual giants whose work was truly visionary. And it was war and the demands of war that brought about some of the key early advances.

The creation of the first computer began as an effort to help American artillery fire their shells more accurately. Before firing a shell, a gunner sets his angle of elevation by calculating many variables: the weight of the shell, wind speed and direction, air density, and others. During the Second World War gunners based their decisions on tables prepared at the Ballistics Research Laboratory at Aberdeen, Maryland.

Creation of these tables was a tedious task that required an astounding number of mathematical calculations. Determining just one trajectory required more than seven hundred multiplications. It was time-consuming work that was done by many young college graduates, math majors most of them, sitting at desks with pencils, paper, and rudimentary adding machines. Determining just one trajectory took three days.

This was not "the highest best use of man's mind to spend lots of time on tedious calculations," wrote Herman Goldstine, an early computer pioneer, in his book *The Computer from Pascal to von Neumann*. "A computer would free the human mind to pursue loftier intellectual goals."

Work on such a machine of liberation, a machine that could create as many trajectory tables as the army could ever need, began in June 1943 at the Moore School of Electrical Engineering at the University of Pennsylvania. The team building the machine was led by two of the most important pioneers in computing history, John W. Mauchly, a physicist and an engineer on the faculty of the Moore School, and J. Presper Eckert, Jr., a graduate student at the Moore School.

Their creation, an electronic numerator, integrator, analyzer, and computer, known by its acronym, ENIAC, was a massive beast comprised of a tangle of wires and metal surrounding more than seventeen thousand electronic tubes. ENIAC stood eight feet high, eighty feet long, and weighed thirty tons. Though it was not completed until the war was over and thus never helped with the creation of gunnery tables, it was, nonetheless, the foundation upon which modern computers were constructed.

From our perspective today, it is a curiosity, a great, hulking dinosaur that deserves its place in the Smithsonian. But when it was unveiled in February 1946, it was a dazzling piece of machinery. During the press conference at which it debuted, Arthur Burks, who was to demonstrate how ENIAC worked, told the assembled reporters that he was going to have the machine add five thousand numbers together. He pushed a button and "ENIAC added the 5,000 numbers in one second. The problem was finished before most of the reporters had looked up!" he recounts in Nancy Stern's book *From ENIAC to UNIVAC*. (In the 1990s, there are computers that, in a single second, can add one billion numbers.)

Though it was too late for the Second World War, ENIAC played an important role in running complex calculations central to the creation of the first hydrogen bomb.

In a strict sense, ENIAC was not a genuine computer. It required the setting of thousands of switches and even the alteration of some wiring to perform a different sort of calculation. A computer, by definition, is a machine that requires no human intervention to perform its functions.

Even before ENIAC's public debut, however, the brilliant Princeton mathematician John von Neumann was writing a paper — drawing heavily on the work of Eckert and Mauchly — that would lead to the creation of the first true computer. As envisioned by von Neumann, this machine would contain a central processing unit that would perform the computational functions. It would have random memory so that any bit of information could be retrieved instantly rather than sequentially. And, crucially, it would contain programs — instructions telling the machine what to do — within the machine itself. This was a dramatic breakthrough. Though the notion of a stored program was not purely von Neumann's creation, he was the first person to articulate this idea so clearly.

In the early years computers were thought of almost exclusively as machines for the military, gadgets that could help create an H-bomb or build a line of defense to guard against a Soviet sneak attack. There was almost no recognition then of their potential commercial value. Thomas Watson, Jr., former chairman of IBM, recalls seeing ENIAC perform within a month or so after its debut. In his book, *Father, Son & Co.,* Watson says it never occurred to him that such a machine might be sold in the commercial marketplace. "I couldn't see this gigantic, costly, unreliable device as a piece of business equipment," he writes. And, although there were "at least nineteen significant computer projects" under way in various parts of the world in 1948, Watson writes that "there wasn't a single solitary soul in IBM who grasped even a hundredth of the potential the computer had."

Again, Eckert and Mauchly were pioneers. As early as 1942, observes Nancy Stern, Mauchly believed there would be commercial value in a general-purpose computer. And in 1946 he and Eckert signed a contract with the National Bureau of Standards to create such a machine for use by the U.S. Census Bureau. The two men formed a company, Electronic Control Corporation. But Eckert and Mauchly proved far more adept at science than commerce — unlike An Wang who would later prove to be the rare exception, a gifted scientist and shrewd businessman. In their new commercial venture, Eckert and Mauchly managed to work themselves into a deep financial hole, which, in effect, forced them in 1950 to sell their company to Remington Rand, a division of Sperry Rand.

But not long after demonstrating their lack of business acumen, they once again showed their scientific brilliance by creating the UNIVAC computer. It was a dramatically better machine than ENIAC, greatly slimmed down (to five thousand vacuum tubes from eighteen thousand), with much more memory and much faster. More important, it was the first commercial machine to employ stored programs — instructions within the machine.

The first UNIVAC was delivered to the Census Bureau in early 1951. The machine gained such a reputation for reliability that the CBS network used UNIVAC to call the outcome of the 1952 presidential election. On election night, various data were fed into the machine and, at just nine o'clock, UNIVAC concluded that Dwight Eisenhower would win in a landslide over Adlai Stevenson. But those manning the machine, mindful that pundits had predicted a very close race, doctored the results and predicted a tight finish. (UNIVAC predicted Ike would win with 443 electoral votes to 93 for Stevenson. The actual count was 442 to 89.)

An Wang was not a pioneer in the same league as Eckert and Mauchly. But three years before the creation of UNIVAC, in May 1948, Wang was fresh from the Harvard classroom and poised to make his own contribution to the world of computers. At the prestigious Harvard Computation Laboratory, he joined a team of engineers building the Mark IV computer, the first all-electronic computing machine built at Harvard. At the lab, Wang was pleased to find another Chiao Tung graduate, Dr. Way Dong Woo, who was also working on the Mark IV. Wang was still uncomfortable with his stumbling English, and he enjoyed speaking Chinese with Woo.

"He was very quiet and very clever," Woo recalls. "He was very smart and did extremely good work."

Charles A. Coolidge, Jr., worked a few benches down from Wang and recalls him diligently winding wire around metal cores, inelegant-looking things that would become part of the Mark IV's memory. Coolidge liked Wang and enjoyed having lunch with him fairly regularly at the Harvard graduate center nearby. Throughout his business life, Wang was referred to as "Doctor Wang," or as "the Doctor," but not at the Computation Lab. Coolidge recalls that when Wang was about to arrive, Aiken, noting Wang's unusual first name, asked others at the lab what they thought the new man should be called. Says Coolidge: "Aiken said, 'Well, we can't call him An, so we'll call him Andy.'"

It was also the last time in his professional life when there was no aura surrounding Wang. "He was just another guy — a very nice guy — working at the lab," says Coolidge.

Wang was given a very specific assignment involving one of the most nettlesome problems with early computers. Though these machines had the bodies of Behemoths, they had the minds — memories, really — of tadpoles. Wang was assigned the task of increasing the computer's ability to store information.

At the time, state-of-the-art computer memory lacked both speed and capacity. Computer information was stored magnetically, but to use it in a computation required clumsy mechanical steps. Wang's assignment was to create a way to store large amounts of information that could be retrieved and used quickly, and to do it all without requiring any mechanical motion within the machine.

For a few weeks, Wang fiddled with a variety of notions, but nothing he tried was quite right. "But then one day while I was walking through Harvard Yard, an idea came to me in a flash. . . . I realized in that moment that it did not matter whether or not I destroyed the information while reading it," he recalls in *Lessons*. "With the information I gained from reading the magnetic memory, I could simply rewrite the idea immediately afterward . . . without any real sacrifice of speed. This concept of rewriting information is the major feature of magnetic core memory."

That Wang's work was a very nice solution was immediately obvious. That he had achieved a breakthrough that would be noted thirty-plus years later in history books about computers, however, was not at all clear. Eventually, Wang would become known as a man who made a significant contribution toward core memory, who played a role in computer history. But there was no such notion at the time.

"When I made my breakthrough, I had no idea of its eventual importance," he writes in *Lessons*. "While it was immensely satisfying intellectually, it did not have the aura of destiny."

But Howard Aiken, the much-feared head of the Computation Laboratory, apparently was pleased with Wang's work and recognized its value. Not only did Wang never incur Aiken's wrath — at least not to his face — but at the end of Wang's first year on the job, Aiken gave him a 23 percent pay raise, an increase Wang says was "unprecedented in the world of the computation laboratory."

Though Aiken may well have been happy with Wang, he was not pleased when Wang sought a patent for his work. In the fall of 1949, while he was still at the Computation Laboratory, Wang applied for a patent on magnetic memory cores. This was directly contrary to Aiken's view that all of the work done at the lab belonged in the public, not the commercial, domain. Wang, unconcerned about Aiken's view, saw a potentially valuable piece of patent property and he pursued it. It was not until a number of years later that Wang finally won a patent, which he, in turn, sold to IBM for the handsome sum of $400,000.

But the whole matter left a bad taste in Aiken's mouth. Peter Brooke, a Wang board member and successful venture capitalist, began his career in the 1950s as a loan officer at the First National Bank of Boston. Brooke was a thorough man who carefully checked the backgrounds of the people in whose companies he invested the bank's money. In the course of his research on Wang, Brooke talked with Howard Aiken and found that Aiken "didn't like Wang much." In speaking to Brooke, Aiken was sharply critical of Wang. Aiken even suggested that Wang "ran away with some of Harvard's stuff and claimed it for his own" when he filed for his memory core patent. Brooke wound up believing it was a case of sour grapes on Aiken's part.

Though he patented it and made a good deal of money from it, Wang's work on core memory proved to have little practical application. Wang later kicked himself for not taking core memory another few steps. That was left to a gifted young scientist down Memorial Drive at MIT. Jay W. Forrester headed the Whirlwind Project, a competing computer-building team, and it was he who took the core memory idea, says Wang, "much further" and "developed a way of using core memory that was far more practical" than Wang's method. Forrester's patent eventually yielded a payment of $13 million, more than twenty times what Wang was paid.

When Wang first learned of what Forrester had done with core memory, he said to his friend and patent attorney, Martin Kirkpatrick, "Why not I think of that?"

But Forrester's work by no means diminishes Wang's efforts. Forrester himself says that Wang's work constituted "a breakthrough." In his book *Creating the Computer,* Kenneth Flamm writes that "the development of magnetic core memory was one of the four 'principal areas of innovation' in the development of computers." Wang, he states, did "seminal work on the magnetic core memory."

An Wang had been in the country for just four years. In that brief time he had received a master's degree from Harvard, earned a Ph.D. in one of the most demanding subjects at the same university, gone to work at one of the most prestigious scientific laboratories in the world, and, on top of it all, made a significant contribution to the advancement of computers.

He was twenty-nine years old.

THREE

A Modest Beginning

S TARTING A COMPANY requires a surplus of self-confidence for anybody. But for a man new to this country, who had difficulty with the language, who had no money (for this was years before his patent settlement with IBM), and who belonged to a race of people subject to widespread discrimination at the time — such a man would need nothing less than supreme confidence. In June 1951, when he formally incorporated Wang Laboratories, An Wang was such a man.

His confidence resulted, in part, from years of extraordinary intellectual success. In the most competitive classrooms in China and America he had excelled, and in Kueilin he had demonstrated a keen practical sense, as well. If he had even slight lingering doubts about his ability, they were dispelled by his work on core memory.

He believed, as well, in his capacity for perseverence. In China, during an age of violent upheaval, he had refused to yield to the weight of great losses. He had steeled himself, refusing to wither and, in the end, drew strength from the fact of his survival.

He believed deeply in his own ability to overcome whatever obstacle faced him, including the widespread and deep-seated bias against Asians. The passage of time has dimmed the memory of discrimination against Asians in the post–World War II period. In fact, it was virulent throughout the war and diminished only slowly thereafter.

History records a rather inglorious past for the United States in its treatment of Asians. The Chinese in America had gained a measure of

economic freedom only a few years before Wang's arrival. Until the outbreak of the war, the vast majority of Chinese living in the United States
were confined to jobs within Chinatown as workers in laundries or restaurants. But the war demanded such prodigious production from American industry that all able-bodied workers, Chinese included, were
welcome. Chinese flocked to the shipyards and factories, where they
eagerly pitched in and proved a valuable asset to the war effort. The war
also afforded well-educated Chinese an opportunity to work in their fields
of expertise, such as engineering.

When he arrived in the United States, Wang was consigned to second-
class citizenship. Under the terms of the Naturalization Law of 1790, naturalized citizenship was restricted to whites only. And the Chinese Exclusion Act of 1882, which remained in effect until 1952, prohibited Chinese
from even entering the country. A few exceptions were allowed under the
law for students, teachers, and others, but the message the law sent was
clear — on American shores, the Chinese were unwelcome. Between 1880
and 1920, the Chinese population in the United States declined from
105,000 to 62,000.

Wang encountered discrimination once when he sought to rent an
apartment in Brighton and the place suddenly became unavailable after
the landlord saw the color of Wang's skin. This bias was an insidious force
that most Chinese in the United States sought to avoid by taking refuge
in academic communities, where there was more receptivity to immigrants. Most of Wang's Chinese friends expected him to continue his
work at a university, as so many other gifted Chinese were doing. But
that was not for Wang.

He explained his reasons to Eugene Linden, his ghostwriter, during a
conversation in 1985: "I say, well if I'm going to leave [the Computation
Laboratory] I think I have enough of my own expertise I think maybe
start own company is a good idea. Because I have some special knowledge
that the outside world is interested in. I have certain confidence because
during that two or three years industry people keep on coming in wants
to talk to me and get my knowledge to tell them what kind of things I'm
doing. Essentially I become one of the experts in that particular field."

Wang's friends advised against starting a business. Paul C. Yu, one of
Wang's roommates at Chiao Tung, had also come to America in the 1940s.
"It was very, very hard for orientals to establish ourselves," he recalls.
After working in this country for two years, says Yu, "I almost gave up.
I was not going to be promoted, I was not assigned to good jobs." He

faced numerous difficulties renting an apartment and, later, buying a house. For Wang to do what he did, says Yu, required "guts and confidence."

None of the discrimination deterred Wang in the slightest. He was never made to feel inferior or forced to question himself or his ability, as other minorities might have been. "Doctor Wang never felt he was a minority," says Peter Brooke. "He acted like he was a white Anglo-Saxon Protestant and just went and did his thing with immense confidence, very quietly."

Wang was proud to be working toward the American dream. And he was determined that he would adapt to American ways, that his would be an American company. By the early 1950s, he was writing in his diary in English, though he still struggled with the language.

It was not uncommon for employees to assume mistakenly that the Doctor was more comfortable with things Chinese than American. Sybil Ashe, Wang's secretary in the early years, recalls practicing how to say good morning in Chinese, expecting that her ability to do so would greatly please her boss. One day, as the Doctor arrived for work, she said good morning to him, in the best Chinese she could muster. He looked very surprised and not at all pleased, replying sharply: "Good morning."

Edward Lesnick, who worked in various capacities at the company for many years, recalls that when new Chinese employees joined the firm, they would often speak their native language to the boss, "and he would ignore them. He would say, 'This is American company and we speak English here.'"

On top of it all, Wang chose his own name for the company rather than taking refuge behind some anonymous high-tech moniker or initials. Later in his life it would become clear that he chose to put his name on the company at least partially out of ego. But he did not acknowledge that in his autobiography and instead said he chose to name the company after himself because he would, in essence, *be* the company.

Occasionally through the years employees would suggest to the Doctor that he change the corporate name. The subject even came up at a couple of meetings of the board of directors, but the directors saw no reason to make a change. One senior official, however, bluntly told Wang that the name should be changed "to something more American." The suggestion was greeted with a prolonged, chilly silence, followed by angry words. "You-you-you," said Wang, stuttering as he frequently did when he was nervous or agitated, "if you don't like name of company you go work for company you like name better."

Although Wang started out in business facing numerous obstacles, he also began with a great deal in his favor. He had Harvard credentials, which he knew instinctively would impress customers. He also did very good work, and he knew it. When he opened the company's doors that first day — June 30, 1951 — his brain and his confidence were the company's only two assets, but they were two very large assets indeed. And though he was confident, he was not foolish. He was, in fact, very cautious. At the Computation Laboratory he had been working on building a computer, but his company would not do that for nearly twenty years. It was not that he saw no commercial potential in computers. He noted with interest the fact that just three months before he founded Wang Labs, Eckert and Mauchly sold their UNIVAC machine to the U.S. Census Bureau — the first commercial sale of a computer ever. But for Wang to build such a machine would have required a large amount of venture capital, and to get that he would have had to cede a portion of his company to investors or to sell out entirely as Eckert and Mauchly had done. Such a notion was — and would always remain — utterly unthinkable to Wang.

Instead of plunging into computers, Wang began doing what he knew best: making core memories, one at a time, and selling them for $4 apiece. For the grand sum of $70 a month, he rented two hundred square feet of dusty office space at the less-than-prestigious address of 296 Columbus Avenue in Boston's South End. He had a phone installed and opened for business in a bare room in a rundown old brick building with, as he put it, "no orders, no contracts, and no office furniture."

But he did have a reputation, and it was not long before customers showed up. One of Wang's first was Bernard Gordon, an extremely bright young engineer who had worked with Eckert and Mauchly on the UNIVAC. Gordon had just designed a dot matrix display system cathode-ray tube and he subcontracted Wang to build it.

"Clearly, he was a very smart guy," recalls Gordon, who explained to Wang what he wanted done and sought Wang's thoughts on how to accomplish it. Wang's enormous self-confidence was immediately evident when he said to Gordon: "First you show me all the ways you know how to do it. After you have done that I will show you how to do it better." Somehow, says Gordon, perhaps because of Wang's humble bearing and his complete lack of bravado, his remark did not come off as arrogant. "He was very quiet, very sure of himself, but very modest in his approach," says Gordon.

Gordon was impressed when Wang did precisely what he had promised. He listened to Gordon's ideas, then provided a better solution than anything Gordon had considered. The result was a patent, held jointly by Wang and Gordon, for a magnetic symbol generator.

Gordon also noticed early on that Wang was no scatterbrained egghead who cared only for science and ignored the realities of commerce. "He was quite business-minded," says Gordon. "He wasn't about to be taken advantage of by anybody. He wasn't a schoolboy engineer who was going to get exploited by anybody. He knew he had something of value and he expected to be compensated for it."

What impressed Gordon most about Wang — what Gordon marveled at, really — was Wang's intellect. "He was a parallel thinker," says Gordon. "His brain could see a whole bunch of things in parallel. Most people make decisions by thinking about A, then they think about B, then they think about C, and draw a conclusion." But there are others, he says, such as Wang, who are able to "think about A and B and C in combination all at once. They say, 'Ah, ha! I see this combination!'"

To have searched for signs of Wang Laboratories' unimaginable success in the late 1970s and early 1980s in the company of the 1950s would have been a futile exercise, for the rather incredible fact is that the company grew less during the entire decade of the '50s than it did during an average week in the late '70s.

Still, in the '50s, the company performed solid work on a wide variety of complicated projects. Wang specialized early on in building digital machines for scientists needing extremely accurate counts and measurements. He developed, for example, a digital device for the United States Air Force that measured the cloud ceiling. The company produced a tachometer that read RPM's in digital form. It built a digital machine that counted red and white blood cells.

Growth was slow and terribly modest, but steady. From the tiny office in the South End, Wang moved the company in 1954 to Kendall Square in Cambridge, now one of the leading high-technology centers in the world. After the tiny, cramped quarters on Columbus Avenue, the new office on the second floor of a two-story building on Hurley Street seemed quite spacious. Wang's operation covered about fifteen hundred square feet — seven times as large as the space in Boston had been — over a rubber cement factory whose fumes wafted up throughout the day. It was an ugly old building made of concrete block, but sturdy and fairly well maintained. It was set in an eclectic neighborhood on the edge of the MIT campus amid pleasant, multiple-family homes, small apartment houses, businesses, and, just across the street, a sprawling, discount department store. On the side streets nearby, MIT was spawning numerous small technology start-ups. Unlike the South End operation, here the Doctor had his own private office. The space was small, about twelve feet square, furnished with a desk, a chair, and a bookcase. And it overlooked an alley and an adjacent apartment house only a few feet away. Though he had the privacy of an office to use as a retreat whenever he wished, Wang spent much if not most of his time at a bench in the main work area designing or assembling products.

By the late 1950s Wang had attracted enough business to have hired a dozen workers. Employees from that period recall a professional though relaxed atmosphere where everyone worked hard. John McKinnon, who started at the company in 1955, recalls that the hours could be long, that working Saturdays was all but expected, and that it was not uncommon for some employees to work Sundays and holidays. McKinnon himself once worked Christmas Day to ship a piece of equipment that a customer needed badly.

The Doctor set the pace and showed very clearly that he was completely dedicated to his work. To all the early employees, Wang was a pleasant though distant figure who concentrated on his business to the absolute exclusion of small talk or any other distractions. Very few employees from any period in the company's history, in fact, can recall even a single conversation — no matter how brief — with the Doctor about any subject other than business. He made no effort to establish personal relationships with any of his employees.

"His only interest was in the work, the business," recalls Prentice Robinson, a designer. "He really worked. He loved to work."

"He was 100 percent absorbed in the business," says Laurence Gosnell, the company's first salesman. "He took a briefcase home and would work all evening. It was difficult for Lorraine to get him to take a vacation."

The rare occasions when Wang made an effort to socialize with employees outside of work were not great successes. Sybil Ashe recalls being invited to the Wang home for dinner one weekend — the only time in the years she worked for the company she received such an invitation — and getting the feeling that the Doctor was happy when the guests departed. Ashe, who always had immense affection for Wang, says she firmly believes that he "had problems getting close to people."

He shared nothing about his personal life with any of his employees. From the very start, he was intensely private. Not only did he tell no one about his first marriage, he never spoke about life in China. His daughter,

Juliette, would occasionally ask him questions about his past and he would offer a nugget or two of information — nothing very personal — and quickly return his attention to the newspaper or his dinner. Fred Wang knew little about his father's life in China until Fred, at the age of thirty-five, sat in on some interviews Wang had in preparation for writing his autobiography.

And though he was pleasant, there was a certain formality to the atmosphere at the company. He was addressed as Doctor Wang by every employee except Ge Yao Chu, with whom he had grown up in China. (Chu and others who knew him from China referred to him as "Wang An," the order of his two names in Chinese. It was spoken rapidly and correctly pronounced by his Chinese friends as "Wong-on.") And the Doctor was hardly known for his sense of humor — very rare is the employee who can recall the Doctor ever telling a joke. When a bit of wit was directed at him, no one was ever quite sure how he would react.

Prentice Robinson remembers one event in particular. Robinson was working alongside an engineer who toiled over a board with electrical components. Commonly, when engineers had trouble with a board, they banged it on the table hard enough to knock loose hot solder. As the engineer was doing just that, Doctor Wang happened by and became agitated.

"You-you-you," he stammered, "do you know how many G's of force you put on that board when you bang like that?"

"If I knew that," the man shot back, "you'd be working for me."

Others found the moment hilarious, but Doctor Wang didn't know how to react, and he walked away. The engineer was convinced he had overstepped some invisible boundary, but Wang never mentioned the incident.

Part of his problem was that he could be painfully shy, so shy, in fact, that Laurence Gosnell says that the Doctor stuttered — often badly — whenever he first met someone. Over time, as he grew more comfortable with the person, the stuttering would lessen in its severity. John McKinnon says that Wang's stuttering was "so bad that I started to stutter." Wang also stuttered when he became excited, beginning his sentence with "you-you-you."

Wang hired a number of Chinese in the early years and would continue that practice as the company grew. While the Doctor may have been slightly more at ease with them, Frank Trantanella, an engineer early on, says, "He wasn't very comfortable with *anybody* as far as I could tell."

                    *   *   *

By 1958, Wang Labs employed twelve people. It had added an average of slightly more than a person per year, and, while it was doing passably well, it had a problem common to expanding firms — it needed cash to grow faster. As was the custom with most growing companies, Wang borrowed operating capital from a bank. But his bankers at the First National Bank of Boston were worried by the amount of Wang's borrowings compared with the size of his company, and they told him he would have to seek some other source of capital, preferably a minority investor. Peter Brooke found a company that wanted to buy a piece of Wang, a Cleveland machine tool company called Warner & Swasey. Brooke thought it prudent that Wang tap into the capital of a large, stable outfit like Warner & Swasey and call on the expertise of the company's chairman, James Hodge, who sat on the Wang board for more than twenty years and who was a wise and experienced adviser to the Doctor.

The arrangement was straightforward enough: In 1959, Warner & Swasey bought 25 percent of Wang Labs for $50,000 in cash and the establishment of a $100,000 loan fund. Warner & Swasey, incredibly, ended up with Wang stock worth $100 million.

Some of the custom design jobs Wang did during the early years drew the attention of major potential customers, including the Air Force, the National Weather Service, and NASA. During the late 1950s and early 1960s, Wang did a good deal of work for the space program. Wang worked with Arthur D. Little, the well-known Cambridge consulting company, to build a system with which NASA could test the reliability of its space suits. Frank Trantanella says that by the middle of the '60s the company was inundated with work. "It was a crazy, awesome workload," says Trantanella, who now owns his own company in Billerica, Massachusetts. "There was a tremendous backlog. We were usually two or three months overdue the day I got the assignment."

Werner Gossells, Wang's first production manager, recalls that it was "always an all-out company. There was a huge amount of work for very few people. There was always a go-go atmosphere. Everybody worked hard, very hard."

The Doctor was, of course, the leader of the business, but there were other exceptionally talented people who helped push the company forward. Dr. Ge Yao Chu was a first-rate engineer; Frank Trantanella and Prentice Robinson were technically gifted, as well.

The company was prospering so much that the Cambridge space became cramped. At the end of 1959, the Doctor moved the company to five thousand square feet of space in a new office park on Huron Drive in Natick. Compared with the company's modest quarters in Cambridge, this was positively luxurious. A cheaply built, utilitarian structure, it was a single-story building in a new industrial park, an amalgam of steel and cement with a huge warehouse space and work area out back and office space up front. Not only did Doctor Wang have an office, but so did several of the other company employees, including Ge Yao Chu. Coincidentally with the move, Doctor Wang hired a sales manager, a bold step for a company that had no product line. Laurence Gosnell, the only salesman, was required to do his selling over the phone because the Doctor thought travel would be too expensive.

In spite of the constraints of a small business, there was generally an atmosphere of cooperation during those days. Vic Neal, who started at the company in 1960, recalls that "everybody worked together, there was no backstabbing. There was nothing political about it. If anybody had a beef with somebody else it'd be ironed out." The Doctor made sure of it.

Through the early 1960s the company's reputation for reliability and first-rate scientific work grew and so did the demand for its services. As more orders came in, more people were hired, and after just four years in Natick, Wang Laboratories had outgrown its third home. In the fall of 1963, John McKinnon, who was searching for new space at the Doctor's instruction, discovered a spot he liked on North Street in Tewksbury, a town about thirty miles northwest of Boston, outside the Route 128 belt. McKinnon found a seventy-two-acre site that formerly housed the Tewksbury poor farm. Seventy-two acres was an awful lot of land for a company Wang's size, so the Doctor asked McKinnon to get a price for only ten acres as well as a price for the entire property. Initially, McKinnon recalls, the Doctor's inclination was to buy the smaller piece, but he decided to buy the whole thing, at $1,000 an acre, and mentioned to McKinnon the possibility that they would rent out space to other companies, perhaps even construct an industrial park.

The building Wang constructed was, with its cheap yellow brick and steel, spare and utilitarian. The Doctor's office was not terribly large, at least not at first. But by then the company was growing so rapidly that new additions were needed every twelve to eighteen months. In all, there were a half-dozen additions to the original Tewksbury building, and with each one, Wang's office grew a bit larger and more comfortable. From a desk, chair, and bookcase, Wang graduated to a spacious, paneled office that included a rather expensive orange leather executive's chair and a conference table at which he did much of his work.

While the Doctor had plenty of space, other employees had little. Almost immediately after each new addition was completed, the place was crammed with workers. It was Spartan and crowded, so crowded that when John Cunningham transferred there from the Chicago field office in 1969, he not only didn't have an office, he didn't even have a desk or a telephone. Though he had an important job as product manager for the company's first computer, he had to check with the receptionist each morning to see if he could use the space of someone who was out sick or out of town. But the overcrowding bothered no one, for the atmosphere was exciting, the company growing, its employees prospering.

"It was very exciting, very busy, and dynamic," recalls Cunningham.

Although the company employed only thirty people when it opened its 14,000-square-foot facility in Tewksbury, any new jobs were welcome in that economically depressed town. And when Wang Labs moved in, the grateful Tewksbury selectmen gave them a welcoming dinner. During remarks, Doctor Wang thanked the town fathers for their kindness. He said that as he looked to the future, he hoped that one day his company might employ as many as one hundred people.

In Tewksbury, Wang established a personal schedule that would not change greatly through the years. Though there are frenzied high-tech wizards who work in wildly creative three- and four-day bursts, Wang was not among them. He much preferred routine. He generally arrived at his office, dressed invariably in a gray suit, white shirt, and bow tie, between 8:00 and 8:30 in the morning and began working immediately. He would huddle with Ge Yao Chu on technology matters, with John McKinnon on administrative problems. When the coffee truck arrived around 10:00 or 10:30, Sybil Ashe, his secretary, would get him a cup of coffee and he would sip it as he wandered through the building working, checking, thinking.

Promptly at noon each day, he headed out for lunch, usually to the Sheraton Rolling Green in Andover, about ten minutes away. His usual dining partners were Ge Yao Chu and Laurence Gosnell, the head of sales. They would settle in at what came to be Wang's table, and engage in discussions about the business. They never talked about topics unrelated to the company. Usually the Doctor began lunch with a glass of scotch. Occasionally, he had two. After returning from lunch, he would work through the afternoon and into the early evening. Often, in the early days, he would work in the evening with one or two other engineers until his office phone rang, around seven or so. When he answered and immediately began speaking Chinese, the others knew it was Mrs. Wang summoning him home. He was still not done for the day, however, when he left the office, for each evening he lugged a bag of work home.

The Wangs had lived in an apartment in Brighton, a largely working-class section of Boston, when Fred was born on September 12, 1950. During the first five years of Fred's life the family lived in Cambridge and then two Boston suburbs, Belmont and Lincoln. After much moving around, Wang would settle in the bucolic bedroom community of Lincoln, where he would live for the rest of his life. Lincoln is one of the most affluent, exclusive, and expensive communities in the Boston area, and home to numerous old Yankee establishment families. With vast, heavily wooded tracts of land, picturesque white clapboard churches, a few gentleman farms, and huge rolling parcels of conservation land, the town felt more like the New Hampshire countryside than a Boston suburb. But for all its seclusion and beauty, the town was just a half-hour commute from downtown Boston.

Wang enjoyed the town and would occasionally stroll in the dense woodland near his home, but his devotion to the company was so complete that he spent little time at home. When he was there, the company was never far from his mind. The company was "like a second marriage" to him, says his daughter, Juliette.

Juliette Wang recalls that when she was growing up her father would leave the house early in the morning and generally return home around seven or so at night. His two companions for the evening were a tumbler of Chivas Regal and a pad of graph paper that was never far from his grasp. Generally, he laid the pad on the dining room table, and walked about the house, drink in hand. When he got an idea, he would freeze, tilt his head upward, think for a moment, and then go directly to the dining room, where he would furiously scribble on his graph paper.

Juliette recalls her father was very easygoing with her and her brothers. He was slow to anger, and there was little that upset him, although Juliette recalls that rollerskating on his tennis court was guaranteed to get him riled. She wishes he had been more available to see her Little League or hockey games. She fondly recalls walks in the woods near their Lincoln home. And she remembers with humor that after she failed a pre-calculus course in high school, he read her math book from cover to cover and then explained the material well enough so that she passed. ("He took the math brains of about four generations," she says with a laugh.)

Sometimes, when he was helping Juliette with her math, she would test his computational ability by firing off questions. She would compute the answer on a calculator while he would do it in his head. "I'd say, 'Eleven times 238 divided by seven. What's the square root of that?'" Usually, her father would beat the calculator.

As precise as he was, and as hard as he worked, An Wang had an absentminded-professor side to him. Before buying the land in Tewksbury, he told John McKinnon that he wanted to walk its boundaries. McKinnon cautioned him to wear boots — it had been raining heavily — but the Doctor showed up in a suit and dress shoes, walked the perimeter, and had mud caked up to his ankles. On another rainy day, Wang went to a meeting at Compugraphic wearing a pair of galoshes. When the meeting was finished, he sat down, took a pair of galoshes belonging to someone else, and put them on over his own, yet did not notice what he had done until it was pointed out to him.

Once, after getting a front fender bashed in on his car, he drove around for weeks without getting it fixed. Someone asked him about it, and he said it didn't really bother him because when he was driving he couldn't see the dent.

Sybil Ashe drove a route to work similar to the Doctor's. On some mornings she would see him driving along at a very slow speed. She could tell when he was preoccupied for suddenly, without warning, his white Lincoln Continental would rocket forward, accelerating as if he were in a drag race.

Compugraphic was a small Cambridge company whose owners had a nice concept for an innovative piece of machinery that would justify lines of text for printing and publishing companies. The idea, if it could be pulled off, would mean faster, more accurate justification. Ellis Hanson and Bill Garth, the owners of Compugraphic, knew what they wanted, but they didn't have the technical knowledge to build it. Hanson and Ge Yao Chu had been graduate students at MIT together, and Hanson asked Chu whether Wang Labs could build a machine to Compugraphic's specifications.

Wang eagerly took on the job. Technical innovation would be Wang Laboratories' trademark for years to come, and this job was no exception.

In 1962, with Chu in charge of the project, Wang Labs built what was called a Linasec machine, which used technology ahead of its time to justify text. The machine Wang built was much cheaper than the competition, and Compugraphic found a good-sized market for the Linasec, mostly among small newspaper publishers. "Technically, Wang Labs did a very good job," recalls Ellis Hanson.

And it paid off financially. Wang's revenues climbed from $427,000 in 1962, the first year of the Linasec, to $643,000 in 1963. In 1964, the company's sales doubled over the previous year to $1.4 million. Though the Linasec was a success for the company, it was a very quiet success. For the name on the machine was Compugraphic, not Wang, and that frustrated the Doctor. But it also taught him that, as successful as his company had been, it would not take off unless it manufactured its own product, innovation to which the Wang name could be affixed. The Doctor was determined to find such a product.

An Wang was never distracted from the work at hand. "The thing that motivated him was his business, his company," says Sybil Ashe. "And there was never mistaking," she says, "that it was *his* company."

During the fifties and early sixties, Wang ended each year with a trip into Boston for a meeting with three close advisers: Charles Goodhue, a lawyer who advised him on a variety of matters and served on the Wang board; Martin Kirkpatrick, Wang's personal patent attorney, a member of the company board, and the trustee of the Wang family trust; and William Pechilis, the family's personal attorney. They would discuss operations and then repair to a downtown bar for drinks. As they drank, inevitably one of the three lawyers would ask Wang: "What if you get hit by a truck?" The notion that Wang might not be around to run the place was alarming.

"He was it," says Kirkpatrick.

Wang was obsessive about control, and he controlled not only the overall direction of the company, but also many of the minute details of its operation. Emblematic of his absolute authority was his habit of reviewing the mail. When it arrived each day, it was sorted, placed in four-foot-long wire baskets, and brought to Doctor Wang's office — *all* the mail, no matter to whom it was addressed. He thumbed through it and read whatever he pleased.

Laurence Gosnell recalls that the Doctor would ride in a car only if he was driving. Wang also exercised a fair degree of control over the lives of his employees. One summer, Stamen Zlatev was working on a project that Doctor Wang badly wanted completed. Zlatev, however, had rented a house on Cape Cod for his family's vacation. Use my house on the Cape instead when you're done with the project, the Doctor told Zlatev. Zlatev stayed to complete the work, but he never did use the house. Ed Lesnick remembers telling the Doctor he had to leave work during a busy session to attend the high-school graduation ceremony of one of his sons. But the Doctor made it clear he needed Ed. Lesnick missed the commencement ceremonies of both his children because of Doctor Wang.

Dale Jelley, an engineer, brought his two huskies to work one Friday before heading to northern New England for the weekend. He left the dogs in a remote corner of the company parking lot tied to his truck. Someone complained that it was cruel, although Jelley explained that the dogs were bred for frigid weather and that they liked being outside. Soon Jelley heard his name called over the plant intercom. He was to call 201, the Doctor's extension. Jelley marvels at the recollection that "a problem like that got to the chairman of the board's office in eight minutes!"

Recalls Vic Neal: "He was involved with *everything*. There wasn't anything that happened without him knowing it."

Work had to be done precisely the way Wang wanted it done, which frustrated those employees eager for some degree of freedom. Laurence Gosnell knew that no matter what he did, at some point in the process of selling Doctor Wang would interfere. But even Gosnell concedes that "in ninety-five out of a hundred cases he'll be right." Wang could "grasp a situation very quickly," says Gosnell. "The man is an artist."

Frank Trantanella says that Dr. Wang "could see things. He could take fact A and fact B — seemingly unrelated — and come up with a really nifty idea."

"He could see the future," said Stamen Zlatev.

Long after the company had grown into a world leader, the Doctor had a meeting with Peter McElroy, a marketing executive, to discuss a product announcement. As they went through the plans McElroy had made, the Doctor said no to point after point. He wanted it done his way. McElroy didn't mind much because each of the Doctor's suggestions had obvious merit. At one point, McElroy asked in mock frustration: "Doctor Wang, when am I going to win one?"

And Wang replied without hesitation: "When you're right."

It would be difficult to imagine an executive more determined to control his company's destiny than An Wang. And Wang Labs' destiny was clear: An Wang would run it for as long as he wished, then he would pass it along to his eldest son, Fred. "As the founder," he wrote in his autobiography, "I would like to maintain sufficient control so that my children might have the chance to demonstrate whether they can run the company without fearing to take a risk or two. . . . I want my children to have the opportunity to demonstrate their skills at management. In fact, I consider it their obligation — rather than their privilege — to do so."

It was a very Chinese notion — one that, many years later, would cause great pain for the company, its shareholders, employees, and the family.

He was shy, and he was brilliant, but he was also a shrewd, hardheaded businessman who could be very tough. Once in the early days he found out that a man he had hired to handle field service work was planning to leave the company and set himself up as an independent field service operator. Wang exploded and fired the man on the spot.

Carl Dantas, who worked at Compugraphic when Wang built the Linasec, says the Linasec production, even though initiated by Compugraphic, was "pretty much done on [the Doctor's] terms."

Sybil Ashe witnessed Doctor Wang chewing out all of his top people at one time or another. During one such session, she heard him repeat over and over: "You should ask me first. You should always ask me first. I will decide when we do this." Sometimes, if he didn't want to deal with a suggestion, he would simply ignore it and walk away. At other times he would cut the person off in midsentence and declare: "No, it is better this way."

Occasionally, Sybil Ashe would hear a plaintive cry of frustration from Gosnell after the Doctor had rejected some plan: "But *why*, Doctor Wang?"

"He was never an easy boss," says Werner Gossells. "He always demanded a great deal."

His toughness at dealing with people hinted at the sort of hardball he was capable of playing and did play in the case of Compugraphic. Linasec sales were strong for several years, but then the competition stiffened. "It became obvious that the price had to come down to create a broader market," says Ellis Hanson. But Wang told Hanson he didn't like the idea of reducing the profit margin on each machine, and that he didn't believe cutting the price would broaden the market. He refused to agree to a lower price.

Hanson and the other Compugraphic people believed it would be sheer folly not to cut the price. They did so, and it did, in fact, broaden their market. Compugraphic also decided to start manufacturing the machines themselves rather than have Wang Labs do it. That news, the Doctor writes in his autobiography, "came as a blow." The company was projecting "about a million dollars in additional revenue from Linasec in the near-term future. Suddenly, any revenue projections based on sales of Linasec looked very shaky. We were about to lose two-thirds of our next year's projected revenue."

So, even though Compugraphic had originally come to Wang with the specifications for the machine, and even though it was sold under the Compugraphic name, the Doctor threatened to sue Compugraphic.

And much to their surprise, the Compugraphic people soon learned that Wang had gone out and patented the Wang Labs design for the machine.

"He talked about bringing suit against us for infringing that patent," Hanson recalls, although Wang never did sue. "We never knew anything about [the patent]. We were very surprised to hear Wang had a patent. . . . I didn't think it was quite reasonable. We had gone to him with specifications, and they had gone ahead and gotten a patent without talking with us, without telling us anything about it. Under that surface, he was a pretty tough guy."

During Wang Labs' first decade in business, the company was "learning and probing here and there," says Ge Yao Chu. But in 1964, An Wang created a product to call the company's own. With Chu having done most of the work on the Linasec, Wang had been free to tinker, and the result was an innovative new desktop calculator. Technically, it was a logarithmic calculating instrument, called LOCI (pronounced LOWsigh).

LOCI was a jet aircraft compared to the gliders that were the mechanical desktop calculators of the day. The true brilliance of LOCI was that it performed calculations previously reserved for mainframe computers, and it did so with far less computing power and far less memory. It could therefore be done much more cheaply. Mainframes cost hundreds of thousands to millions of dollars, while the LOCI was only $6,500. It was immediately clear to the scientific and engineering communities that the LOCI was faster and more sophisticated than competitive machines made by companies such as Olivetti and Monroe.

By the standards of today, the LOCI is a quaint, clumsy old machine. But in its day, it was the sleekest thing around. The LOCI covered about a quarter of the surface of an average desktop. It looked as if a typewriterlike keyboard had been welded to the front of a rectangular box about a foot high. About eight inches above the keyboard, the LOCI displayed a single row of numbers, which the user punched in to perform calculations. For anyone other than a skilled engineer, scientist, or mathematician, the LOCI's keyboard would range from intimidating to utterly incomprehensible. It consisted of some forty keys and a dozen switches to solve an almost infinite variety of mathematical problems.

The key to creating the LOCI lay in the manipulation of logarithms. When he set out to create a calculator, Wang believed that if he could easily calculate the logarithm of a number he would be able to build a calculator capable of various mathematical functions "without going through the endless steps of the other methods then in use."

And that is precisely what he did. He found a simple method of generating logs and then made it work electronically. The machine was aimed at scientific users, engineers principally, and it required that the user understand logarithms. Nonetheless, it was much easier to use than previous machines. It was, in fact, the first in a long line of user-friendly products — well before the term had even been coined — that distinguished Wang Laboratories through the years.

The LOCI was a forerunner to the modern calculator. It could raise a number to any power or calculate its root and do it digitally. And it was precisely accurate.

LOCI went to market in January 1965, and in that year the company sold twenty calculators at $6,500 each to scientific laboratories and engineering firms. By 1966, Wang was selling ten LOCIs a month. Suddenly, Wang had what it had lacked its first fourteen years in business — a product of its own. No longer would the company rely on piecemeal jobs for its principle income. Now it was a genuine manufacturing company.

During the first week of January 1966, Doctor Wang was conducting an interview with Frank Chen, a marketing specialist. Chen had a technical background, having done his undergraduate work in physics. As they talked, the Doctor, wearing his trademark starched white shirt and bow tie, suddenly asked Chen if he would like to see something. Sure, Chen replied. The Doctor left his paneled office and returned a moment later with a small device. He placed it in front of Chen, who saw that it was a calculator. He saw the E to the X power key and said to Wang, "You mean this thing can generate logs?"

Wang nodded. Chen began fiddling with it and couldn't believe his eyes. This little machine, barely a third as large as LOCI, could generate natural logarithms with ten-digit accuracy in a matter of milliseconds.

"What do you think?" Wang asked.

Chen was speechless. "Wow!" was all he could say.

The Doctor smiled.

"It was revolutionary, positively revolutionary," says Chen, who knew at once that this was an amazing machine. But not so much for what it could do, but for *who* could do it. While using the LOCI required an understanding of logarithms, using the new 300 calculator required only rudimentary mathematical ability.

The 300 was a much more modern-looking instrument than the LOCI. For one thing, the 300 was smaller, at least the portion that appeared on the desktop — about nine inches wide and seven inches deep. Above the keyboard was a display screen. Most of the circuitry for the machine was tucked away in a box that could be placed under or behind a desk. With only about half the number of keys as the LOCI, the 300 console was less cluttered than the LOCI.

The 300 was not only more compact than the LOCI, it was also faster and cheaper. And it was possible to attach as many as four keyboards to a single electronic control package — the heart of the machine — allowing four different people to use the 300 simultaneously.

Production of the 300 began in earnest in the winter of 1966 and it was an immediate hit. It sold well to the traditional Wang customer — scientists, medical researchers, educators. In fact, it was not long before the company proudly proclaimed that the 300 was at work on one hundred different college and university campuses.

For fourteen years Wang Laboratories had never dared venture outside scientific fields. It had grown respectably, though slowly. But now, with the 300 calculator, Wang had found, in banks and insurance companies, a massive new market for its product.

It was on the strength of the 300 that Wang began a period of explosive growth. Revenues climbed from $2.5 million in 1965 to $3.8 million in 1966 and to an incredible $6.9 million in 1967. In just three years, the company's revenues had nearly tripled! And with the revenue growth came a huge jump in the number of employees, from just thirty-five in 1964 to more than four hundred in 1967.

So great was the selling power of the Wang 300 calculator that in just five years the company grew tenfold — from under $3 million to $30 million.

The now rapidly expanding Wang sales force was finding that the quality of the 300 easily overcame misgivings customers had about a company of which they had never even heard. Ted Goodlander, the Wang salesman in Orange County, California, joked with some customers that the name Wang was an acronym for Wild Ass Number Grinders. Goodlander sold the image of Doctor Wang as "a mysterious Chinese gentleman. The great genius." He would describe Wang Labs as a "high-growth company in high technology founded by the man who invented core memory and sold it to IBM. I would sell the Harvard Ph.D., always hit the Harvard button." The Doctor's having sold his patent to IBM, says Goodlander, "made them feel comfortable with the company, and Harvard made them feel comfortable about the man." Goodlander had great success selling to a variety of customers including universities, real estate appraisers, actuaries, financial people, and the government.

In retrospect, it is easy to see that there was a huge market for the 300, but that was not so easily discernible at the time. For the Doctor to have oriented the company so heavily toward calculators was risky, says Frank Trantanella. "I was in awe of the guy," he says. "He took chances. Launching the calculator against that competition. I thought the odds were unworkable. He was very brave to do that."

Wang Labs was growing so fast during the late 1960s and its appetite for capital was so voracious, that its bankers began to worry about the size of the company's debt. In 1967, Wang Labs had a net worth of about a million dollars while it owed the First National Bank of Boston more than that. The bankers suggested Wang go public.

Though the Doctor considered finance a kind of hobby, he was far from being the financial expert he would later become. To prepare for going public, Wang began reading about finance. Usually when he went to bed at night, he would read something entertaining — he was partial to Agatha Christie mysteries — but if he was to sell shares of his company to the public, he wanted to understand what that entailed. Instead of Agatha Christie, Wang took up reading a stock market handbook, a thick, heavy, tedious tome. But he worked his way through it. Each night he would read awhile, fall asleep, and the book would tumble to the floor with a thud. Finally, he worked his way through it.

Wang took the company public on August 23, 1967, with the intention of raising about $2.5 million. The price of the initial public offering was set at $12.50 per share. When trading on the company commenced, however, the price went berserk. By the end of the day, Wang Labs stock closed at an incredible $40.50 a share, and this company worth a million dollars the day before suddenly had a paper value of $70 million. Doctor

Wang was financially comfortable prior to the stock sale. After it he was fabulously wealthy. His family's shares were worth $50 million.

The public offering was a time of great excitement at Wang. Overnight, the company was one of the darlings of Wall Street. "Everybody was very much surprised," recalls Laurence Gosnell.

Employees had paid one-tenth the day's closing price for their options. "It was ecstasy," says Prentice Robinson. "I was very young and naive. All of a sudden I was worth a couple of hundred thousand dollars. It was beyond belief."

FOUR

"I Have to Do This to Save My Company"

T HE COMPUTER PIONEERS of the 1940s and '50s concentrated the bulk of their efforts on hardware, on the steel and wires that comprised the body of a computer. But by the 1960s, there was a crying need for people who could create software, the set of instructions that tell a computer what tasks to perform. If hardware is a computer's body, software is its mind.

Software is now a huge worldwide industry, but in the early 1960s, when there were few people who understood computers well enough to write programs for them, the software business was in its infancy. Predictably, some of the software pioneers were nurtured in the Cambridge of MIT and Harvard.

And of all the small companies spawned in that area during an explosion of scientific creativity, Philip Hankins, Inc., was one of the best. The company took its name from its founder, a bright young man whose passion for computers drove him to work seven days a week. PHI, as it was known, was located in Arlington, Massachusetts, near Cambridge, and it attracted some very gifted young people. It began operating in 1958 and within only a few years had gained a reputation within the elite computer world as a first-rate operation.

PHI's client list was a Who's Who of technology companies and government installations, from the consulting firm Arthur D. Little to NASA and IBM. PHI engineers, in fact, bailed IBM out of what might have been a humiliating moment. Just a few days before IBM was to unveil a new computer, IBM officials discovered that their new machine wasn't working properly. IBM brought the machine to PHI's ramshackle offices, and a band of rumpled young PHI specialists worked nonstop for four days until they got it working.

There was a pioneering sense at PHI, a "terribly exciting" atmosphere, recalls Bob Plachta, a PHI vice-president, a sense that they were operating on a new scientific and commercial frontier. Computers were massive, powerful beasts at the time, and the PHI people showed they could tame those beasts, that they could create programs to make the machines do whatever people wanted them to do. The company started in an old house, absorbed the house next door, annexed a garage, and finally spilled over into an old funeral home. Hankins expanded his business by leasing a powerful new IBM 360, the pioneering line of mainframe computers that would set the industry standard. He turned an old hearse barn out back into a computer center, and PHI rented time on the machine to a variety of different businesses who needed the use of a computer, but couldn't afford to lease or buy a machine of their own. It was the right move at the right time for PHI. So great was demand for time on PHI's machine that the center had to be kept open twenty-four hours a day.

But PHI's business truly took off when the company's designers created software that enabled a computer to do the entire payroll for the Marine Midland Bank in New York. In retrospect, it was as simple and basic as a software package could be, but at the time it was an exciting breakthrough with virtually unlimited commercial application. In the 1960s, the tedium of producing a payroll every week or two was a burden for every company and government agency in the world. Anyone who could computerize the task would make a fortune.

Many of the PHI people, more oriented to science than commerce, didn't see the commercial potential. But a young PHI salesman, John Cullinane, saw it clearly. Cullinane later left PHI and founded his own software outfit, Cullinet, which was, at one time, the most successful company of its kind in the world.

PHI sold enough payroll packages to grow into one of the largest software companies in the area. "PHI was probably the most fantastic business atmosphere I had ever seen," recalls Bob Plachta. "It was almost like magic. I remember we were at our Christmas party one year, and a young man just wandered into our party. He was a Harvard Business School grad and he wound up talking to me and Phil, and he said, 'What are your company's problems?' And we looked at each other for a moment and shrugged and said, 'Well, we don't really have any problems.'"

One of Plachta's jobs was to make sure the bright, sometimes eccentric young programmers were happy with their environment. "We turned the bedrooms in these old houses into programmers' offices," he says. "They were quiet, wall-to-wall carpeting, good lighting, and a kitchen downstairs where they could go get coffee anytime they wanted. That's all they wanted. They were there day and night. Christ, they were like mice. We kept them happy."

Long after PHI was gone, Phil Hankins was remembered for the generosity and thoughtfulness with which he treated employees. Hankins distributed PHI stock not just to his top designers and executives, but to every employee, from keypunch operator to janitor. "PHI was very casual, but everybody was very professional," recalls Dale Jelley, who worked at PHI as a programmer and systems analyst. "Phil was a down-to-earth, bright guy. He was a father figure, very well liked."

And Hankins loved his company. He had been told over and over again that his was an extremely attractive acquisition and that he ought to shop it around. In fact, during 1967, he had listened to a half-dozen suitors. Any of the deals would have made him a great amount of money, but he didn't sell. He cared too much for the company, and "there weren't very many other people I wanted to work for."

Wang Labs had plenty of people who knew hardware, but no experts in software. The problem was particularly acute because Wang himself was a software novice, and he knew that to be a successful computer company he needed top-flight software talent. To get it, he enlisted the aid of Peter Brooke, his banker. In early 1968, Brooke called Hankins, whom he knew slightly. "He said, 'Do you know Doctor Wang?'" Hankins recalls. "I said, 'No.' He said, 'You should either do business with him or sell him your company.' I said, 'I don't want to sell my company.'"

To satisfy Brooke, Hankins and Wang chatted in May 1968, and Hankins was struck by lightning: He experienced an immediate and instinctive attraction to the Doctor.

"When I met Doctor Wang," says Hankins, "within a matter of days, maybe hours, I decided that I could work for him the rest of my life. . . . He was clearly a significant person; he was not trivial. I had an immediate respect and admiration for him."

On the day before he met the Doctor, Hankins was sure he would not sell his company. A week later, after what Hankins calls a "whirlwind romance," he sold PHI — to An Wang.

Not all the PHI people were happy about the new union. Some were skeptical of Wang's assertion that he would let PHI operate pretty much as a separate entity. David Moros, an engineer who would go on to play a key role in designing one of Wang's greatest products, says PHI people were suddenly well-off thanks to the transaction. In some cases, their PHI shares, which were converted into high-valued Wang stock, were worth a small fortune. But beyond the money there was little enthusiasm for the marriage. PHI was a growing company with a superb client list. Moros himself, while at PHI, had worked on both the Apollo and Gemini missions through PHI's contracts with Draper Labs. Worst of all, says Moros, he and the other young engineers at PHI had never even heard of Wang, and when they discovered that Wang was essentially a calculator company, they were very disappointed. There was, however, a certain mystery surrounding Wang, this distant figure who had been involved in the early stages of core memory, that intrigued some PHI people.

The deal was one of the best moves An Wang ever made in his life. "The greatest gain to Wang was not the profit we could produce," says Plachta. "The asset he got was our people." With PHI, Wang got people who would play lead roles in creating Wang Laboratories' finest products. In addition to Moros, PHI brought Robert Kolk and Robert Siegel to Wang Labs, and the contributions of these men would mean literally billions of dollars in revenue over the years.

The acquisition of PHI provided Wang Laboratories with the software talent it needed to reach the Doctor's next goal, building a computer. For Wang was not diversifying so much as he was radically shifting the direction of his company. In 1971 An Wang made one of the truly visionary calls of his life: He decided to pull his company — Wang, the calculator company, as it was known — out of the calculator business. He would not do it overnight, but within a few years he would have Wang out of calculators entirely.

To some of his top people, it was insanity. Calculators accounted for nearly three-fourths of the company's business. But to Wang, the decision was perfectly rational, for when he looked toward the future he was disturbed by what he saw. The calculator business was changing rapidly at the time. Companies such as Bowmar and Texas Instruments were becoming intensely competitive, and the Doctor saw the Japanese coming. He predicted to his top managers that within just a few years calculators would be smaller, faster, more powerful, and cheaper. He foresaw the day when, through the miracle of the semiconductor chip, there would be cheap pocket calculators more powerful than the best machines then on the market. "It was certainly not obvious at the time that it was the correct thing to do," says Bob Siegel, one of Wang's brightest young stars.

Once he had made the decision to turn away from calculators, An Wang moved on to computers.

In 1968, Wang held a series of meetings in his Tewksbury office to discuss the development of a computer by Wang Labs. The meetings, held around the conference table across from his couch, were attended by Phil Hankins and Dave Moros, the PHI software expert. During one of these meetings in 1968, Hankins mentioned an article he had read in a technical journal about the innards of the IBM 360. Soon thereafter, Moros found that Wang had read and absorbed the article and had come up with some ideas of his own on how to build a smaller, simpler machine. And he assigned a team to begin work on it immediately. The team included Moros, Phil Hankins, and a new Wang employee by the name of Harold Koplow. Doctor Wang had quickly found that Koplow possessed a remarkable natural talent for programming. To get the new computer going, Wang used a management style he would use for years to come. He pitted the three men against each other in a contest to see who could microprogram instructions for the new machine most economically. Koplow was competing against two men with a great deal of experience on computers, yet Koplow won.

The work was progressing well when it came to an abrupt halt. Hewlett-Packard had announced a new, programmable calculator that was so much better than the Wang 300 that HP would capture Wang's market unless Wang responded. While it was true that the Doctor wanted to get out of the calculator business, he intended to do so slowly. And he wanted to do it on his own terms, not by getting shoved out by a competitor. To pull out precipitously or to get pushed out would threaten his business with collapse.

Koplow remembers that when the Doctor heard about the new HP product he was "ashen-faced. He said, 'Let's chop up what you have done with the computer and make a calculator.'" Recalls Moros: "Wang was very, very scared of HP."

Moros, Koplow, and the others threw themselves into the new project. "After about three months of working mostly day and night," says Koplow, "I felt confident we could build the beast." Confident, but not positive.

Nonetheless, when Koplow told the Doctor that he thought they could do it, Wang replied: "Good, we announce."

It was a gamble. Long before their machine was even close to being ready to manufacture, Wang announced the product and promised, in December 1968, that it would be ready to ship the following June. But it was not ready. The company needed something to show at a huge industry trade show in June, however, or it would fall hopelessly behind the competition. Not being ready to manufacture was one thing. Not being ready even to display a demo was truly terrible. Doctor Wang ordered Koplow to put something together and to get out to the trade show in L.A. On the eve of the show, Koplow gathered the machine's various parts together and headed for the West Coast.

In California, Wang wrote in *Lessons,* Koplow "bolted the console to the top of a bridge table and then ran wires from the console through a hole in the table to a second table underneath, where the electronics were located. Our relieved customers saw a working calculator that was very much more powerful than the Hewlett-Packard machine." Most 700s were contained within a cream-colored shell and looked somewhat like a large version of today's laptop computer. From the side, the 700 had a profile similar to that of a very large electric typewriter. The keyboard, which was built into the unit, contained nearly ninety keys for an incredible array of calculating functions. Just above the keyboard, where the screen is located on a laptop, was a lighted display of numbers. The whole mechanism rested upon a heavy metal base that anchored the machine to a desk.

"The 700 was really a computer, not a calculator," says Moros. "It was a tiny computer masquerading as a calculator." Wang, in his annual report to shareholders that year, boldly described the 700 as "significantly more sophisticated than any other calculator on the market."

When it was introduced to the market in January 1969, it was immediately clear that the 700 was a truly marvelous machine. For, unlike any of its predecessors, it could be used by people who were not expert in computer languages, and it could perform many of the functions previously reserved for mainframe computers.

Wang aimed the 700 at engineers and scientists, and they loved it. Geophysicists at the Manned Spacecraft Center in Houston used it to compute the angular orientation of the moon. It was used to control dosages of radiation therapy, to perform statistical analysis in a crime laboratory, to design ball-bearing assemblies for steering gear, and much more.

The success of the 700 was attributable not only to the quality of the product, but also to the way the company positioned it in the marketplace. Wang was smart enough to peddle it as low high technology, as a calculator rather than a computer. "It is a lot easier to sell a calculator — even an expensive one — than it is to sell a computer," Wang wrote in his autobiography. "For one thing, we could sell a calculator directly to the user, and we were good at that. In contrast, in the late 1960s and early 1970s, the decision to buy a computer would involve top management at most corporations. . . . There would be committees and meetings with the company's data processing people and a great deal of deliberation about the machine's compatibility with IBM and which languages it supported. . . . The decision to purchase a calculator could be made at a much lower level and much more quickly."

The machine was so powerful and fast that the Wang sales force found the 700 incredibly easy to sell. "It was just a fantastic product," recalls salesman Ted Goodlander.

The scientific markets for the 700 were large and profitable, but the big breakthrough came when Wang Labs discovered a commercial market for the machine.

Ken Sullivan, a salesman in the Wang Chicago office, had a notion that the 700 might be programmed to handle the mass of paperwork required after the federal Truth in Lending Act became law and obliged auto dealers to provide customers with a large amount of information. Dealers were buried in an avalanche of paper until Sullivan's theory proved to be correct. The 700 was easily programmed to suit car dealers' needs perfectly.

"It allowed the dealer to compute monthly payments for an auto loan on the spot," says John Cunningham. "If a customer said the payments were too high, the dealer could refigure the contract instantly."

Being able to do it right away was crucial, according to Cunningham, who knew the auto business from having grown up watching his father work part-time as a car salesman. Before the Wang 700, it took a couple of days to get the paperwork together on a sale. "A lot of people do the deal, shake hands, and never come back to sign the papers," says Cunningham. "They rethink it in the days that it takes to get the paperwork ready. Some dealers were losing 25 to 30 percent of their business that way. The 700 put the paperwork in front of the buyer instantly."

The dealers package signaled an important shift in the company. No longer was Wang Labs a firm that dealt primarily with scientific customers. Now it was a company selling to business people, and huge new markets would soon open up. The machine was so hot that it soon became an astonishing 70 percent of Wang's business!

Already, the 700 was being used to do sophisticated and specialized work for bond traders, surveyors, insurance companies, and structural engineers.

Though there were snags, the development of the 700 showed that Wang was adept at rapid, innovative product development. There was no company bureaucracy to stifle creativity or slow a project down, and what creative tension there was among the development people was channeled constructively by the Doctor.

"That project, as these things go, went very, very smoothly," recalls Dave Moros.

So smoothly that after only one year of production, the 700 became Wang's most important product and what Wang described as "the basis for the most powerful calculating systems in the world." So popular was the 700 that by 1973 the company was able to boast that "Wang calculators are the most widely used programmable calculators in the world."

The company had become a force, and one of the first analysts outside Wall Street to take note of it and to see its enormous potential was John Adams, at Adams, Harkness & Hill, a Boston investment advisory firm. In a report to clients of his firm written in May 1972, Adams wrote that Wang was "the leading factor in programmable calculators, with an estimated 30–35% share of market." Adams expressed concern about what he saw as the company's greatest weakness — dependence on new products — but praised what he called its greatest strength — "its ability to develop new products both quickly and economically."

And he made it clear that his confidence in the company depended on his confidence in its CEO. Doctor Wang, he wrote, "is very much in charge of the whole operation," and he added: "Over the long term, we believe that Wang has the opportunities and, in the personality of its founder, the vision to become a far larger company."

Hewlett-Packard had only delayed, not dashed, the Doctor's hopes of creating a computer, but the company's initial pass at building one was a bust.

The 3300 was Wang Labs' first real minicomputer. But, like so many computers of its time, the 3300 was clumsy and difficult to use. It employed a teletype and a fragile paper tape that took forever to load and needed to be reloaded if even the most minute detail went awry. It was so bad that the sales force quickly stopped even trying to sell it.

In 1970, Doctor Wang gathered a design team headed by Bob Kolk, who had come to the company from PHI, and began again. He said he wanted a machine that would be fast, efficient, and powerful. But, above all, the machine had to further Wang Labs' reputation as a company that made easy-to-use products. The Doctor wanted this machine to fill what he saw as a gaping hole at the low end of the computer market, a crying need among small businesses for an inexpensive computer that was easy to use. Wang's success with its fast, powerful, and user-friendly calculators convinced the Kolk team that they could build a machine that would fill that market niche.

Kolk and his team of Bruce Patterson, Dave Angel, Joe Wang, and Horace Tsaing dumped both the teletype and the paper tape right away. In place of the teletype, which had been used to load data and tell the machine what functions to perform, they used a small cathode ray tube screen, which was easy to read. Rather than a paper tape, which frequently broke, they used a cassette tape. They produced a machine that was fairly powerful, quick, and reliable. But the feature that would insure its success was ease of use.

"You'd turn it on and go," says Kolk. "It was as easy to use as a calculator. It was incredibly user-friendly and very easy to program." Users liked the 2200 because it was so simple to operate. It relied upon BASIC, the easiest computer language, and it performed an amazing array of functions. It worked well and reliably on routine business problems such as accounts receivable and inventory and could also perform with speed and ease advanced math problems for statisticians and engineers.

And, on top of all that, it was about half the price of the cheapest machine from Digital Equipment Corp., which were much cheaper than IBM's products. In the late 1960s, the least expensive computer cost between $15,000 and $20,000. The 2200 sold for about $8,000. When deliveries of the machine began in May 1973, it was an immediate hit.

And, crucially, it was a hit with office workers as well as scientists. Among scientists and engineers, Wang Labs was well known and respected, but while the scientific market was very large, it was dwarfed by the office market. Getting a toehold in the office market with the 2200 would prove decisive for the company.

No sooner did the 2200 hit the market than the company was jammed with a backlog of orders. It was so popular that in fiscal year 1974 — which ran from July 1973 through June 1974 — it accounted for half of all Wang Labs' revenues. For years after Wang was deeply into the computer business, it would still be known as a calculator company, even when the 2200 managed within a couple of years to capture 17 percent of the small-business computer market. Maybe the world didn't know it yet, but Wang, the little calculator company, was now a growing computer company.

Wang Labs had done well in selling innovative calculators to engineers and scientists, but the Doctor had seen that the scientific market was minuscule compared with the commercial office market. Wang knew there were hundreds of thousands of scientists and engineers who needed a sophisticated calculator, but he also saw that there were millions of office workers throughout the world who needed similar help. It was clear to Wang that a great deal of money could be made selling machines that eased the workload of workers in offices stacked in tens of thousands of buildings across America, indeed, across the world. After all, IBM had proven throughout most of the twentieth century that huge profits could be made selling and servicing office machinery.

With the 2200 computer, Wang had broken into the office market, and he could plainly see that the potential for his company was unlimited.

Wang was particularly interested in a machine made by IBM. Called the MTST (magnetic tape selectric typewriter), it was one of the only word processors in the world and by far the most successful. It was little more than a glorified typewriter with a bit of memory that allowed it to store documents and print them with the push of a few buttons.

In 1969, Wang told his people that he believed that the innards of the 700 calculator could supply the basis for a word processing machine. Wang leased an MTST, took it apart, and found that his company had what it would take "to devise a better machine."

Harold Koplow, leader of the team that had developed the 700, examined the inner workings of the MTST and pronounced it a "real clunker." Koplow's idea was to "take the 700 and put a typewriter on it and make it do everything IBM's does only better."

Koplow did just that — modifying the 700 and hooking it up to an IBM Selectric. Suddenly, Wang Labs was in the word processing business with the 1200, a machine the company described as "a typewriter with a 'brain.'"

The operation of the 1200, which was announced in late 1971, was described by the company this way in its 1972 annual report: "A secretary using the 1200 can type at her fastest speed. Simultaneously, the letter is tape cassette recorded — ready for changes or final typing. With the draft copy on his desk, the author has ample time for 'second thoughts' and changes. To make such changes, the secretary 'instructs' the 1200 to find the required line by simply typing-in the first few characters of that line. Uniquely, the 1200, scanning at the rate of 330 lines per minute, searches to the exact line. No need to retype the entire letter. Only the line or portion requiring change is retyped. Then, upon signal, the 1200 automatically types out the final corrected copy from the taped recording with absolute accuracy and at the more than human speed of 175 words per minute." The 1200 was cheaper than the IBM machine, and, Wang claimed, easier to use. By Wang's estimate, use of the 1200 could cut the cost of an average business letter in half.

It was, in the estimation of analyst John Adams, "by far the most important new product at Wang" and "the most important variable in the Wang picture."

It appeared, initially, that Wang had hatched yet another hot product. Wang assistant Ed Lesnick bought a big motor home, outfitted it like an office, and took the word processing show on the road. He pulled up to office complexes throughout the Midwest and along the East Coast, demonstrating the 1200 to scores of enthusiastic secretaries, who would finally be free to throw away all those annoying little bottles of whiteout. Though the system took some getting used to and was rather complex to manipulate, it seemed clearly superior to a typewriter. Ironically, success for the 1200 would accrue somewhat to IBM's benefit, for Wang bought IBM Selectric typewriters — at full price — to go with their machines.

Orders for the 1200 were strong from the start. But the early euphoria ended abruptly, for no sooner had the machines been shipped than angry customers began complaining that the machines couldn't print properly. "The carrier with the ribbon and ball was hopping up and down," recalls Lesnick. At times, the typewriter ball on the Selectric would seem to go berserk, randomly typing some letters while skipping others.

Complaints mounted. Customers liked the idea of the machine, but more and more were complaining that the thing simply didn't work, that it was totally unreliable. The machines started coming back in massive numbers. Soon, an astounding 80 percent of all 1200s ordered had been returned. Many more trucks backed into Wang loading docks to dump 1200s than left to deliver new ones. The consequences were potentially catastrophic. The Wang people scoured the machine looking for the problem. Finally, it was discovered that a small spring intended to stabilize the typewriter's carriage was missing from the Selectrics that IBM had sold Wang.

Lesnick was enraged. He went to the IBM people, who denied that the spring was a standard piece of equipment. He didn't believe them. For two weeks, Lesnick traveled eastern Massachusetts checking Selectrics in every IBM installation he could find. He checked Selectrics used purely as typewriters, Selectrics used as terminals on 360 computers, Selectrics used for word processing, Selectrics used as input-output devices on mainframes. He checked about twenty different applications of the Selectric. Every single one had a carriage-stabilizing spring.

"I called the guy at IBM and I said, 'You told us we didn't need the spring, and it's in every machine you have,'" Lesnick recalls. "He called me back and said he would have a team in the next day." Ten IBM service people showed up and repaired every Selectric.

But for the Wang 1200, a machine that could have successfully launched the company in the word processing market, it was too late.

The failure of the 1200 was a terrible blow to the company, and it could not have come at a worse time. Wang had grown steadily and resolutely for twenty straight years, but now, in 1972, the company suffered its first earnings decline. And, though he was loath to do it, Wang was forced to conduct the first layoff ever at the company, in which forty people lost their jobs.

But the failure of the 1200 word processor was not the company's only problem. Wang was battered during the early 1970s far worse than most companies. The OPEC oil embargo was a disaster for Wang. Rising gasoline prices ordinarily would have little effect on a high-technology company, but it just so happened that Wang relied heavily on automobile dealers and, from coast to coast, auto showrooms were empty.

John Cunningham recalls that before the embargo, Wang had revenues of $1.4 million a month on the auto dealer business. Just three months later, after the embargo began, that had tumbled to just $200,000 a month.

"From about 1971 through 1975 Wang was poorly thought of," says Cunningham. "It was a bad company. DEC and Data General were hot companies then, but Wang was a very sick company. It was doing awful."

In addition to the disaster of the oil embargo, Wang was groaning under the weight of hefty bank debt. After Wang's borrowings leaped from $12 million to $29 million in fiscal 1974, analyst John Adams noted that Wang's balance sheet had gone "from strong to weak" in just a two-year period.

In 1975 and early 1976 company officials sought investment dollars from major private insurance companies to replace the bank debt, but there were no takers. And this was the company that had just a few years earlier been the darling of Wall Street — whose stock had rocketed out of sight the first day it was offered.

Now Wang Labs was confronted with the word processing disaster, the auto business crash, and a recession.

An Wang believed that in such a time of crisis the best man to call upon was himself. He would dig down deeper and fight for his company. He would will it, if need be, to survive. The Doctor told Koplow, whom he had placed in charge of marketing, that he would be moved; that he had failed to do the job. An Wang himself, in addition to being president, CEO, head financial man, and many other things, would also run marketing.

He told Harold Koplow: "I have to do this to save my company."

FIVE

"Like Selling Sex on the Beach"

I N THE MID-1970s computers lay far beyond the reach of the masses. The use of these wondrous new machines remained under the control of a select few, a kind of computer priesthood that had access to computers by virtue of their lofty positions within major corporate, academic, or government institutions. They understood how the machines operated, and they could speak the obtuse languages in which computers conversed. With their forbidding, space-age appearance and their mysterious whirs and hums, these machines were lodged in sanitary, glass-encased rooms, on raised floors that acted as altars. The ultimate barrier was their extraordinary cost. "Only the largest institutions — universities, corporations, research institutes, and government agencies — could afford them," writes Stan Augarten in his book *Bit by Bit, An Illustrated History of Computers*. ". . . Big and costly, they were the very symbols of entrenched and centralized power — arrogant, haughty, impersonal, inefficient, and inaccessible."

Augarten cites John Kemeny, former president of Dartmouth College and co-author of the computer language BASIC: "For the first two decades of the existence of the high-speed computer, machines were so scarce and so expensive that man approached the computer the way an ancient Greek approached an oracle. . . . Only specially selected acolytes were allowed to have direct communications with the computer."

But Wang Laboratories was about to change that for hundreds of thousands of office workers throughout the world. Before the term "user-friendly" existed in the computer lexicon, Wang Labs was building machines that fit that description. The company's strength, says John Cunningham, was understanding "how users interact with a system, understanding how to take the technology and make it easy to use."

The 2200 was among the most user-friendly small computers ever built. And it had sold well. But the Doctor saw a much larger market out there. Office automation, he believed, was the next technological wave. Wang saw that while computers were widely used in offices for a variety of data processing applications, they had not been used to ease the burden on most office workers.

He believed offices would soon be largely computerized, and he had hoped his company's word processing system — the ill-fated 1200 — would free office workers from a great deal of drudgery. Though it was not to be, Wang was far from ready to concede the office market. Wang Labs, in fact, was on the verge of a breakthrough that would bring computing power to the office masses.

Wang's greatest technological breakthrough began with a demotion, or, more accurately, two demotions. Harold Koplow and David Moros, two talented young designers who had worked together on the 700 calculator, were assigned by Doctor Wang to work on word processing.

Koplow, a particular favorite of Doctor Wang's, was of average height, with bushy dark hair, a pleasant smile, and glasses that gave him a bookish aura. To the Doctor's secretary, he looked like a techie nerd. His words carried an air of certainty that, when he was challenged, came across as abrasive. He spoke deliberately and punctuated his discussions with laughter at ideas he found amusing or absurd.

For his work on the 300 and 700 calculators, two of Wang's most successful products, Wang had rewarded Koplow by making him head of marketing. It was a very odd appointment, for Koplow was a technical expert, not a marketing man. Though Koplow was determined to do his best, it was quickly apparent he was in the wrong job. During one of his first meetings as the new marketing chief, Koplow stood before a room full of expectant salespeople, held up a textbook — a basic introduction to marketing — and said, "I don't know much about marketing, but I read this." *This* was the man who had replaced John Cunningham as head of marketing.

The salespeople thought him utterly bizarre, and it was not long before he amply demonstrated his assertion that he really didn't know much about marketing. But he worked so hard he made himself sick and depressed and was unable to work for a month.

One day in 1975, Doctor Wang summoned Koplow to his office and said: "You no longer in charge marketing. You do long-range planning."

Koplow was stunned. "I thought I was doing a damn good job," he says. "I hated the way he threw me out."

And he was sure he was gone, for at Wang, long-range planning was a euphemism for getting kicked out of the company's mainstream. Generally, people who had been sent to long-range planning found themselves with nothing to do and, eventually, left. So sure was Koplow that his days at Wang were numbered, that he began searching for a new job. Fortunately for Wang Laboratories, however, he did not find anything that quite suited him. Harold Koplow was not an easy man to please. Former colleagues describe him as sometimes egotistical, abrasive, obnoxious, disruptive, and intolerant.

"He was crazy, hyperemotional, erratic, volatile, vitriolic, given to explosions of anger," says Dale Jelley, who worked with Koplow. "Once, he had a huge fight with somebody over the question of whether a computer should have a light on the console to determine whether it was on. Koplow was screaming."

Whatever anybody at Wang thought of Koplow personally, however, it was clear, and certainly Doctor Wang knew, that Koplow was a truly gifted young man. John Cunningham, who would go on to form a friendship and successful business relationship with Koplow, says Koplow was well liked by the people who worked for him. "They had tremendous respect for his ability and they learned a lot from him."

Moros says Koplow was "really a difficult person to get on with, but Harold is extremely intelligent and he's very good with his people, a good team leader."

Koplow was an unlikely success story at Wang for he had begun his professional career as, of all things, a pharmacist. "I never liked it," says Koplow. "I had flat feet and my feet used to hurt. The pay was bad, the hours were long." He often worked until closing, and late one night after he had locked up the store, he was walking home with a bag of Popsicles for his pregnant wife when he was held up at gunpoint and forced to fork over the bag.

He soon decided that the life of a pharmacist wasn't for him and started working toward a Ph.D. in physics at Tufts University. But that didn't suit him, and neither did his next venture, teaching high-school physics.

One day, as he searched the newspaper Help Wanteds, Koplow saw an ad for computer programmers at a small company called Wang Labs.

The extent of his experience with computers had been sitting in on a graduate-school lecture about the machines. But computers intrigued him and he applied for the job. In September 1968, at the age of twenty-seven, Koplow joined Wang.

His lack of formal computer background gave him an odd approach to the business. "Harold is a very disarming guy," says Ed Lesnick, who had long favored the company's moving forcefully into the word processing market. "He's not into computerese at all. In describing the electrical current within a system he would stand up at the blackboard, in front of a diagram, and talk about 'these guys coming down this path, and then these guys go up this and turn that on.'"

There was an irreverent side to Koplow as well. After only a month on the job he completed all the assignments he had been given and went in and told Doctor Wang he was bored, asking impatiently: "You got anything else for me to do around here?"

Koplow found that his office was uncomfortably warm in summer. To remedy that, he took a hacksaw one day and diverted some of the flow in the air-conditioning system that fed into the Doctor's office.

That Koplow was irreverent or sometimes difficult mattered not the least bit to An Wang, for Wang saw that this man was gifted. Koplow was so crucial to the success of the company that Lesnick says Wang Labs would have gone nowhere without him.

But Koplow's days as the Doctor's pet seemed rather distant when he was assigned to long-range planning. He arrived there to find that his friend Dave Moros had been exiled as well.

But, for Moros and Koplow, winding up together was some consolation, because the two men had great mutual respect. Koplow described Moros as bright and perceptive, but something of an absentminded professor. "He can forget where the hell he is," Koplow says of Moros.

Moros can, in fact, appear remote. He looks at first, in his rumpled corduroys, like an academic specializing in Middle English. He is of medium height, somewhat stocky, with powerful shoulders. His dark hair, swarthy complexion, and dramatic good looks lend him the air of a patrician prizefighter. While Koplow could be loud and aggressive, Moros was reserved, a reflective reader of Socrates, something of an aesthete.

Moros's father had fought with the White Army in Russia against the Bolsheviks in the 1917 Revolution and was forced to flee the country after the Communist triumph. He escaped to Tel Aviv, where Dave was born in 1936, two years before the family settled in the United States. After studying math at Tufts, where he was in the Reserve Officer Training Corps, Moros went on active duty as a computer specialist, and worked for a time on a UNIVAC. Moros earned his master's degree in business administration from American University and, in 1964, joined Philip Hankins, Inc., where he worked on the Apollo and Gemini space projects.

Moros had not been happy with the Wang-PHI merger. Although he had immense respect for Wang's professional ability, Moros was not enamored of what he considered the paternalistic atmosphere at the company. "The place always ran like a Chinese family," says Moros. "He was the father. He knew best. You did what you were told. I didn't like that at all."

Moros was sent to long-range planning, he joked, "for having disturbed the peace of the Middle Kingdom" — in this case, that meant having gotten caught in the crossfire of company in-fighting.

And so Koplow and Moros, two men who grew to be, in John Cunningham's words, "like a long-married couple," were thrown together, castoffs within the company.

An Wang dispatched Koplow and Moros with the instruction that they try to do something with the company's word processing mess. "So in a very relaxed, unpressured, and who-cares kind of way," says Moros, "we worked on word processing."

They began with a series of unhurried trips to see what the state-of-the-art word processing machines could do. In their travels, they were guided by Ed Lesnick, who had a longstanding interest in word processing. As early as 1969, Lesnick, in fact, had gone so far as to write specifications for a word processing machine. Lesnick monitored technological developments at other firms and, in 1975, he led Koplow and Moros on an inspection tour to companies, some of them tiny start-ups, in Washington, D.C., California, and Canada. Each new machine had at least one strong feature, and most had major weaknesses. The Wang team wanted to build a machine without any of the weaknesses, but with all of the best features they'd seen on other machines.

When they returned from their scouting trips these men were more convinced than ever that Wang could break new ground. "I was *sure* we could do better," says Koplow.

Moros is a relaxed man who loves the intellectual side of science, but who is not in the least like the hackers who work nonstop for three or four straight days and nights. Moros prefers a far more civilized pace and it was at his pace that he and Koplow proceeded as they sat down to begin their project.

"We did it almost as therapy" to soothe the pain of having been shunted aside, says Moros. "We were doing it because we were good at doing it."

They began with an interesting approach. Moros suggested that rather than starting with the design of the machinery, that they write a manual for the ideal word processor, a manual that would place the technology, as Moros put it, "at the level of the user." Step one would be to write the manual; step two, to see if they could bring to life the wish-list that the manual would embody.

Though Wang's first entry into word processing, the 1200, had been a disaster, it proved to be useful experience for the Koplow-Moros team. "With the 1200, when you wanted to do something sophisticated, the user would go bananas," says Moros. "It was too complicated. The important thing was to think about the person who's going to use the tool."

They worked in Moros's cramped, inglorious office, an eight-by-twelve-foot cell cluttered with fat computer manuals and furnished with a cheap gray metal desk, a metal bookcase, and a large blackboard. They would begin work around 9:30 A.M., sometimes later, with Moros pecking away — ironically, given their task — on a manual typewriter. Moros would sip from one of the seven or eight cups of coffee he would consume during the day and puff on his pipe. Koplow would pace back and forth nervously, squinting as ideas came to him and as the two men chatted — or argued — about various aspects of the machine. Their intellectual battles were spirited, but always pleasant. They would give vague shape to an idea verbally, then add a bit more precision as they committed it to paper and sketched out schematics on the blackboard. By 1:00 or 1:30 in the afternoon, Moros was through for the day. He would then take his brain home for a rest. With that, Koplow was out the door in search of a new job. But as he traveled the high-technology corridors of the East Coast for interviews, he found himself more interested in finding out what various companies were doing technologically than in landing work. He left one interview after another with an understanding of where other companies were. He went to companies such as Vydec, Exxon, Xerox, and found that he and his friend Moros were doing better work.

After six months of labor, they completed a ninety-six-page user's manual, and gave it to the Doctor. He reviewed the document and said: "I like. You build."

Koplow immediately set about trying to create the machine their user's manual described. It was one thing to write a manual for the ideal machine, and quite another to be able to create the hardware and the software for such a beast.

The architecture of the machine — a patented design that would win much praise later on — was determined at a meeting in Doctor Wang's office on September 28, 1975. Initially, the Doctor — who became a key player in the development of the machine after the manual was written — wanted to power the machine with a new minicomputer the company was in the process of building and that would eventually be called the VS. But he, Koplow, and Moros eventually felt it would be too slow and cumbersome, and Koplow argued for placing a microprocessor — a tiny computer on a chip — in each workstation. It was a notion that could hardly be more commonplace today, but was radical back then.

This crucial element meant that the machine would not be hooked into a time-sharing system — it would not be connected to a mainframe computer that it would have to share with many others. "On an IBM mainframe, you'd type in your stuff, hit Enter, and then you would wait," says Moros. "You would stand in line waiting for a mainframe to deal with requests ahead of yours."

The Doctor gave the go-ahead to use a microprocessor in each word processing station, making each machine a computer unto itself. Koplow and Moros designed a system wherein groups of word processors tied into a powerful server that would store much of the data used by the machine. With this design there was no waiting in line. The machine responded instantly.

In fact, the design was years ahead of its time. The computing rage in the early 1990s has been local area networks — different machines tying into each other and into printers and computer file servers that store and transmit data to various workstations. The Wang design was, in effect, an early local area network.

To build the machine, a team consisting of some of the company's most talented people was assembled under Koplow. The fourth key player was Don Dunning, who was in charge of putting the hardware together, and whose name is on the patent for the machine along with Wang, Koplow, and Moros. Dunning was an impressive man who, with the aid of Ed Wilde, turned the hardware specifications of the Koplow-Moros manual into reality while Koplow and Moros worked on the software. Dunning skillfully made a hardware pipe dream work. The team had it all solved, with the exception of one problem. For the system to work, it needed an extraordinary degree of speed, and Koplow had not figured out how to engineer that into the exchange of information between the file server and each workstation. During the September 28 meeting, Doctor Wang mentioned an idea that he and Dunning had come up with. He said they thought a particular type of cable would provide the speed necessary. They would use a collection of microprocessors connected with a coax cable.

When Jake Jacobson was only in his mid-twenties he was one of Wang's best salesmen. A native Californian, he was a brash, affable young man with beachboy good looks who absolutely hated to lose a sale. Jacobson worked out of the Wang New York office, where he was striving mightily to crack major accounts in the city. In the fall of 1975, when he tried to make a sale to Touche Ross, the big accounting firm, he was told thanks, but no thanks. Touche Ross wanted word processing, and all Wang had to offer was the 1200, which, even with its repaired printing capability, already seemed like something of a dinosaur. Jacobson didn't know the specifics of the work Koplow and Moros were doing back in Tewksbury, but he had heard talk that they were up to something.

"We got blown out of Touche Ross because we didn't have a competitive product," Jacobson told his boss in New York. He said that if there was better material back in Tewksbury, now was the time to show it.

Word of the problem reached Koplow. He did not have a finished machine, but he had made enough progress with the hardware to be able to demonstrate some of the machine's capabilities. He invited the Touche Ross people to Tewksbury for a demonstration.

"We started the day with an informal meeting with Doctor Wang and several development people and Harold and Bob Doretti [head of the New York office] and myself, and, after the normal niceties, Doctor Wang left the room," Jacobson recalls. "Harold got up in front of the blackboard and started to draw out what the thing looked like. He listed its features. As he continued listing them, the Touche Ross people became more and more enamored. They kept asking, 'Could you do this?' and the answer was 'Yes' and 'Here's how we can do it.' It was being enhanced by Touche Ross right there. We went into the R&D labs and there was a breadboard of the machine. The cathode ray tube (CRT) was enclosed in a red plywood box. Harold showed them some word processing things on the screen, and you could see: It's for real!"

Koplow recalls that when the top Touche Ross executive on the trip went into the lab and saw what the machine could do, "his eyes popped. He had never seen anything like it."

In the ensuing weeks, Jacobson shuttled back and forth between Tewksbury and New York answering questions from Touche Ross. They wanted to buy, but Wang Labs was hardly IBM. In fact, in the competitive world of high technology, Wang was a small, unknown player. The few people who knew about Wang knew it as a calculator company. Touche Ross insisted on numerous safeguards in the contract so that if Wang went belly-up or somehow failed to deliver the goods as promised, Touche Ross could back out of the deal. "Wang's size and position in the marketplace dictated that the management of Touche Ross say, 'We'll take the risk, but we want to get out of it if this small company can't perform.'" The machine was simply too good to pass up.

In the winter of 1976, Wang got a signed deal from Touche Ross for $142,000. It was one of the biggest orders the company had ever received. And the machine had not even been finished or announced yet.

The word processing system had received its private debut during the Touche Ross sale. Its public debut was scheduled for June 1976 at a major trade show in New York City. The Syntopican show was one of the biggest and most important of the shows that companies looking to make major computer purchases attended to examine the latest technology. Koplow and his group worked frantically during the weeks prior to the show to prepare four word processing machines for display. The beast was doing beautifully, but with one glitch: Koplow simply couldn't get the printer to work. The truck was backed into the loading dock ready to haul the machinery to New York the night before the show was to open. Koplow would not give it up. He kept working on it until, less than an hour before the truck had to leave, he finally got the printer fixed.

The show had completely taken over the vast New York Hilton on the Avenue of the Americas between 53rd and 54th streets. In the hotel basement was a cavernous display area where hundreds of computer company products were exhibited. The place was packed with rows of booths from which salespeople for every major and many minor companies demonstrated their wares. On the floors above, scores of companies had taken suites of rooms where they displayed their wares for serious customers. Wang had two of the new machines on the display floor and two more upstairs in a suite. The show was only a few hours old when it became clear what a phenomenon little Wang Laboratories had produced. As the day wore on, the cluster around the Wang display grew until the line snaked around and into the booths of other companies.

"Would you like to see a demonstration?" someone at an adjoining booth asked a man standing in line in his display area.

"No thanks," he replied, "I'm waiting for Wang."

As was everyone else. And when they saw the new machine, they loved it.

"It was an instant ah ha!" recalls J. Carl Masi, who was then a Wang marketing executive. "People would say, 'My God, look at this!' Everybody walked away shaking their heads as though they couldn't believe what they saw."

Koplow smiles at the memory and says, "It was a killer machine." And indeed it was. For one thing, this was the first major successful use of microprocessors in the commercial computer industry.

It began with the kind of screen common on today's personal computers. CRT screens were something of a novelty then. The screen would allow the user to see about a half page of text at once. On the old screens, only a single line, sometimes a few, were visible. And the new machine was goof-proof.

The true beauty of the machine lay in its simplicity, for it was vastly easier to use than any computer ever built. From the moment the switch was turned on, the user was presented with straightforward choices at every turn. The choices were offered in plain English, not computerese. Koplow and Moros knew users lived in mortal fear that if they pressed the wrong button by mistake, an entire file would disappear into the stratosphere. So they made the machine immune to such errors.

What Wang Laboratories had done was to take the power of computing out of the priesthood and place it into the hands of average high-school graduates who didn't know the difference between a megabyte and a dog bite.

"With ten minutes' training you could use the machine," says Koplow. "It was just intuitive. There was nothing like it in the world."

If there was any doubt about the machine's ease of use, it was dispelled that night when salespeople from the New York office were brought in to relieve the exhausted Wang sales force on the floor of the show. The job of the fresh troops would be to demonstrate the machine the following day, and even though none of them had ever before laid eyes on it, their training session that night was remarkably brief.

In the stifling heat and humidity of an early New York summer, the lines grew. Throughout the hotel word passed. It was *the* machine of the show. The scene in the suite upstairs was pandemonium. "You couldn't move," recalls Koplow. "They were gushing over it." Huge potential customers — Mobil, Citicorp, Chase Manhattan, and others — were demanding to know how soon the word processor could be delivered. The Wang people had no idea. Every machine they had produced was right there under the Hilton roof!

Jacobson had struck a deal with Exxon in advance of the show, but, for dramatic effect, he had worked out an arrangement where they would actually be signed up right on the floor of the show. It only added to the magical aura of the moment for Wang Labs.

The Doctor appeared stunned by all of this. "He was as nervous as I had ever seen him," recalls Masi. Mostly, the Doctor wandered around in a kind of daze, puffing on his cigar. By the end of the three-day show, "we had a stack of press clippings that would choke a horse about how great this new product was," recalls Masi. And the Doctor was in ecstasy.

The third night, with the show over, the Doctor told everyone he was taking them out to dinner. Would it be Nathan's? The Doctor had been rather parsimonious when it came to expenses. But no, on the recommendation of John Cunningham, Doctor Wang led his triumphant brigade to Perigord Park at 61st and Park, one of the most elegant and expensive restaurants in Manhattan. There were about two dozen people in all. The bill came to more than $2,000.

Doctor Wang looked at it and pulled out his American Express card as a broad smile broke over his face.

The word processing system held great promise, but as of 1976 it had not yet made a dollar for Wang and money was what the company desperately needed. In truth, Wang Labs was in serious financial trouble. The company was deep in hock to its banks with more than $50 million in outstanding debt. For a company with revenues only twice that, such a level of debt was onerous. The bankers didn't like that ratio at all. They told the Doctor that additional equity would have to be raised, and the most obvious way to do that was to sell stock. But the Doctor was extremely reluctant to do that. The sale of more public shares would only dilute his ownership and weaken his grip on the company. Unthinkably, it might lead one day to his losing control of Wang Laboratories.

Wang told his friend and board member Ge Yao Chu that he wanted to bring the company from $100 million in revenues to $1 billion. Recalls Chu: "But he said, 'By the time $1 billion my holdings will be diluted to 10 percent of the company. By that time I'll be successful in the business but I lose my company.'"

In 1976, when a five-year revolving credit arrangement with several banks came up for renewal, the banks insisted that Wang reduce his debt with them. Unless he wanted to sell a minority share in the company to another corporation, which he was loath to do, his only alternative was to sell stock.

For An Wang, this was cutting to the bone. And he put his considerable intellect to devising ways to raise the capital he needed without diluting his ownership.

Naturally, he thought of a solution. Wang thoroughly enjoyed the intricacies of finance and, through the years, had become an expert on the subject. He became so good, in fact, that Dave Moros believed Wang was even better at financial matters than technical ones. Having little choice but to sell more stock in his company but fearful of losing control, An Wang concocted a scheme that could accomplish both: He would sell a second class of stock — B stock — that would have full equity in the company. And he would create yet another class of stock, C stock, primarily for the Wang family. And the family would control the company through its shares, which would carry ten times the voting power of B stock. Under this arrangement, the family would choose a majority of the members of the board of directors. Thus, no matter how many publicly held B shares existed, Wang would always control the company.

The biggest problem was that the New York Stock Exchange, the most prestigious U.S. exchange, would not permit the listing of two classes of stock for any company (except Ford, which had established a second class of shares in the 1940s before the prohibition against dual classes of stock went into force). Wang executives argued vehemently with the Doctor that being kicked off the New York exchange would psychologically reduce the value of the shares. But Wang didn't care. He was willing to do it for the control. The company was indeed demoted to the American exchange, but Wang had achieved his objective of locking in his absolute control over the company no matter how big it grew.

The Wang Word Processing System did not merely boost the company, it transformed it. When the machine was introduced in 1976, Wang's revenues were $97 million. Over the next three years Wang rode word processing sales to revenues triple that. The machine was so hot that by 1978 Wang was the largest supplier in the world of CRT-based word processors.

Dick Connaughton, then manager of Wang's operations in Australia, recalls that the response from customers was "unbelievable. People were flocking to Wang." Connaughton quickly sold the system to the Australian government as well as to the five largest companies in the country.

That many customers thought of the beast as a word processing machine rather than as a computer was a great advantage, says Bob Ano, then a marketing manager who was a rising young star at Wang. "In those days you didn't want it to be a computer because computers were big, scary, expensive, and hard to operate. This system was intuitive, menu-driven. Selling it was easy. It was like falling off a log."

In the past, Wang had been unable to break into the Fortune 1000 companies. Normally, winning the business of those corporations took years, but within weeks of the New York show, Jacobson had signed major accounts such as J. C. Penney and the United Nations. The mainstay of Wang's business had always been small accounts. The company would sell a few calculators to a university or engineering firm, a 2200 computer, maybe two, to a small business. But now they were looking at the possibility of selling dozens — in some case *hundreds* — of word processing units to a single corporation. The possibilities seemed incredible.

"The Doctor liked the fact that we were not selling one and two 1200s," says Jacobson. "All of a sudden we were doing $400,000 and $600,000 deals. It didn't take Doctor Wang long to figure out that the future of the company was in information processing."

When the company began manufacturing large numbers of word processors — around the end of 1976 — its sales force began aggressively pursuing new accounts. Because Wang was a very small company compared with the industry giants, potential customers were wary of signing big contracts right away. They wanted to make sure the machine was as good as they thought it was and that the company backed it up with service. Wang salespeople offered free trial periods of sixty days everywhere they went.

"We were aggressive [with trials] because we knew we had a fantastic product," says Jacobson.

Within just a couple of years, major accounts went from being a very small part of Wang's business to being 40-plus percent. Many of the accounts that started out as free trials grew into large, lucrative pieces of business. Wang had gone from selling calculators one at a time up and down the street to selling truckloads of word processing equipment to some of the largest corporations in the world.

Trying to enter the word processing market at the time was very bold indeed. "IBM had 100 percent of the market" with its MTST, says analyst John Adams. "To take on somebody of that caliber with that kind of market share is not trivial."

Says Wang engineer Bob Siegel: "At the time he made the decision to get into word processing, 90 percent of the company thought he was crazy. IBM was the competition. People said, 'Who the hell are we to do this?'"

But Doctor Wang believed that IBM was not strong in this area and that it was not a priority for them. "I framed the competition in such a way that our greatest strength was pitted against their weakness," he wrote in *Lessons*. IBM, he continued, was "formidable and aggressive, [but] they are highly bureaucratic, and as a result they are sometimes slow to react. . . . By not developing their own word processing technology, they provided us with the time to learn from our mistakes and correct them."

Crucial to the success of the word processing system was the combination of having the best product on the market *and* having the sales and distribution network capable of getting that product to customers. Though the 1200 had been a flop, it had led to the creation of such a network, which was ready for the new word processing system.

Nobody at Wang had envisioned the machine's spectacular success. Even Koplow and Moros — though they believed in their creation — never expected the level of sales that followed. But, ironically, the Wang official who was most skeptical ended up having as much to do with its success as anyone outside the design team. John Cunningham, who was running sales, service, and marketing worldwide when the word processing system was introduced, "thought the company would screw it up same as they had screwed up the 1200."

Cunningham had suffered with the 1200. He had set up a system to train the sales force on the intricacies of the machine. He had established distribution channels for the machine. And he had watched as his salespeople took angry calls from customers sending back the 1200s, reversing the distribution channels he had so carefully established to send out 1200s.

Perhaps it was understandable when Cunningham greeted the new machine with acute skepticism. And his skepticism turned to cynicism when he saw that Koplow hadn't been able to get the printer to work on the eve, literally, of the New York show. Rather than go to the New York show, Cunningham had said: "You guys will fuck it up. I'm going to play golf with my father and my brothers." (However, when he heard how the first day had gone, Cunningham hopped the shuttle to New York.)

It was mostly the new technology that had made the celebration possible, but it was not the only reason. The importance of the sales infrastructure was emphasized by Thomas Watson, Jr., in *Father, Son & Co.* "In the history of IBM, technological innovation often wasn't the thing that made us successful. . . . Technology turned out to be less important than sales and distribution methods. Starting with UNIVAC, we consistently outsold people who had better technology because we knew how to put the story before the customer."

Amazingly, Wang had the field to itself for nearly three years before IBM responded with a product even close to being competitive.

In a business that, within just a few years, would become arguably the most competitive industry in the world, that was a remarkable bit of luck. Wang took full advantage of it.

"By being slow to respond," the Doctor writes in *Lessons*, "IBM gave us the time to invade this marketplace."

"We put the processor in the secretary's hands," says Moros. "It broke the central priesthood. You no longer had to go to a central, holy place. You had your own microprocessor under your fingertips."

"Wang word processing was a huge breakthrough," observes George Colony, president of Forrester Research in Cambridge, a firm that analyzes computer companies and equipment for major corporate customers. "Wang defined that market. They freed the masses."

Not only did Wang have what was now the hottest product in office computing (Cunningham described it as "like selling sex on the beach to teenagers"), the company also had a hit with the 2200 computer. In early 1977 analyst John Adams wrote that "the company is now positioned in two markets with exceptional growth prospects — small business computers and word processing systems." Wang Laboratories was poised for one of the most spectacular periods of growth in the history of modern industry.

SIX

John Cunningham: An American Son

T HE FOURTH of five children born to a Boston public school-teacher and his wife, John Cunningham grew up in West Roxbury, an Irish-Catholic neighborhood of Boston. The area was populated by many public employees — teachers, firefighters, and policemen — and workers at the electric and gas companies, as well as a few politically connected lawyers.

John was fair-skinned, a freckle-faced redhead who spent his childhood wrestling with his brothers and playing baseball, football, and hockey. His parents sent him to St. Theresa's, a Roman Catholic primary school, where it was obvious that he was unusually smart.

"He was an independent little one," recalls his mother. "You couldn't talk him out of what he wanted. He always knew what he wanted and he got it."

What he wanted, from an early age, was money. And he had the drive and discipline to go out and earn it. "The snow would come down and while everybody else was in the house relaxing, John would already have done four walks," says Bill Dixon, a boyhood friend.

He took math and science courses at Boston College High School, a prestigious institution run by Jesuit priests, and scored well with minimal effort. If the other students were smart, and they were, he was smarter; if they were ambitious, and many were, he was more so; if the other boys were determined, young John Cunningham was doubly so. He wanted a car and was willing to work hard to get the money to buy one. During his last year in high school and his first couple of years in college,

Cunningham would buy old cars, steam-clean the engines, turn the odometer back, put on new seat covers, paint them, and sell them at a substantial profit. In all, he sold thirty-five used cars in that way.

He inherited the work ethic from his father, who not only taught school, but also worked part-time as a car salesman, coached various sports, and picked up extra money officiating at high-school games. Paul Connelly, a lifelong friend of Cunningham's whose father was a Boston juvenile court judge, recalls that whenever his parents wanted to make a point about hard work, they pointed to the Cunninghams. "In my house they were always used as an example of how people can raise their status by good hard work," says Connelly.

Young John Cunningham worked during school vacations and summers at a variety of jobs. He drove a truck, delivered flowers, sold cigars, and loaded trucks at a bakery. In 1960, when he was a freshman in college, he was one of a very few students with a car. He didn't have just any car; he tooled around in a sleek Triumph TR3. His parents had been dead set against his buying it. Didn't he realize that the car's price equaled the cost of a year's tuition? Yes, he knew that. But he wanted it. He was determined to have it. And he bought it.

"He was different from other boys his age," recalls his wife, Ellen, who grew up less than a mile from Cunningham in West Roxbury, and who met him at a party crashed by Cunningham and his friends. "He did more than other kids. He had all sorts of jobs, majored in math and physics. He packed a lot in. He was very ambitious. He seemed to have a lot of drive."

It was not easy making enough money to support his lifestyle at the time, but Cunningham was clever and fearless. While working at GTE Sylvania on the night cleaning crew, he discovered a lucrative sideline for himself. In the early '60s copying machines were rare, but there was a Xerox copier at GTE. It gave Cunningham the idea to make fake IDs. He would cut, paste, and photocopy various official documents and then forge the name of Clement A. Riley, the Massachusetts registrar of motor vehicles. Finally, he would run it through a laminating kit and sell it for $15. His forgeries were not restricted to driver's licenses. In college, he also sold forged stickers to the faculty parking area, but he was forced to discontinue that when he was caught.

Ellen Condon was a senior in high school when she met her future husband, who was then a college freshman. Around girls he was shy and awkward, and therefore not very popular. Around his male friends he was wild. "He had a car, and he always had a can of beer in the car," recalls

Ellen. "He was known for acting up. He was a real party boy with the guys."

Cunningham loved to drink, and he played hard every chance he got. During the summer before his senior year, he worked nights at a warehouse where he would get off at 3:00 A.M. and immediately go drinking. It was nearly impossible to find cold beer at that time of night, but Cunningham could be very resourceful when it came to liquor. The United States Open golf championship was held that summer at The Country Club in Brookline, a five-minute drive from West Roxbury. Upon leaving work, Cunningham would head immediately for The Country Club, park in the woods nearby, and sneak into the concession stand on the golf course, where he would liberate three or four cases of cold Budweiser. Unfortunately for Cunningham and his pals, the tournament and its festivities lasted only a week. But, in a pinch, he could always be relied upon to produce something from his emergency stash in the coal bin of his parents' house.

Cunningham would use any excuse for a party. One year during high school, his Catholic Youth Organization baseball team was headed for the New England finals in Hartford. "As we were wrapping up practice the day before the game," says Paul Connelly, "I look out to center field and John is out there, and he had this briefcase he opened with VO, plastic cups, stirrers, ice, soda water, and ginger ale. He was setting up a bar in center field!"

There were dozens of escapades, including the night on Cape Cod that Cunningham and his troops, after many beers, attempted to visit — to the dismay of the United States Secret Service — Jacqueline Kennedy at the Hyannis Port compound. Another time, again on the Cape, Cunningham and company broke into a lobster pound at 3:00 A.M., fell into the lobster tank, and stole lobsters for the group dinner. But the lobsters weren't enough. They needed to watch television while dining, so they liberated a TV set from a nearby motel. And, at daybreak, they dined on lobster at the cottage they had rented and watched the tube. (The TV set was returned.)

"We did some dumb things," says Paul Connelly. "But we never did anything really evil or vindictive. It was kids having fun. We never, ever were vicious."

Petty thievery was common among Cunningham's crowd. They stole food, mostly, steaks and salad makings from supermarkets. But they would also occasionally take someone else's gasoline.

"We were siphoning gas out of someone's car so we could go out for a night," recalls Bill Dixon, "and John was sitting as the gas was being transferred, scanning a theology book for an exam the next day. And I pointed out to him the irony of our situation. He laughed."

His drinking did not go unnoticed by his mother, and she didn't like it a bit. She was so enraged one night when he came home obviously drunk that she yanked a vodka bottle out of his coat pocket and poured its contents over his head.

But Cunningham was shrewd. To get his mother to lay off him, he wrote to the Catholic Archdiocese of Boston requesting information about entering the priesthood. He knew that his mother carefully scrutinized each day's mail. He also knew that she was, above all else, a devout Catholic. Just as he expected, when the mail arrived she was simply ecstatic to see her Johnny inquiring about a vocation.

In the new, postwar prosperity, the Cunninghams lived a pleasant life. Their home at 40 Tennyson Street was by no means huge, but with its dining room, living room, kitchen, and three bedrooms, it was spacious enough. And, each summer, the family rented a house on Cape Cod. Essential to their lifestyle was Mrs. Cunningham's ability to stretch a dollar. Each year before Easter she would venture downtown to the department stores hunting for bargains. She would go out with $20 or so and return with five new outfits for her children.

The crowd with which Cunningham grew up was far from disadvantaged. His pals were the sons of lawyers, teachers, and policemen. One friend's dad was a juvenile court judge. Another's had the most glamorous job in all of West Roxbury — traveling secretary for the Boston Red Sox. Cunningham and his friend Tom Dowd, son of the Red Sox man, enjoyed playing golf, but not at the public golf courses where others from West Roxbury went. Instead they would go to the Dedham Country and Polo Club, a beautiful and exclusive private facility, where, with free Red Sox tickets for the greenskeeper, they would bribe their way onto the course. They even had the temerity to march over to The Country Club in Brookline, the most exclusive club in Greater Boston, and boldly tee it up. Members of the private Catholic clubs swore at them and chased them off the course when they were caught playing there. When caught at The Country Club, however, they would be coolly but civilly asked to leave the course upon completion of their round.

When he looked around at the way these crusty old WASPs lived —

at their gorgeous clubs, exclusive private schools, their stunning homes in the very best areas — he knew that that was how he wanted to live his life. There was nothing wrong with homes close together on a side street in West Roxbury, or working for the school department and hustling cars on the side; there was nothing wrong with earning a modest income, with renting a summer home on the Cape. Nothing wrong with any of it, except it wasn't for him. He wanted not a pleasant home, but a sprawling mansion; not an average job, but a lofty position in American industry; not a steady income, but wealth — great wealth.

His parents and older siblings looked around at West Roxbury and saw a life that was far better than that of many other city dwellers squeezed into apartments or housing projects in South Boston or Charlestown. When young John looked around, he saw not that he was better off than many people, for he did not compare his status with that of most people. He compared himself with the most successful people. He looked around and saw that his life was far inferior to that enjoyed by the Yankees living in rambling mansions in exclusive Chestnut Hill. While his mother and father looked down the economic ladder and were thankful for what they had, John looked up and focused on what he didn't have.

"Class was always an important issue to me," he says. "I wanted to rise up. I wanted more. To an extent, I was jealous. I liked the other things."

He was determined to break out, and one way he saw to do that was to go to an Ivy League school rather than Boston College, which was then populated almost exclusively by working-class Catholic kids who commuted each day. "Catholics were not integrated into Boston society at the time," he recalls. "Catholics were encouraged to go to Catholic schools. The feeling I had was BC was an inferior school. There was a real split between BC and the Ivies. BC at that time was all commuters. People who came up through BC always felt inferior to the Ivy guys. The First National Bank of Boston was all Dartmouth guys. There weren't the same opportunities for a BC grad."

He applied to BC, but only as a backup in the event that his first three choices — Dartmouth, Harvard, and the University of Pennsylvania — turned him down, which is precisely what happened. In spite of his having been a top student at a demanding school (his combined SAT scores exceeded 1400), he was refused admittance by all three. Privately, he suspected that the Jesuits at BC High had undermined his applications to the more prestigious schools because they wanted him at BC, where he would continue studying under Jesuits.

And so he was off to BC, following in the footsteps of his father and two older brothers. He was undeterred. If he couldn't go to the Ivy League as an undergraduate, he would do it as a graduate student. If anything, going to BC spurred him on, for his daily route to school was through the heart of the most affluent area of Chestnut Hill, smack in the belly of the WASP establishment.

"There was something inside him," says his brother Bill, "that said, 'I'm going to go get something somebody else doesn't have.'"

And what he would get would be an MBA from one of the nation's top business schools. He was admitted to Harvard, though his admission there was deferred a year so that he could get some real-world business experience. But John Cunningham was in a hurry and he wasn't about to wait around for anybody, even Harvard Business School. He headed instead up to Hanover, New Hampshire, and the Amos Tuck School of Business Administration at Dartmouth College, where he was not only admitted, but offered a generous fellowship as well. His two years in Hanover were a glorious experience for Cunningham, who had never before lived away from home. He loved dorm life there, recalls his wife. He also enjoyed the small classes and thrived in the intellectual stimulation that played to his math and marketing strengths.

But the crucial event at Tuck was Cunningham's realization that he could compete against classmates whose undergraduate degrees were from Ivy League colleges. John Cunningham had never had a low opinion of himself. He had always believed, in fact, that he was rather smart. But he arrived in Hanover convinced that he was inferior to his fellow students who had gone to schools such as Harvard and Princeton as undergraduates. He was certain that they possessed some mystical qualities that would always elude him. At Tuck, his most important lesson was that that belief was wrong.

After he had been there long enough to get the measure of his classmates, he thought: "I could eat these guys for lunch if I get out into the business world and hustle."

While at Tuck he also learned to calm down. He realized that if he continued the drunken, crazed social life he had led with his pals, he could wind up hurt, an alcoholic, or worse.

"I decided, 'I can't live like this or I'll be dead,'" he recalls. He decided to get married.

In the spring of 1966, a week after he received his MBA, John Cunningham married Ellen Condon at St. Theresa's Church in West Roxbury. The reception for three hundred and fifty was held in the main ballroom at the Copley Plaza, an elegant old hotel in Boston's Back Bay. They honeymooned in Bermuda, and then it was off to New York for a training program at the Chicago-based Oxford Paper Company. Soon, John settled into his job at Oxford, in Chicago, and they moved into a house in Highland Park.

Within six or eight months of starting his job at Oxford in July, Cunningham realized he had made a mistake. The paper business wasn't for him — the pace too slow, the products uninteresting. And, as he looked ahead, he saw limited chances for advancement. He needed a far more dynamic atmosphere with far greater opportunities to move up. He was also interested in working his way back to Boston at some point, and Oxford didn't offer that. But since he had made a commitment to the Oxford people, he hung in there for a while before looking around.

One day he saw an ad in the *Wall Street Journal* in which Wang was advertising for a salesman in its Chicago office. Cunningham knew that Wang was a hot company because he had bought a few shares of Wang stock when it had gone public. Although he was earning $14,000 a year at Oxford, and Wang was paying salesmen only $4,000 plus commissions, he wanted the Wang job for the opportunity it presented. It was clearly a gamble, but he felt it was worth it. Though he intensely disliked selling, he saw it as a route up and a prerequisite to future advancement. He started with Wang as a salesman in the Chicago office in October 1967, the youngest salesman Wang Labs had ever hired.

The popularity of the 700, Cunningham's natural sales ability, and a great deal of hard work combined to make him one of the company's outstanding performers. Cunningham was extremely successful as a salesman, and within nine months of having joined Wang he was promoted from salesman to manager of the Chicago branch, where several salesmen worked for him. Six months later, Cunningham was promoted to district manager with responsibility for several states and eight salespeople. When company officials were looking for someone to manage the marketing of what would be Wang's first real computer — the 3300 — they reached out to Cunningham. In October 1969 he was brought to Tewksbury and began what would be his meteoric rise to the top of the company.

It was a rise that must have surprised the outside firm that evaluated Cunningham when he first started work at Wang. Cunningham was given grades of B-minus in both sales and management and was only "mildly recommended" in either category. His evaluator wrote that he "may prove to be adequate, or perhaps better, both as salesman and manager."

*   *   *

Back in January 1968, only three months after John Cunningham began work for Wang Laboratories, Ellen had given birth to a son, Christopher. But when the baby was just a year old, Ellen was involved in a bad automobile accident in which her VW bug was hit and she was crushed under the steering wheel. Ellen suffered spinal injuries and was hospitalized for six months, but, miraculously, the baby was uninjured.

In June 1972, after the family had moved back to the Boston area, the Cunninghams suffered another misfortune — this one an unspeakable horror. The Cunninghams sold the house in which they had been living in the small rural town of Harvard, forty miles outside Boston, and purchased a home in Wayland, a suburb somewhat closer to Boston. It was moving day. While John and Ellen were in the house, Chris was outside in John's brother's Mercury station wagon, which John had borrowed for the day. Chris, who was four at the time, was playing in the back of the car, leaning out over the rear gate. The window closed. His neck was caught, his windpipe crushed. He was rushed to the hospital, but little could be done. He lay in a coma. Doctors ran one test after another. Thirteen days later, they told John and Ellen that Chris's brain damage was irreversible. He would remain in a coma, they said, a vegetable, for years to come until, one day, he would quietly die.

The Cunninghams were devastated.

"We lost our youth that day," says Ellen. "All of a sudden, you look at everything differently. You lose your carefree attitude. John clammed up. He couldn't talk about it."

The doctors advised them to start over again. John took the advice. Ellen couldn't. "I wasn't ready to say goodbye," she says.

Ellen visited Chris daily, but John could not bring himself to go nearly as often. That summer, John, Ellen, and their infant daughter, Erin, moved in with John's brother Bill and his wife and three girls. They couldn't bear to be alone. Bill and his wife were a great help. Having lost a son three years earlier to spinal meningitis, they understood the unrelenting nature of the pain.

For a long time, John wanted to escape the thoughts of Chris's accident that invariably came during any quiet moment. He needed distraction. He wanted to be out mixing and mingling all the time, with hardly a rest — Friday night, Saturday night, Sunday. It exhausted Ellen. She became terribly depressed.

Hurting badly, John looked for anesthesia and found it at Wang Laboratories. Others would go home at a reasonable hour in the evening, would try to take weekends off, would avoid too much travel. Not John

Cunningham. No hour was too late for work. Saturdays were no different from Tuesdays. And travel — he would go anywhere they wanted, at any time, with no notice whatsoever.

"It was the right answer for him," says Ellen, a pretty, petite woman who looks ten years younger than she is.

Says his brother Bill: "Work was how he was going to burn this off. He was going to make a name for himself. He dedicated himself to being awful goddamn successful."

In some respects, the elements of success were in John Cunningham's genes. His father, Bill, had been a natural salesman. Though he was a professional educator and served as teacher and headmaster of several Boston public schools during his career, he worked part-time at a Chevy dealership in Boston to earn extra money. He would do little things after the sale that might make customers think well of him and draw them back when they bought their next car. He collected empty baby-food jars, washed them out, and, whenever he made a sale, filled the jar with the precise color of paint on the customer's new car. That way, if the car was nicked, the customer could do a touch-up job himself. Growing up in Dorchester, Bill had been a soda jerk, the kind of man, says son Bill Jr., who could have "six people in line, wait on one at a time, and keep the other five happy."

John Cunningham inherited that ability from his father. And some of it may have been passed down from his maternal grandfather, an executive at Boston Edison who was on track to becoming president of Edison when he died at age thirty-five from diabetes.

The combination of inherited talent, sheer brainpower, and the prodigious amount of work he had put into the company caught An Wang's eye. Wang liked this young Cunningham, liked him very much. Wang and Cunningham, in fact, had a relationship that was unique within the company.

It would be difficult to imagine a less likely combination. An Wang, a product of wartime China. John Cunningham, a Boston Irish Catholic. Together, they looked like Mutt and Jeff: Cunningham was a florid-faced, jowly Irishman, well over six feet tall, slightly overweight. He smiled often and sometimes spoke out of the side of his mouth, giving him the air of a wisecracking street kid. He moved quickly without seeming hurried and he had a remarkable knack for lightning-fast thinking on his feet. He was so articulate that he was able to speak, extemporaneously, in what sounded like complete, polished sentences and paragraphs. He had the kind of personality to which people warm quickly. The Doctor, in contrast, was short, trim, and noticeably uncomfortable in almost any social setting. He was terribly inarticulate and spoke in fragments of poor English, sometimes punctuated by a stutter.

Ironically, the success of their relationship lay in their marked differences.

"John was everything the Doctor wasn't," says Bob Ano, who worked as an assistant to Cunningham. "It was a very good, dynamic relationship."

Cunningham did not leave the success of his association with Doctor Wang to chance. "I worked hard to build a relationship with him," recalls Cunningham. "He's hard to follow, has difficulty communicating. For three or four years in the early '70s, when he would tell me to do something, I would say to him, 'Would you please explain that again to me. I want to make sure I do what you want me to do.' So he would explain it to me again, and I'd go off and do what he really wanted me to do." Others in the company were fearful of asking Wang too many times to clarify his meaning. Instead, they guessed what he wanted. As a result, they did some of what he requested, or even most of it. But they would be off — sometimes by a lot, other times by just a bit. Because he questioned Wang so closely, Cunningham was almost never off.

By the middle of the 1970s, there was genuine trust between Wang and Cunningham, a greater level of trust than Wang had in any other non-Asian. Perhaps the only person at the company to whom Wang was closer was Harry H. S. Chou, the company comptroller, who was Chinese, about Wang's age, and a personal friend.

Cunningham adapted a style with which he thought Doctor Wang would be comfortable. "I was very quiet, very careful about what I said," he recalls. "I did not show much emotion. I tried to be as Chinese as I could. I was the inscrutable Irishman. I was as Chinese as a kid from West Roxbury could be.

"Harry and the Doctor thought I was a good listener, a good compromiser," he says. "They thought I was not a loud-mouthed American."

Others at the company marveled at the Wang-Cunningham relationship. Theirs was an "incredible combination of respect and trust," says Peter McElroy, a marketing man.

A key moment in Cunningham's rise to power came in the spring of 1975 after Gerry Jones, a bright Harvard Law School graduate who had represented Wang on Wall Street, left the company. Before the initial public offering of the B stock, several company officials had gathered together to prepare for an important meeting in New York with analysts at Moody's Investors Service. Cunningham was involved in the preparation session but he was not scheduled to go to New York. He worked sales and marketing, not finance. But as they prepared, it became clear to Cunningham that he would be able to help at the presentation, that perhaps he could fill a void left by Jones's departure.

He said to Harry Chou, who was leading the Wang team to New York: "Why don't I put together five or six flip charts explaining our technical and company strategy and our distribution strategy, and go with you?" Chou thought it was a good idea. Cunningham went along and his presentation was a hit. He appeared relaxed standing in front of a room full of financial analysts. He was a natural politician who could work a room with ease. Cunningham made sure he was always available to Wall Street financial people looking for an understanding of the company, and he quickly gained credibility among analysts, many of whom developed a personal liking for him as well as professional respect.

It was a perfect match for the Doctor, who hated going down to Wall Street. He neither liked nor trusted the financial community, and feared they would try to get their hands on part of his company. He saw them as a threat to his control of Wang Laboratories.

It was very unusual for a small and growing company's CEO not to attend such Wall Street meetings, but Doctor Wang hated them so much that he happily accepted Cunningham's offer to stand in for him. Cunningham even managed to turn the Doctor's absence to an advantage. Invariably, analysts would ask who the CEO was and where he was. Cunningham would fill them in on the Doctor's background, mentioning his work on core memory at the Harvard Computation Lab. And he would say that Doctor Wang was unable to be present because "he's in the back room with a soldering iron inventing the next new product." To the analysts, the image of a mysterious Chinese genius in the lab was irresistible.

In 1976, the Doctor put Cunningham in charge of all the company's external communications — advertising, public relations, dealings with financial analysts.

Perhaps the best measure of how trusting and close a relationship existed between Cunningham and Doctor Wang was Mrs. Wang's reference to Cunningham as "our American son."

Though Fred Wang never considered Cunningham his American

brother — far from it — even he reserved high praise for Cunningham's ability: "John was terrific at growing the sales force at a time when we couldn't get the best people. The company was small and the top college graduates chose IBM. John created an organization that was very good for what it needed to do. He had the personality, that glib style of his. He captured customers, the press, and analysts. He was into sound bites before they were popular. He's a very intelligent guy."

And he worked his way up in the company in an intelligent manner. Both of Cunningham's older brothers, Bill and Paul, had worked at Burroughs, the big computer company, and his brother-in-law was at Honeywell. John constantly quizzed them about the business until he felt he had a fairly keen understanding of Burroughs, a company for which he had never worked a day in his life. And he took the lessons of Burroughs and applied the best of what he had learned to Wang Labs.

If there was a crucial asset that allowed Cunningham to climb the ladder at Wang, it was range. He understood and was comfortable not only with sales, but also with marketing, finance, distribution, and even research and development. He could glad-hand with the sales guys, peer into the future with the marketing people, speak the language of the techies, and talk the intricacies of the financial world on Wall Street.

"He can charm a venture capital audience; he's terrific with people on the Street," says David Fine, a former IBM vice-president who later worked as a consultant in the computer industry and got to know Cunningham while he consulted to Wang Labs. "John understood like few guys in sales the technical side, pricing, and economics. He understands the total business. He's one of the smartest guys I've met."

"You won't find anybody who is as bright and as good with people," says Bill Dixon. "You'll find people who are brighter and you'll find people who are better with people, but you'll never find people with both."

In the fall of 1981, Cunningham was offered the job of president of Prime Computer, a fast-growing Massachusetts-based maker of minicomputers. It was a very big deal, indeed, for a thirty-eight-year-old man to have a chance to take over such a dynamic company. But Cunningham was so confident of his relationship with Doctor Wang and believed so strongly in his future at Wang Labs that he turned the job down. The Prime board wanted him badly enough that they approached him again with a sweetened offer. But, again, he turned it down. His future was at Wang Laboratories.

"I was in a good position with Wang," says Cunningham. "I liked the way the Wang stock looked for '82 and '83. I had a lot of loyalty to Wang. I felt in his debt." Much of the loyalty stemmed from Doctor Wang's generosity in establishing a trust fund to help care for Chris Cunningham for the rest of his life. "It was very private," says Cunningham. "He never told anybody. It was personal funds from he and Mrs. Wang. It made the company a special place. Doctor Wang was a kind of father figure to me."

Besides, Wang was a hot company and Cunningham was having fun "riding a boat traveling fast and high in the water."

When he turned down the job, the *Boston Globe* reported the story and portrayed Cunningham in a very favorable light, stating that he was "the architect and developer of the company's marketing and sales success. . . . Since joining the company in 1967, he has become the senior Wang's closest business adviser."

He stayed because of money, as well. He could make a great deal at Prime, he knew, but he could make more — probably much more — at Wang. He wanted financial independence, and by that time he had $10 million in Wang stock. "I didn't like growing up in West Roxbury and having no fucking money," he says. "If my parents ever had to write a $500 check, they wouldn't have been able to do it. They never had $1,000 in their savings account. You never had any reserve kitty on a teacher's salary.

"Money means independence. It means being able to do pretty much anything I want to do. And there's a certain amount of scorekeeping. 'Hey, you've done pretty well.'"

Jack Connors, CEO of Hill Holliday Connors Cosmopulos, Boston's largest advertising agency, is one of Cunningham's closest friends. "To John, money is life's report card," says Connors. "John just wanted the money early. He learned early on that the next generation may not happen."

Cunningham was also enthralled by the perquisites of the executive suite. Bob Ano recalls that "he liked to play at being big-time executive. John enjoyed the trappings of office — fancy cars, private planes, helicopters."

The offer from Prime was public affirmation of Cunningham's value as a corporate leader. He was very close to the top of one of the great business success stories of the time. His relationship with Doctor Wang was superb; he was recognized outside the company as a major player. And his family had survived the trauma of Chris's accident and the ongoing pain of his continued existence in a vegetative state. Time had helped heal the terrible wounds inflicted by that event on both him and Ellen. The Cunninghams had had another baby, a girl, and their two daughters were growing up into healthy, happy kids.

But there was something nagging Cunningham. It wasn't a big deal, but it did bother him. And that was Fred Wang. The Doctor had said he was going to put Fred in charge of the product-planning section of R&D. Cunningham was concerned about that. It was clear to him that Fred wasn't up to the task.

During the summer, Cunningham told the Doctor of his concerns about Fred. "You can't do this unless you're there watching over him," Cunningham told Wang.

The Doctor promised Cunningham that he intended to keep a very close eye on Fred. Reassured, Cunningham felt free to take off and plunge into the company's European business. Domestic operations were in terrific shape and things were going very well in Australia, South America, Canada, and Asia. Europe needed work, and Cunningham headed over there. But this would be no ordinary business trip. This would be different. Ellen Cunningham had always wanted to get a taste of European life, and her husband was about to give it to her.

During the first week in September 1980, the Cunninghams, their two daughters, Erin and Trisha, and a baby-sitter flew to Paris, where they took up residence in not just any hotel, but the elegant Hotel Crillon. And in not just any room, but the suite of eight rooms that Richard M. Nixon had occupied while, as president of the United States, he had visited Paris. A suite that cost Wang Laboratories $700 a night.

Ellen recalls that although the company could hardly have been enjoying more success, Cunningham worried on and off while in Paris that fall. Sometimes he was comforted by the Doctor's promise to watch closely over Fred; sometimes the prospect of Fred running the product-planning section of R&D terrified him. It got to the point where Cunningham decided he had to sell some stock, to set aside some cash for the family just in case the company went bad. Not a lot of cash, maybe a half million dollars. It became an obsession with him, yet he was reluctant to sell because he thought the Doctor would see it as an act of disloyalty. Normally very decisive, Cunningham wavered. By late fall he was worrying about it constantly. It was so bad that one night in Paris, he began having heart palpitations. Ellen was terrified. Just do it, sell it, she told him. John sold it.

Cunningham would work during the week — in Stockholm, Vienna, London, Frankfurt — and return to Paris on weekends to be with his family. When the weather in Paris grew chilly in mid-November, the Cunninghams moved down to Monte Carlo. They remained in Europe until just before Christmas, when they returned home.

It had not been your average business trip. In fact, it had cost Wang Laboratories more than $70,000. "I could do anything I wanted to do. Business was cranking good; my career was cranking good."

Cranking good was an understatement.

SEVEN

The Runaway Horse

ALTHOUGH Wang had made huge strides during the mid-1970s, the company was still largely unknown. Among those few who recognized the name, it was still widely thought of as "Wang, the calculator company." But advertising was about to relieve Wang Labs of its anonymity.

The hiring of an advertising agency was accomplished in a characteristic Cunningham fashion. In 1974, when it was obvious the company needed a professional agency, Cunningham invited two of Boston's most prominent agencies to pitch the business. On a whim, he threw a third company into the competition. Cunningham had been at a planning meeting for his Boston College tenth reunion and had heard a fellow alumnus who happened to be in the advertising business make an impressive speech. Cunningham told his secretary to track the man down and offer his agency a chance to pitch the Wang account.

In search of the BC adman, Cunningham's secretary found Jack Connors, president of Hill Holliday Connors Cosmopulos. She told Connors that Cunningham had seen him speak at a BC reunion meeting and wondered whether Connors would be interested in coming in to discuss the account. Connors, who had graduated from BC a year before Cunningham, was surprised by the call because his agency, which billed only $8 million annually, was far smaller and younger than the other two Boston companies going after the business. But Connors was also delighted because he very badly wanted a piece of business in the computer industry.

A meeting was set up and on the appointed day Connors was shown into Cunningham's office. When Connors walked in, Cunningham looked at him and realized he had never laid eyes on him before in his life. He asked Connors, "Who are you?"

"I'm not the guy you thought I was because I've never spoken to a BC reunion meeting," said Connors with a smile.

They laughed about it and talked anyway. It would have been difficult to imagine two men who would hit it off faster and better than Cunningham and Connors. Both were BC grads, both were Irish Catholics. They were smart, engaging men only a year apart in age, and it turned out that they had grown up within about a half mile of each other. Now, both were ambitious young businessmen on their way up. Connors saw the Wang account as a way to boost his agency's prestige in the Boston advertising community, and he desperately wanted to win it. Weeks later, after the three agencies had made their pitches, Cunningham called him.

"Humphrey Browning gave a better pitch," Cunningham told Connors. "They were more professional, they did a better job, they're bigger."

But Cunningham told Connors he needed someone with whom he felt comfortable, someone he could trust. He also wanted control. This was essential to Cunningham. Although he was then head of marketing — and therefore in charge of the company's advertising — he was about to be moved out of that job to head up sales. As the leader of the sales organization, he would not have line authority for advertising, but he was confident that he understood better than anyone else at Wang what the company's public themes should be.

"Nothing's going to happen unless you check it through me," Cunningham told Connors.

"Trust me," said Connors. "If we get this, I'll check everything through you."

Connors got the account.

Before Jack Connors, Wang's advertising program was standard for a computer company, with the great bulk of its advertisements concentrated in trade journals. In 1976, survey research found that the campaign wasn't working very well. On an unaided-awareness scale — in which an interviewer from a market research firm asked people chosen at random to name as many major computer companies as they could think of — Wang was mentioned by only 3 percent of those surveyed. On an aided-awareness scale — in which the interviewer read off a list of companies and asked the respondent to identify which were computer companies —

Wang was recognized by 10 percent. Put another way, 90 percent of those surveyed had never heard of Wang Labs.

Connors concluded that Wang Labs could not break out of the pack without a dramatic shift in its advertising strategy. He was struck by how extraordinarily competitive the computer business was and how rapidly things changed, and he made the case to Cunningham that Wang should do something radically different: advertise on network television.

On its face, the idea was crazy. Wang's advertising budget was all of $400,000. For that kind of money, you couldn't make much more than a short-term dent in a local television market, never mind a network. But Connors believed that the advertising was being asked to accomplish far too much and with the wrong tools. When Wang salespeople got in the door, their products all but sold themselves. The problem was getting in the door. That prospective customers didn't know the Wang name meant having to spend more time breaking down initial barriers. Cunningham wanted the advertising to pave the way for his sales force, but Connors said that if the company continued to rely on print ads, the Wang name would become known much too slowly, and Wang would be left in the dust of the coming computer industry frenzy.

"You'll never do it this way, there's not enough time," Connors told Cunningham. "You've got to jump-start this sucker. It will be easier for your salesmen to close a deal. They can't love you unless they know you. This is a very fast track. The fastest way to get known is television."

The only computer companies advertising on network television were the giants — IBM, Xerox, and Honeywell — and most of their money went into sponsoring public service programs. It was years before all the major computer companies began selling their products on the networks. His idea was a gamble, but Connors convinced Cunningham of its merit, and Cunningham, in turn, persuaded the Doctor that television advertising made sense for Wang because "TV could make a little company look big-time."

Wang was persuaded. The company could afford to produce one spot only and chose the Hill Holliday idea of a spoof on a corporate David versus Goliath.

The scene is a boardroom. The fat-cat president stands at the head of a long conference table surrounded by obsequious staffers who nod agreement at his every word. He leans across the table and says: "Let's buy our small computer from the giant computer company." And as he looks down at a slight young man at the other end of the table, he adds: "You can't beat Goliath. Right, David?"

Smiling, spunky David disagrees. "Sir, let's go with Wang. Nobody makes a better small computer or word processor. They're giant-killers!"

And as the rock from David's hand causes the entire boardroom to shake and knocks paintings off the wall, a voice-over says: "It happened before. It can happen again. Because nobody's hungrier than Wang."

It was a fiesty, attention-grabbing spot that industry people found titillating for its direct assault on IBM. Hill Holliday wanted to air the commercial during the 1978 Super Bowl, but it was far too expensive. Instead, Connors bought thirty seconds on the Super Bowl pregame show for $150,000 — $5,000 per second. The people at Hill Holliday also pushed their contacts at CBS to air the commercial as close to game time as possible. On Super Bowl Sunday, the Wang brass sat back to watch, and they could hardly believe what they saw. The commercial didn't just run close to the beginning of the game; it was the very last spot during the pregame show! It was like getting the first commercial during the game and vastly better than having it run later in the game, when the audience had dwindled. A mammoth audience — tens of millions of people — was watching when the Wang commercial aired. And the effect was dramatic.

"Everybody in the fucking world saw that spot," recalls Cunningham.

The Wang sales force was ecstatic, and customers were impressed. The spot ran periodically in the following months, and research showed it had been an overwhelming success. Unaided-awareness of Wang increased from 3 percent to 14 percent. Aided-awareness jumped from 10 percent to an impressive 35 percent. The Wang people had only one fear — that other computer companies would quickly catch on to how effective television advertising was for them. In fact, Ken Fisher, then CEO at Prime Computer, would run into Cunningham from time to time and ask how the TV advertising was working. Cunningham would innocently reply that it really hadn't worked and was a mistake. In truth, of course, it was working beautifully.

"That TV advertising put Wang on the map," says Cunningham. "It was a nothing company everybody thought was a big deal."

The advertising was timed perfectly to open doors for the salespeople. And once a Wang salesperson was face-to-face with a prospective customer, the rest was easy, for the truth was that Wang Labs was offering some of the finest computer products in the world, products so good that one industry analyst heard numerous IBM customers telling Big Blue, when it was about to come out with a new product, to "build it like Wang."

These superb products triggered a period of growth so spectacular that in July 1979 analyst John Adams observed, "Wang's growth is now the fastest of any major [company] in the business. Moreover, we believe it will continue so for the next 12 months at least. Our confidence is based on the company's product line. . . ."

Like other analysts, Adams greatly admired the stars of the Wang line, the 2200 small-business computer and the word processing system, which was jumping off the delivery trucks. In 1978, another blockbuster was added to the Wang line: the VS minicomputer.

By the late 1970s, minicomputers were taking a sizable bite out of the mainframe business. Companies and government offices found that minis efficiently performed many of the functions previously reserved for mainframes at far less cost. "Minicomputer" was a misleading description. The image it conjured up was of a small, even tiny, machine, a meek little box with modest ability. In truth, though they were small compared to the massive mainframes, minicomputers could be as large as a refrigerator — and they were surprisingly powerful.

Doctor Wang and John Cunningham were eager to enter the minicomputer sweepstakes, where profit margins were fat and where the market was easily large enough to accommodate Wang, along with Digital Equipment Corporation, which dominated the mini market, and other small but hard-charging contenders such as Data General and Prime.

A Wang Labs development group headed by Robert A. Siegel, a brilliant, abrasive young designer with shaggy hair, a mustache, and glasses, had been working to build a minicomputer since the early 1970s. Siegel was very much like Harold Koplow — a creative genius with a gargantuan ego. He was a wunderkind who joined PHI as a programmer when he was barely twenty-two. In his rumpled corduroys, Siegel looked like a man who had lost count of how many Grateful Dead concerts he had gone to. At Wang, he was known to be brilliantly creative, but he was also an absolutist with little willingness to compromise. Siegel's attitude was that he was right and anyone who disagreed with him was not only wrong but probably stupid as well. A native New Yorker with an extraordinary competitive instinct, he had little respect for opinions that clashed with his. He was an intense and deadly serious young man.

He had made enough progress on the new Wang mini that some company officials believed the machine should have been announced much earlier. But Siegel would not allow it out the door until it was perfect, strange as that was in an industry where incomplete products are commonly announced. However, no one within the company wanted to trifle with Siegel. The talk around Wang was that once, when Siegel was passionately making a point during a meeting, Doctor Wang and Fred Wang entered the room — and he ordered them out.

The computer that Siegel's team produced was called the Wang VS. It had many of the characteristics of a mainframe computer because it was essentially modeled after the popular IBM 360.

"The VS was very easy to operate," says John Cunningham. "There were a lot of minis for scientific and engineering purposes from DEC, HP, and Data General. The Wang VS was one of the first minis for commercial application."

The toughest test of the VS was competition from the now legendary VAX computer, which was announced by Digital only weeks after the debut of the VS in October 1977. In sales, the VS more than held its own against the VAX, and for business needs, the VS proved vastly superior to the VAX.

When the VS fully hit the marketplace in 1979, it gave Wang its third hot product. The 2200 small-business computer continued selling well, and the Wang Word Processing System had become an industry phenomenon. Most high-tech companies would have been more than delighted with a single product as popular as any one of Wang's three top sellers. Collectively through the years, the 2200, the VS, and the word processing system would yield *billions* of dollars of revenues for Wang Laboratories. These three remarkable products were attributable to four men. Thousands of Wang employees contributed to the cause, of course, but the success of these three offerings could be traced back to the three technology team leaders who, along with Doctor Wang, had developed the products. Bob Siegel guided the VS team. Koplow led the word processing group. And Bob Kolk guided the 2200 development.

Kolk was very different from Siegel and Koplow. He was older by a half-dozen years, and he more readily listened to others' views. He had graduated from MIT in 1958 and had gone to work for North American Aviation, the company that would later become Rockwell International. He earned a master's degree in engineering from the University of Southern California and joined PHI in 1966 when it was the hottest software house around. While Siegel shunned social activities at PHI, however,

Kolk participated enthusiastically in company softball games and beer parties.

At Wang, Kolk gained a reputation as smart and reliable. Though he wasn't considered as flashy an intellect as either Koplow or Siegel, he was respected for his steadiness. Kolk was particularly popular among the salespeople, who appreciated his willingness to listen to what customers wanted in products. Kolk, in fact, was quite skillful in his dealings with customers, far smoother than most R&D people.

Other than their success, the three men held in common only one thing: a mutual enmity. At times, hostilities even broke into the open.

But that problem was solved by the fourth man to whom the company's technological success could be attributed — An Wang.

During the early glory years, from about 1977 through 1981, An Wang was as untraditional a CEO as there was at an American company. For he was not only CEO but he was also chief of development — the man who presided, day-to-day, over the R&D operation. Throughout the company's most successful years, An Wang was intimately involved in the running of his company, but he paid vastly more attention to R&D during the early part of that period than he did during the later part. John Cunningham estimates that before 1981, Wang spent fully 65 percent of his time working on development projects. This is one of the reasons the products were so good. He didn't merely assign a product development task to a team and forget about it for six months; he worked with the team day in and day out. He moved from one development meeting to the next, listening to plans and ideas, tossing out comments here and there. He spent endless hours in meetings with Harold Koplow, working on refinements to the word processing system; he worked with Bob Kolk to develop a personal computer; and he labored extensively with Bob Siegel on the original VS and its subsequent generations.

Up until about 1981, when the company rose from its extraordinary success to become some sort of phenomenon, the Doctor spent about 20 percent of his time on corporate matters such as the company's finances, the marketing and sales plan, and so on. Only about 15 percent of his time went to various functions with employees and customers. These lunches, dinners, and cocktail parties were not the Doctor's strength, and he did his best to avoid them. But when his sales managers from throughout the world or the country gathered in Boston or Lowell, he felt compelled to show up. With regular meetings of manufacturing managers, distribution managers, sales managers, and others, the Doctor spent at least two nights a week on the Route 128 rubber-chicken circuit.

Largely because of his fear of flying, the Doctor did very little traveling during this period. His annual vacation to Europe was on a cruise ship, and his irregular forays from Lowell to New York were by limousine.

On an average day, the Doctor would arrive at work at about 8:30 or 8:45 A.M., ride the elevator from the basement of the building where his driver kept the car, to his penthouse office, where he would immediately plunge into a day's worth of meetings. Most included development people and involved the nitty-gritty of how to make products better, bigger, faster, and more salable. He was rarely far from a blackboard and thoroughly enjoyed the intellectual give and take with the likes of Koplow, Siegel, and Kolk.

He met daily with Cunningham and Harry Chou to discuss financial matters, and to talk over any major decisions or to deal with any problems. He customarily lunched alone at the Lanam Club in North Andover, and he headed home at about 6:00 or 6:30 with a full briefcase. He worked a slightly shorter day on Saturdays, and he generally avoided going into the office on Sundays, although of course he worked at home.

The Doctor was the key to the company's success. But the Wang Labs' secret was not only An Wang's visionary technical ability. It was the combination of that ability and his remarkable skill as manager of R&D. As Wang Labs grew into a huge worldwide company, it became more important that Doctor Wang manage the technology groups than that he do the development work himself. One of the most difficult tasks facing the leader of any technology company is determining which R&D projects of the dozens or hundreds proposed get pursued. Even in a company Wang's size, there were only so many projects that the company had the money and brainpower to undertake. In a business in which bad R&D decisions could be calamitous, Wang was a genius at identifying the right projects.

Perhaps most important, Doctor Wang had an uncanny knack for managing the design team leaders. Whether they were arrogant or abrasive, as Koplow and Siegel were capable of being, or quiet and restrained, as Kolk so often was, the Doctor knew how to draw great work out of them. He had, says Cunningham, "a unique ability to manage crazy people." He kept Koplow, Kolk, and Siegel apart while setting them in competition with one another. Wang believed that this sort of intensely competitive, two-scorpions-in-a-bottle management would result in the best products for the company.

"The Doctor let Siegel, Kolk, and Koplow fight," says Dale Jelley, an engineer. "He encouraged them to fight. The way he managed it, it was a productive conflict."

Kolk says the Doctor gave plenty of freedom to each of the development groups. As a result, quality work was produced, and "within each one there was an awful lot of esprit de corps."

Because the Doctor was himself an inventor, says Siegel, "he knew you weren't going to win every time. He knew that if you don't take risks you get left behind because the world is changing so quickly. Under Doctor Wang you could reach and stretch and push."

Siegel looked the part of a slightly mad scientist, and that's what the Wang atmosphere allowed him to be. When he came to Wang in the late 1960s after the company acquired PHI, he was immediately enchanted with An Wang. "He was an inscrutable oriental," says Siegel. "He was not talkative. You had to figure out what he wanted. He would sit back, puffing his pipe and listening. I wanted approval for something and I explained my idea. He listened and said nothing. The meeting broke up and Harold Koplow said, 'Congratulations.' I said, 'For what?' He said, 'Doctor Wang approved your project.' I said, 'I didn't hear him say that.' And Koplow said, 'Well, he didn't say not to do it.'"

What thrilled Siegel most about Wang Labs during the 1970s was its emphasis on merit. "Doctor Wang loved the blackboard," recalls Siegel. "He always had one or two in his office. In the early days, I was a young kid with no power. But it didn't make any difference. Anybody with an idea could jump up to the blackboard, grab the chalk, and start drawing. It didn't matter who you were. It was the idea. With a good one, he'd get very excited. And, of course, he was brilliant and would grasp things right away. It was very easy for good ideas to surface."

Though Wang Labs was an intellectual meritocracy, the truth during the early and mid-1970s, when the VS was being developed, was that Wang was a financially strapped company, and decisions about which development projects to fund were not at all easy. But An Wang believed in the VS. He was convinced that the company could compete effectively in the minicomputer market, and he bankrolled the VS development project through some thin times. It was a visionary decision.

During the late 1970s, Wang was breaking out of the pack of high-technology companies so fast and with such style that the news media couldn't help but notice. By December 1979, it was becoming clearer that Wang was on the cutting edge of the computer revolution. The *Boston Globe*'s well-respected business writer, Robert Lenzner, looked at Wang and liked what he saw.

> Move over, Digital Equipment. Get going, Data General.
>
> Here comes Wang Laboratories, around the turn, making a hell of a run.
>
> Sales of word processors and minicomputers have risen spectacularly from $75.8 million in 1975 to $321.6 million last year. Profits per share have done better, from 16 cents a share five years ago to $1.17.
>
> The future may even be better. Revenues were up to 70 percent in the three months ended Sept. 30, on the way to $510 million for 1980, in the opinion of Adams, Harkness & Hill, the Boston brokerage that follows Wang. Profits of $1.90 a share are expected. . . .
>
> . . . Wang's performance is amazing when you consider their competition. In the computer area are [IBM], Hewlett-Packard, Digital Equipment and Data General. Wang's success in word processors has been against the likes of IBM, Xerox and Exxon. It is no small feat that the Wang technology is revolutionizing office work.

Not quite two months later, the *Washington Post* weighed in with its ode to Wang:

> To hear a lot of people these days, American business is in deep trouble. The auto and steel industries are in a slump. The United States is falling behind on new technology. Competitive spirit is on the wane.
>
> Not at Wang Laboratories Inc.
>
> While some U.S. firms may be fighting desperately to stay alive, the big problem here at Wang is how to slow the company's explosive — and admittedly unmanageable — growth pace:
>
> Since 1977, the Lowell-based computer maker has been growing at an average 67 percent annual rate — a staggering pace that company executives concede is unsustainable and must be arrested in the next two or three years.

It was August 1979 and Ted Leonsis was ecstatic at how well the announcement of the Wang Integrated Information Systems (IIS) had gone. The function room at the Marriott Essex House Hotel on Central Park South had been full of analysts and reporters bearing witness to the debut of the IIS, the latest Wang offering. Though IIS was not a landmark or breakthrough the way the word processing system or the VS had been, it was a nice addition to the Wang product line, for it combined those two wildly popular machines into one product. It seemed to Leonsis, a Wang public relations man, that the company had no end of superior products.

On the warm summer evening after the IIS announcement, Leonsis and Courtney Wang, the second Wang son, younger than Fred by six years, headed to the Marriott bar overlooking Central Park. Courtney, who had joined the company a year earlier, fresh out of Tufts, was flushed with excitement from the event.

Leonsis, who wasn't much older, was excited as well. After a drink or two the young men began talking about the future of the company. The more they talked, the more convinced they became that Wang Labs would eclipse IBM one day in the not-too-distant future. So sure were they of this vision that they took a large Wang envelope and wrote down the prediction that Wang would be the largest computer company in the world by the year 2000. Both men signed it.

"We believed it," Leonsis recalls.

They were not the only ones who embraced this astonishing goal. It was sometime in 1979 that Wang Laboratories became infused with an almost mystical belief in itself, when employees began to believe that there was something magical about their company. They looked around and saw competitors struggling mightily to find one hot product while Wang had three. Wang people saw that they were competing head on in two major markets with none other than IBM, and they were winning!

That pleased An Wang immensely, for he had never much liked or even respected IBM. Long after IBM had bought his core memory patent, he was left with a sour taste about the company. In later years he would make statements about IBM that would eventually prove to be embarrassing. He said that IBM was "not innovative" and that IBM was "not that formidable." Wang was rarely an emotional man, yet IBM seemed to reveal what little irrationality lay within him. He never would forget the extreme scrutiny to which IBM had subjected his core memory patent, and the way in which IBM had used its enormous resources to squeeze a lone man, who had just started in business with nothing. Wang always believed his patent was worth far more than the $400,000 he was paid, but at the time, believing he had little chance of getting any more money from IBM, he had accepted the offer.

Later, after Wang Labs began to take off, IBM — as it had done with every other major computer company — requested that Wang pay a fee for a license to use certain technologies on which IBM owned the patents. Other companies had routinely signed the agreements and paid IBM a small fee. IBM wanted only a couple of hundred thousand dollars from Wang, and Wang's lawyers urged the Doctor to sign. But Wang resisted. He wanted to give IBM neither satisfaction nor money. His lawyers told him he had no choice. And they pointed out that the amount of money involved was a pittance for a company Wang's size.

Reluctantly, Wang signed. Soon after he had done so he received an invitation from Frank Carey, then president of IBM, to lunch at IBM. Carey's interest was in having a pleasant chat about the industry and in thanking Wang for working out the licensing arrangement. It was more a social call than anything else. Although an invitation from Carey, chief of the world's largest computer corporation, was a coveted item, Doctor Wang told his people he had no intention of traveling all the way to New York for the lunch. In one of the few acts of petulance in his career, Wang said he would do it only if Carey met him halfway. And so they dined in Hartford. As it turned out, Wang found Carey a charming lunch partner, and the Doctor thoroughly enjoyed their visit.

But the lunch did nothing to diminish Wang's ambition. Jack Connors remembers being in Wang's office one day when the Doctor pulled out a chart on which he had plotted Wang's growth and projected that Wang Laboratories would overtake IBM sometime in the middle of the 1990s. "He had kept it for a long time," says Connors. "And he *believed* it."

IBM was forty times Wang's size, but that didn't matter to the Doctor, says Cunningham. "He thought we could grow 25 percent a year and in something like 1999 we would pass IBM."

Wang believed it so intensely that at one point he wanted to place an ad in the *Wall Street Journal* comparing the growth of Wang and IBM. Staff members stonewalled and he eventually dropped the idea.

There were other true believers at the company as well. "We were going to beat IBM," recalls publications manager Karen Smith Palmer. "We were going head-to-head with Big Blue, and we were going to win! We really believed it. It seemed as though anything was possible."

Who was going to tell An Wang and his acolytes that it couldn't be done, that the notion of overtaking IBM would one day seem laughable? In the late 1970s and early '80s Wang Laboratories was, after all, racking up growth numbers the likes of which had rarely been seen as the company doubled in size every other year! Wang was proving itself one of the greatest business success stories ever. "Wang seized an opportunity and did as well with it as any company I've ever seen," says George Rich, a consultant to high-technology companies who had experience at IBM,

Digital, and Hewlett-Packard. Rich, who was also a member of the board of Amdahl, a manufacturer of mainframes, spent most of 1979 through 1982 consulting to Wang.

The explosion was touched off by the Wang Word Processing System in 1976, when the company's revenues totaled $97 million. By 1978, revenues had more than doubled, to $198 million. They doubled again two years later, and again two years after that. It was hard to believe, but true: From just 1977 to 1982, Wang Laboratories grew nearly tenfold!

In November 1979, John Adams's enthusiasm was unbridled. "For the past five quarters, the demand for Wang products has been nothing short of incredible. . . . We are aware of no company which has crashed the half billion dollar mark while growing at a rate in excess of fifty percent."

The number of employees had grown so fast it was hard for company officials to believe what was happening around them. From 1978 to 1983, the head count went from 4,000 to 24,800.

Karen Smith Palmer joined the company in late 1981. She recalls huge waves of new employees cascading into the company's offices for orientation classes each Monday morning. Some weeks there would be literally hundreds of new people charging in to join the ranks. When Beth Riley joined Wang in 1980, there were thirty people in her group, but, after just a few months, there were one hundred and fifty, and, after that, they stopped counting.

"It was very upbeat, very exciting," says Palmer. "There were lots of new, bright, young people. We were in the eye of the storm. Just to *be* there, to walk around, was a very heady feeling."

So rapidly had the company expanded that it was not long before thousands of employees were crammed into space intended for half their number. The company's efforts to build enough work space were utterly futile, for people poured in much faster than workers could build. It meant that there were two, three, sometimes four employees shoehorned into a small office meant for one person.

But nobody cared. They were working for the hottest, most exciting, and fastest-growing company in the hottest, most exciting, and fastest-growing industry on earth.

Amidst all the growth the Wang work force had quickly outgrown even the company's greatly expanded Tewksbury facility. From the original building, the Doctor had built seven major additions in just eleven years. But he needed still more space. Wang considered building yet another addition at Tewksbury and found that a 60,000-square-foot warehouse would cost $1.3 million. Company officials checked prices in Lowell and discovered they could buy excellent space for much less money. The Lowell building the company found, in fact, would give Wang Labs five times as much space for about the same price as a Tewksbury addition.

Lowell city officials had been looking to take advantage of the high-technology boom in Massachusetts, but their hopes had been pinned on a big company such as DEC or IBM, which could come in and instantly solve the city's economic problems. Wang wasn't DEC or IBM, but it wasn't bad.

As Wang Labs thrived, so did the city and its people. Generations before An Wang arrived, Lowell had been as prosperous a city as any in the United States. Its massive red-brick factories were bursting at the seams with tens of thousands of New England farm girls diligently working their looms and turning out more textiles than any other city in the country. It was here, with the Merrimack River powering dozens of mills along her shores, that the American Industrial Revolution was born. When Francis Cabot Lowell appropriated the design for a power loom and brought it to America, the city was ready. In the middle of the nineteenth century, Lowell began what would be a near century-long period of prosperity.

When the Great Depression struck, however, the immigrants who had replaced the farm girls in Lowell's mills demanded higher wages than the cheap labor in the South. And in a great, heaving rush, the mill operations, one after the other, pulled up stakes and headed south. By the outbreak of World War II, there was no use for the Merrimack's hydro-electric power, nowhere for the immigrants in search of the American dream to work.

When the textile industry that had been its heart and soul departed, the city of Lowell collapsed. Long after the Depression had ended, Lowell seemed to retain its woeful tenor. Frozen in time, the city was a kind of modern industrial Pompeii, where an antique way of life was preserved forever. When Lowell fell on tough times, it fell hard. By the middle of the 1970s, Lowell was afflicted with the highest unemployment rate — 13.8 percent — of any city in the United States. But thanks in large measure to Wang Laboratories — and to the drive and work ethic of the people of the city — Lowell, Massachusetts, in less than a decade, would boast the *lowest* unemployment rate in the country.

The products of Lowell's terrible depression — its ample supply of energetic workers willing to toil for relatively low wages and its surplus

of cheap land — made it attractive to Doctor Wang when he went looking for space in which to expand in 1975.

The company bought sixteen acres and a 350,000-square-foot building
for the extraordinarily cheap price of $1.85 million and only $50,000 down
in cash. The Doctor turned Lowell into his corporate headquarters and
kept Tewksbury for manufacturing.

As had been the case in Tewksbury, Wang outgrew its Lowell space
quickly. When Wang moved into Lowell in 1976, it occupied only half of
its space and so rattled around in the building that Harry Chou suggested
to Doctor Wang that they rent out the rest of the property. But within a
year it was filled with Wang employees. By the late 1970s, Wang's growth
was so explosive that the company believed that it would have to build
up rather than out to handle future expansion. However, finding a building taller than a few stories in the Lowell area was all but impossible at
the time. But city officials moved mountains to clear the path for Wang.
They not only approved a zoning variance that allowed the construction
of tall buildings, but they also gerrymandered the boundaries of the city's
urban development district to enable Wang to benefit from attractive
financing rates under a federal Urban Development Action Grant, loans
designed to improve the economic health of urban areas.

When Wang set about constructing a tower, he charged his architect
with the task of building a cheap, utilitarian structure. There were to be
no extra expenses, no flourishes of any kind. Doctor Wang was a man
who had bought real estate in Tewksbury in part because massive, ugly
high-tension wires bisected the property, driving down its cost. If such
cables could be run through a building to lower its price, Wang would
have been delighted. But there were no unsightly cables to mar the opening of tower one in April 1980. The event was so significant that it
attracted both the Massachusetts governor, Edward J. King, and Senator
Paul Tsongas, a Lowell resident who would later serve on the Wang board
of directors. Company officials were delighted with the building. Though
it had been constructed quickly and cheaply, it lent the company an air
of prominence and solidity. "It was a big deal," recalls Cunningham. "It
was a building with elevators. It looked like we had real jobs. We all had
pretty nice offices" with gorgeous views. On a clear day those looking
eastward could see all the way to Boston, while those on the north side
could see the rolling hills of New Hampshire.

It was a strikingly incongruous building, twelve stories standing
naked, dwarfing the one- and two-story structures nearby. Framed against

the sky, the tower was an enormous, hulking thing that was about as well-suited to its surroundings as a geodesic dome would be in Manhattan. It was gray cement, and functional. The only grudging bit of color appeared at the top of the tower in a bright blue Wang logo.

Just two years later, the company opened tower two and almost immediately filled it with workers. Tower two appeared to be an exact replica of tower one although it was 25 percent larger. And it was crowned with a penthouse for the Doctor and a handful of top executives. These were not simple utilitarian spaces, but huge, beautifully furnished offices, every one with a superb view.

"The penthouse was a big deal," says Cunningham, "because if you were there, you were important. They were better facilities, beautiful views, great sunsets."

Naturally, the Doctor had the finest office, eighteen hundred square feet of sprawling space in which Wang was completely dwarfed.

Architecturally, the towers gave off a somber air when all-out celebration would have been more appropriate, for Wang Labs was nothing less than the savior of this soulful old mill city. By the time Wang was done expanding, it would go from occupying 350,000 square feet of space in Lowell to nearly two and a half million square feet. And, in the process, it would play the lead role in cutting the city's unemployment rate to a mere 3 percent.

As the 1970s drew to a close, it was clear that stories like Wang's resuscitation of Lowell were emblematic of something taking place throughout Massachusetts. In February 1979, an article in the *Boston Globe* read:

> Born and bred in Massachusetts, the computer industry has become a giant of this state's economy and is growing like the proverbial beanstalk. From the seeds of a science fertilized in Cambridge laboratories, the industry has grown in a quarter century from a fledgling whose functions were as incomprehensible as its jargon to a key medium for the United States in world competition. Likewise, the industry is now at the epicenter of Massachusetts' vitality in the national marketplace.
>
> The pace of the computer age has been characterized by startling technological advances and markedly decreasing unit costs. The work of a machine that 20 years ago filled a room and cost several million dollars is now done by a chip the size of a matchhead that sells for 30 cents. It has stimulated the productivity of an area that not so long ago seemed cornered by increasing energy costs, depleted natural resources and a declining labor pool. . . .

In 1976 Wang Labs wasn't even in the top 50 of *Datamation*'s list of the country's major computer companies. By 1979, it was number 25. Just two years later, it had leaped up to number 11.

Leading all the growth indicators was the company's stock. Its increase through the years testified dramatically to the company's spectacular success. From 1976 to 1983, the effective price of Wang Laboratories stock climbed from $6.75 per share to more than $800 per share. An investment of slightly less than $8,000 in 1976 would have appreciated in 1983 to $1 million.

The Wang sales force that helped drive the company to such great heights had a gypsylike character. These were men and women who were not cut out of the prim-and-proper corporate mold. They were a colorful group, many with less than stellar résumés. The legend around the company was that Cunningham had taken a group of former venetian blind salesmen and turned them into a formidable high-tech sales force. The Wang people were misfits, distinctly different from the well-trained, white-shirted, stiff-collared IBM crew. Exuberant Wang staffers in the company's support group, comprised mostly of women, printed T-shirts with the message: "If you have a Wang you need support." Not to be outdone, the service group printed T-shirts reading: "My Wang is always up."

They were their own brand of entrepreneurs, hard chargers who worked until the point of exhaustion and who then played, often with an *Animal House* mentality, as hard as they worked. During one meeting in Phoenix, a group of salespeople sat around listening to a manager drone on. A salesman grew bored. He raised his hand, and asked for permission to pull up his socks. Of course, the annoyed manager replied. The salesman smiled, stood up, dropped his pants, and pulled up his socks as his colleagues roared their approval.

Cunningham recruited the most aggressive, hungriest salespeople he could find, loaded them down with sizzling products, and shoved them out the door. They were unstoppable. As a reward, he paid them better than any other computer company in the country. While IBM paid its salespeople commissions under 2 percent, Wang salespeople got 5 percent on sales (up to a limit). It was far easier for Wang salespeople to reach an annual income of $150,000 than for salespeople at any other company in the industry. Earning much more than that was difficult because of ceilings Wang imposed. Nonetheless, some salespeople made $200,000 and $250,000 in a year.

When word got around the industry of the money that could be made at Wang, salespeople flocked to the place. Though it was never terribly difficult to get a sales job at Wang, it was hard to hold on to one. People would be trained for a week or so on the Wang product line, thrown into a territory, and told to perform. Those who consistently met their quotas — which were extremely high — were kept. Those who missed their quota for a quarter were placed on probation; those who missed a second quarter quota were fired.

Dick Connaughton, who became one of the youngest vice-presidents ever at Wang, started as a salesman in 1972 when he was hired in a group of one hundred other salespeople. Three years later, only five members of that group remained at Wang. And two years after that, Connaughton was the sole survivor.

The quota policy was not an arbitrary one. Cunningham had done research that showed it was extremely rare for a poor producer in the first six months to become a good producer two years later. "We found that anybody who was marginal at six months was also marginal at two years," Cunningham recalls. "So we lost nobody good by blowing them away after six months."

Cunningham pressured salespeople to get into the Fortune 1000 companies because it was there, he believed, that the company's future lay. "To break into the Fortune 1000 was a very big deal," he says. "There were only a few vendors for these companies, and it takes many years to get on their approved vendor lists." What had taken other companies a generation or more took Wang Labs a matter of months.

The Wang sales force was comprised of "probably the most down-to-earth, least pretentious, self-satisfied people" that George Rich, a consultant who had worked with a number of big computer companies, had ever encountered. "The tempo of the business was very great and add to that an unstructured environment where there were very few ground rules. It encourages individual initiative and a certain degree of wild behavior."

They were a ragtag collection who did nearly everything to excess and who "thought they could get anything done," says Cunningham. "They honestly believed they could take on IBM and kick the shit out of them."

Before taking on IBM, they practiced on each other. At sales gatherings where liquor was served, Cunningham would invariably look up at some point and see a couple of Wang salespeople squaring off — half drunk or more and ready to punch someone's lights out. There was an outlaw flavor that only added spice to the Wang experience.

"At times half the organization was screwing the other half of the organization," says Cunningham. "It was a party, a hot place to be."

"We were all caught up with it," says Dale Jelley, an engineer who came to Wang as part of the PHI acquisition in the late 1960s. "We worked, we made money, we fucked, we drank. We did it all to excess."

At IBM, sales managers were forbidden to buy employees a beer on the expense account. At Wang, managers competed to see who could add the most expensive bottle of wine to a dinner check.

These sorts of activities were hardly reflective of An Wang, but he tolerated it because he believed that the expense money was well spent. It never got out of hand, certainly not compared with the company's staggering revenues. As long as Cunningham believed that the expense policies made sense, that was enough for the Doctor.

Then, too, the wild, free-spending atmosphere didn't entirely exclude the Doctor. In 1982, the company's top managers planned an all-day meeting in Boston to review progress and look ahead to a very bright future. To add some fun to the day, it was arranged that the morning session would take place on a 110-foot yacht that would cruise Boston Harbor.

On the appointed day, a group of several dozen Wang executives spent the morning in serious discussion at the Doctor's floor-through apartment in the Harbor Towers condominium complex on the Boston waterfront. At noon, they boarded their chartered boat and cruised out on to the breezy, sun-drenched harbor for drinks and lunch. Doctor Wang joined enthusiastically in the party as the Chivas Regal flowed. It was a lovely summer afternoon, and the group was relaxing and basking in their phenomenal success.

As it turned out, the Doctor became a bit too relaxed. After the boat had docked, Wang walked down the gangway, lost his balance, and plunged into Boston Harbor. He was quickly fished out and placed on land. Trudging back to Harbor Towers in sopping wet shoes and suit, the Doctor looked as ridiculous as anyone had ever seen him.

Meanwhile, the nonstop party at Wang Labs broke up only for furious periods of work. "It was almost a fanatical thing," recalls Sam Gagliano, who ran product-planning and development. "We were on a mission, and it was tremendously satisfying to be a successful underdog."

It mattered not at all what was required to get the job done. There was no ceiling on the number of hours to be worked. Carl Masi, who supervised operations in Europe, spent so much time on transatlantic 747s that he gave his address as seat 2A, TWA.

There was a price for it all, of course. "There were a lot of screwed-up personal lives," says Gagliano. "A lot of divorces." But it all seemed so very worth it. There was not only a great deal of money to be made, but there was the recognition that came with being successful within the company. And no computer company was better at creatively rewarding its people than Wang Laboratories. One of the greatest rewards of all was Wang's achievers' trip.

These gatherings were legendary. Each year, the company threw a party for all the salespeople who had met their quotas, but these were no ordinary parties. They were million-dollar-plus blow-outs in Acapulco, Bermuda, London, Hawaii, Mexico, and Rome.

The achievers' trips were Cunningham's idea. He invited both the salesperson and his or her spouse, and he spared no expense. The company paid for two airline tickets from the salesman's home city; when the achievers arrived at their destination, they were pampered at every turn. During the five days of the trip, the company paid for everything. Cunningham didn't want his people to have to take out their wallets at all.

"The achievers' trip was the most visible recognition within the company," says Cunningham. "People would kill for it."

Every achiever received a plaque and had his photograph taken with Doctor Wang. Cunningham delivered a speech that was invariably greeted with a stomping ovation. The trips were so popular that he found, through the years, that wives (the great majority of the salespeople were men) put pressure — sometimes subtle, sometimes not — on their husbands to make their quota so they could go on the trip.

"In 1978 in Acapulco it was like spending millions of dollars on a party for five hundred of your best friends," says Dale Jelley. "They'd hire a whole hotel, Ricky Nelson and his band — no expense was spared. In London they bought a whole theater, a whole restaurant, bus tours. The last night of every achievers' trip was called New Year's Eve and that's what it was like. There was a black-tie dinner, dancing, the Doctor, the Doctor's family, the board of directors." Perhaps the most memorable was the 1984 achievers' trip to Rome, where the company spent $6 million on a four-day toga party that became so wild it made the Rome newspapers.

Even during the rest of the year, Wang executives were sometimes just as extravagant as they were during achievers' trips.

"There were some tremendous excesses," recalls Dale Jelley. "A dinner check for $1,600. Limousines, helicopters, jet planes. Nobody could do anything wrong."

Expense accounts would roll in with charges for a bottle of wine — one bottle — for $220. A sales manager signed up for a box at a National Hockey League rink for $50,000. "It was kind of like a drunken spree," says Dale Jelley. "There were no controls. It was rollicking, out-of-control spending."

It was not totally out of control, however. Doctor Wang knew that the achievers' trips were a motivational tool worth far more than they cost. He also knew that letting employees feel like they were running up huge expense account bills — when, in fact, they amounted to a pittance of the total company revenues — was good business. Wang never let it get totally out of hand, and, indeed, he occasionally looked over expense accounts to see where his money was going. Once, Jake Jacobson, one of his best and favorite sales managers, was working on a deal in Hong Kong. On the third night there, Jacobson went out to dinner with his Chinese hosts and faced yet another banquet at a fashionable Chinese restaurant. For many people this would have been a delightful prospect, but Jacobson was a red-blooded American who liked his steaks and wasn't the least bit fond of squishy, hard to-identify Chinese food. He was also sick of chopsticks. Jacobson had had enough. He told his hosts he was sorry, but he wanted a steak and a knife and fork. Though eyebrows were raised at this offensive breach of etiquette, Jake got his beef and utensils.

Months later, toward the end of the calendar year, Cunningham was going over bonus payments to various members of the organization with Doctor Wang. They came to Jacobson's name on the list, and Cunningham recommended a generous figure, something in the neighborhood of $20,000 to $25,000. In most cases, the Doctor merely nodded his assent. But when Jake's name came up, Wang, angry that Jacobson might have offended his Chinese hosts, told Cunningham to cut the bonus by $10,000.

"Tell Jake," the Doctor said to Cunningham, "that the steak cost him $10,000."

For many top executives, and for star salespeople, expense accounts were all but unlimited. It had not always been that way. Until 1976, the only employee with a company car was Doctor Wang. In the late 1970s only a half-dozen Wang executives, the Doctor included, had them. After the Doctor's absentminded style of driving caused a minor accident, company officials insisted he be chauffeured. He started out with a Cadillac limousine, but then moved up to a Mercedes stretch limo. When he did, other top executives, Cunningham included, got Mercedes-Benz sedans.

But in 1981 the Doctor's security people said he was too visible in the Mercedes limo and would be safer in a Mercedes sedan. Although there had never been any threats against Wang or his family, Wang liked the security of having guards around and took their advice. Cunningham, to his eternal delight, inherited the Doctor's limo.

Cunningham was picked up at his Weston home each morning and, during the twenty-five-minute drive to Lowell, he would breakfast on coffee and a muffin while he perused the *Boston Globe,* the *Wall Street Journal,* and watched the *Today* program on television. He was not yet forty years old, and he was being delivered to smart downtown restaurants in a Mercedes-Benz limousine. This man, who had snuck on to exclusive country club courses as a teenager, relished pulling up to clubs minutes ahead of his tee-off time and watching the gawkers as he emerged like a head of state from his magnificent vehicle. "I was the only kid from West Roxbury driving around in a Mercedes limousine," he says with pride.

The one thing on which the Doctor would not budge was a company jet. Cunningham badly wanted one, but Wang thought it too expensive. Almost as compensation, Cunningham was allotted $250,000 a year to lease all manner of flying machines. He got a Sikorsky eight-seat helicopter for a six-month free trial on the pretext that Wang was considering buying the craft. Buzzing around eastern Massachusetts was great fun, but, as much as he liked the chopper, he truly loved jets. Why his fixation with planes? "If you're at a cocktail party, everybody's got a house on the Cape, everybody's got a Mercedes, everybody's got a house in Brookline, Wellesley, or Weston, but not everybody has a jet."

Cunningham once flew off to Tarpon Springs, Florida, for a game of golf. While in Puerto Rico on business, he decided to take a detour on the way home. He stopped in Bermuda for an ice cream cone. Another time, he jetted off to New York for the Heisman trophy dinner, where BC's own Doug Flutie received the award for the best college football player in America.

On one of his more memorable trips, Cunningham and his wife took off in a Falcon 50, a sleek, speedy, three-engine twelve-seater that sold for $14 million. The Cunninghams touched down in London for meetings, visited Paris for more meetings and some shopping, swung over to Scotland for the opening of a Wang facility at which Cunningham presided and where Prince Charles was the guest of honor, and finally headed home. The six-day trip cost Wang Laboratories, for the jet alone, $60,000.

The executives were not the only ones to benefit from company lar-
gess. In January 1980, long before it was the fashion, Wang opened a
state-of-the-art child-care facility for employees' children. Just a couple of
months later, the company went so far as to buy the Groton Country
Club for the exclusive use of company employees. It wasn't a private jet
to Bermuda, but it wasn't bad.

The greatest perk of all would not be purchased until later, when the
peak years were all but over. It came when the Doctor changed his mind
and decided, out of the blue, that he wanted a corporate jet after all. For
many years, the Doctor's fear of flying had kept him off planes, but now
the company bought one of the best small jets in the world, a Gulfstream
III. It was an elegant plane that comfortably seated twelve passengers,
who were served food on china bearing the Wang logo. The company
built a hangar for the plane at a cost of $1.2 million, which, added to the
$14.8 million purchase price of the jet, brought to $16 million the amount
Wang Labs paid for its executive air service.

When Doctor Wang returned from a long trip — across country or
abroad — the plane would land at an airfield not far from his home. He
would walk off the plane, get into the car his driver would have waiting,
and motor home in minutes.

During the glory years, the company was run by An Wang, John Cunningham, and Harry Chou, An Wang's friend, contemporary, and the
company comptroller. Chou, a small man with a pleasant smile, played
an important role in the company's operations but had little influence on
its strategic direction.

That task was largely the province of Wang and Cunningham. Theirs
was a unique relationship, particularly since Wang trusted so few people.
"John Cunningham helped Wang develop a marketing strategy and exe-
cute that strategy," says Peter Brooke, the venture capitalist and Wang
board member. "Wang gave Cunningham high marks for developing that
strategy with him and executing it properly. He was the only outside guy
who had any impact with the old man."

Cunningham and Wang's strategic planning was accomplished privately during small, closed-door meetings. This was difficult, crucial
work, especially given the rapidly changing world business environment.
There were manufacturing decisions such as whether to build the machinery in-house or to farm it out; distribution decisions, such as whether to
sell the equipment through a Wang sales force or through retail distri-

bution chains; and other decisions involving R&D, marketing, finance, and human resources.

Cunningham's most visible task within the company and the role for which he was best known was leading the Wang sales force. "John was driving the sales force," says consultant George Rich. "John was excellent at keeping in personal touch with area directors and district managers. There was unbelievably high morale. It was very exciting. Decisions were made very quickly, unlike places like Xerox and DEC. . . . There was very little bureaucracy or delay."

In the late 1970s, analyst John Adams observed that the company's growth placed great strain on the organization's ability to cope with the avalanche of orders. It put terrific pressure on the field service organization even as it required greater sophistication from the sales force. "The fact that management could respond well to two such disparate challenges," Adams wrote, "is a far more substantial accomplishment than it might appear to the casual observer."

Cunningham was also the company's financial point man, the spokesman responsible for selling the Wang story to Wall Street. It was a task he took very seriously, for it was worth huge sums of money to the company. During Cunningham's years there, Wang Laboratories raised more than $1 billion from investors who believed in the Wang story, who were convinced, more often than not by Cunningham, that Wang was traveling the correct strategic path.

"The Doctor and John were a very strong team," says George Rich. "John was treated by Doctor and Mrs. Wang almost as if he was a member of the family."

Cunningham believes he reached that position of trust because he listened carefully to what Wang wanted, because he did high-quality work, because his strengths complemented the Doctor's weaknesses, and, finally, because the competition wasn't very tough. Cunningham points out that he was the only graduate of an Ivy League business school at Wang until 1974. Hotshot graduates of the best business schools ignored Wang in those days, if, that is, they even knew of its existence. Cunningham says he would not have climbed as high at a company such as Digital or Data General. Whether that is true, the fact remains that Cunningham brilliantly led the Wang sales and marketing forces.

"Everybody in the company saw him as the reason for the company's success," says Carl Masi, who was in charge of worldwide sales under Cunningham. "He was *the* leader, no question."

John Cunningham's reputation was important to him, and he was bothered in the fall of 1983 that although he had accomplished a good deal at Wang Labs, people outside the company "didn't know what I'd done."

He was bothered, as well, by Fred Wang's increasingly important role in the company. Agitated as he was, Cunningham knew it would be unwise to speak with Doctor Wang about his concerns. Instead, he sat down for a quiet chat with Harry Chou.

"I wasn't happy, and I told Harry," says Cunningham. "I had a motivation problem. I told him, 'This thing with Fred is not working.' I wasn't happy with Fred, with his involvement in decisions, and with what was happening in R&D. Harry would tell me, 'You have to make it work. It's your job to make it work.' He told me I didn't understand the family issues in a Chinese family, that they were carrying on a Chinese tradition, that it was probably more important than the enterprise itself. I didn't know whether I should start looking around.

"Harry would take my straightforward, blunt emotional message and sift it and present it to Doctor Wang."

Within ten days of Cunningham's discussion with Chou, Doctor Wang sat down with Cunningham, smiled, and said he would like to make him president of the company. Cunningham was a bit surprised. He truly had been worried about Fred's ascendence. And even though the Doctor told him that day that Fred, too, would be promoted to a position as executive vice-president, Cunningham was extremely gratified. "I'm very, very pleased that you think that much of me," he told An Wang.

Cunningham was pleased, indeed, for although his responsibilities would remain essentially the same, the title of president would dramatically boost his status in the industry, and in the Boston community, where he lived and had grown up. Everyone would now know that John Cunningham from St. Theresa's and BC had made it, and made it big.

"Psychologically, it was a big deal," says Cunningham. "It was the culmination of what I was looking for in my career. It was perceived on the outside as a big deal. It was perceived as a big deal to employees, to customers. The perception was that it was a significant accomplishment in a very difficult and complex business. I was by far the youngest president of a multibillion-dollar technology company in the United States. I was thirty-nine years old and president of a $2 billion-a-year company. I was making six hundred grand. I was one of the top ten paid people in high tech. The presidency exposed me more. The outside perception was 'this is the guy who runs the show.'

"But, functionally, my job didn't really change."

Why did Wang give Cunningham the new title if his actual job wasn't going to change? To keep him, says Fred Wang. "John had done a good job developing the field organization. John was very comfortable with outside analysts, the press. My father was worried about losing him."

To Cunningham, the presidency meant money, prestige, recognition, and the satisfaction of knowing he had done well. But it was also his ticket to whatever it was he would do next in his life. "John wanted to be president," says Ellen Cunningham, "so he could turn it into something else later."

For even as he took over as president, Cunningham knew in the back of his mind that it would not last forever, that it might not even last very long. He had heard Harry's message about the family and Chinese tradition. And he understood it very well.

Cunningham was clearly the second most important person in the company, and reporters with questions about Wang Labs invariably sought him out. He was knowledgeable, entertaining, and eminently quotable. But journalists seeking to learn the secret of the company went to An Wang. To understand the Doctor, they reasoned, might be to understand this phenomenal company.

However, every writer who journeyed to Lowell in search of the Doctor's soul was disappointed. So protective of his privacy were company officials that reporters were told prior to interviews with the Doctor — interviews that were grudgingly and infrequently granted — not to even ask personal questions.

In late 1980, writer Joseph P. Kahn of *Boston* magazine, after negotiating for months to win an audience with the Great Man, finally sat down in Wang's office. Before the session, he was warned — as usual — not to ask Wang about his personal life. Kahn plowed ahead, nonetheless. He quickly learned of the extraordinary jealousy with which An Wang guarded his privacy. Wang's utter unwillingness to make even an effort to respond to mildly personal questions was purely consistent with who he was and had always been — a man who would share little about himself with anyone; a man who did not even reveal to his closest associates, or even to his own son, that he had been previously married.

When Kahn asked Wang about his life, Wang replied: "I don't think we need to talk about me personally. It is not important."

Kahn persisted, however, and asked about the Doctor's "hopes, dreams, desires." When he did so, An Wang's "eyes become hooded, the gaze vacant, the distaste apparent."

Like others who had come looking to peer within An Wang and to learn his secrets, Kahn returned to his typewriter in frustration.

Through the decades during which An Wang's company changed dramatically, the man himself changed little. Despite the money, notoriety, and success, his passions were work and control of his company. His material demands remained modest. Outside work, he continued to enjoy a game of tennis, an evening of bridge. He liked watching baseball on television occasionally, and he was fond of sitting down in the evening and reading a stack of newspapers. He owned two identical gray suits. He indulged himself with a membership in the Lanam Club, an exclusive suburban dining club housed in an elegant old Victorian home with dark wood paneling, leather armchairs, and white tablecloths. It was located in North Andover, about a twenty-minute drive from the towers, and Wang fell into the habit of having lunch there nearly every day, occasionally with others but often, increasingly as the years passed, alone. He would enjoy a Chivas or two before lunch, and dine on soup and scrod as he pored over several newspapers, invariably leaving lunch with his hands covered in black ink. His wealth certainly did not turn him into a gourmet, for his evening meal was usually no grander than a bowl of rice with small side dishes such as shredded pork.

Though *he* was the same, a great deal had changed around him. By the early 1980s, he had taken on an aura of greatness — much more than the aura surrounding the superwealthy; more than the aura surrounding genius; more than that which cloaks the establishment figures with whom he rubbed elbows on the Harvard Board of Overseers and the board of directors of the Bank of Boston; more even than that which comes with a couple dozen honorary degrees. He was not only a genius and one of the world's wealthiest men, he was also a bona fide member of the establishment and a philanthropist. He seemed to be a humble genius who wasn't quite fallible. He was a visionary, it was said; a man who could peer far off into the future and see where the world of technology was headed. He would not err in these matters; if he made a slight mistake or miscalculation, he had the wisdom and vision to perceive it quickly and correct his course. Press reports about him from the 1970s and early '80s are more often than not reverential.

He had become a sort of deity.

It began within the company. When Wang Labs was small, he had contact with many employees, but with its subsequent explosive growth, he suddenly sat atop a sprawling, worldwide corporation that was on its way to employing more than thirty thousand people. To the vast majority of those employees, Wang was a distant figure, elevated in the towers, removed from the jostle of daily commerce. The talk around the company was of his having survived the turmoil in China, having triumphed at Harvard, and "invented" — his contribution was always exaggerated by employees — core memory. And he had not only made himself wealthy, he had brought prosperity to thousands of families. Employees who had bought or been granted fifty or one hundred shares early on found their stake grown to the point where it put a son or daughter through college.

Because the Doctor said so little for years, remaining a mute public figure who bowed stiffly at the applause as he gave millions to charitable causes, he took on an air of mystery. Major customers had the same reaction when granted an audience with the Doctor. "He was like a Thomas Edison," says Bob Doretti, who was head of U.S. sales during some of the glory years. "They were in awe of him when they saw him."

The image grew as Wang spent more of his time on charitable work. He founded an elite graduate school called the Wang Institute for computer software engineers. He bought an old mansion in the Massachusetts town of Tyngsboro, not far from Lowell, located the institute on its lovely grounds, and lavished tens of millions of dollars on it.

By the early 1980s, Doctor Wang had begun to withdraw somewhat from the day-to-day fray. He did so in part because Fred Wang wanted to run his own show without interference from his father when he took over as head of R&D. The Doctor took the fifteen to twenty hours a week he had devoted to managing development and focused them elsewhere. He continued to take a keen interest in pet development projects of his own — he would never stop being an inventor. But he spent more time on the Wang Institute, and on charitable causes, politics, and outside boards. He devoted some time a few years later to work on his autobiography.

By 1983, he sought to leave day-to-day management of the company in the hands of a troika: Cunningham, Harry, and Fred.

He became involved politically by donating to a variety of office-holders, including Congressman Barney Frank and Senators Paul Tsongas and Edward M. Kennedy. In presenting Wang with the state's "Outstanding Democrat" award in 1982, Senator Kennedy described the Doctor as "a one-man Marshall Plan for Massachusetts." Wang also gave to President Carter. In the Massachusetts gubernatorial campaign of 1982, he endorsed Michael S. Dukakis over incumbent Governor Edward J. King, who had appointed Wang to the state board of higher education. He sat on the board of trustees at Boston College. The company gave $3 million worth of computer equipment to public colleges and universities in Massachusetts.

By far his most celebrated gift was to a performing arts center in Boston that was on the verge of collapse. The Metropolitan Theatre had once been among the grandest cultural settings in Boston, a home for theater and ballet, movies and music. But this majestic old building, which had reminded so many cultural mavens of the Paris Opera House, had fallen into disrepair. So acute were its problems that shortly before a show in 1982, a section of the ceiling plunged to the seats below, exposing a hole in the roof. The theater was forced to close, and leaders of the city's cultural community scrambled furiously to find money for repairs.

The place was rescued by An Wang.

Having spent millions on the Wang Institute and millions more on the Massachusetts General Hospital, Wang was already big in education and medicine. This was a chance, says Cunningham, for the Doctor to establish his name in the arts, as well, and for what to Wang was very little money. Says Cunningham, "I sold it to him as a PR deal."

Cunningham approached the Doctor, who listened carefully to the pitch. The center would be named after anyone contributing $5 million, Cunningham told Wang. Would they do it for $4 million? asked Wang. They did.

In December 1983, an elite crowd of three thousand Bostonians rose to their feet in thunderous applause as An and Lorraine Wang appeared on stage during the dedication of the Wang Center for the Performing Arts. It was at this event more than any other that Wang was publicly deified. The press coverage of him was even more glowing than it had been before. A Boston television station piece on the Doctor was indicative. It ended with the reporter stating that there was "at least one smash hit class act in town — Doctor An Wang."

The deification suited this man, who was, in John Cunningham's words, a "humble egomaniac."

"This was a man," says Peter Brooke, "with an immense ego. He wanted his name on everything. The impact of the man was immense, really, really immense. He had a desire to be a very big man. He wanted to be an important man, and he wanted to be recognized as an important man."

Though he was not a saint, few employees saw anything but his saintly demeanor. Only a handful of senior executives witnessed how demanding he could be.

He grew increasingly remote, especially after 1980 when he became almost obsessed about security. Ken Olson, president of Digital Equipment Corporation, who lived down the street from Wang, was the apparent target of a small bomb that detonated near his home. But nothing else ever happened and Olson carried on without security.

After the explosion, however, Wang Laboratories instituted round-the-clock security for the Doctor and his family members. The grounds of Wang's Lincoln home were covered by infrared sensors that could detect the presence of an intruder. Security protected Wang's Cape home and the homes of Fred and Juliette Wang. Wang was so fearful of being harmed or kidnapped that neither he nor any members of his family attended the achievers' trip in Rome. The security for Wang and his children cost the company close to $2 million a year.

The existence of the security suggested that this man was so great he had to be protected from some unseen force of evil by men with powerful weapons. The feeling toward the Doctor came to be a kind of reverence. It was a great plus in developing loyalty among employees, but it also had the potential to be troublesome, for there can be danger for a company that is overly dependent upon a single, mortal, being.

If there were any problems during the company's growth years, they did not appear, on the surface, anyway, to be terribly serious. John Adams followed Wang as closely as any analyst, and in April 1978 Adams observed that "Wang's only problems appear to us to be the function of extraordinary prosperity . . . clearly, most companies would like to have 'problems' of this ilk." In January 1983 Adams indicated the level of the company's success when he wrote that "some day Wang will do something wrong. However, the person who knows what or when has a lot more insight into the business than we do."

It was true that the company had long been dogged by a reputation for poor service. The problem was caused in part by the difficulty of keeping pace with the rapid flow of products. Though the company took some flak for this, it didn't seem to matter all that much — Wang machines were so good that customers tolerated the poor service to get Wang technology.

It was also true that some basic management systems that were well established at other major companies didn't even exist at Wang. There were no budgets, for instance, until 1980. Department heads weren't given annual allotments of money to carry out their programs. They spent as much money as they felt necessary. New executives hired from other companies found this particularly hard to believe. A large corporation with no budgets at all?

"Our weakness was growing so quickly that there was no real infrastructure," says Fred Wang.

The joke around the company was that a management consultant came in one day to try to decipher the Wang organizational chart. The consultant asked how many of the employees reported directly to Doctor Wang, and a company official replied. "All of them." Employees took solace in the notion that these administrative problems could be explained by the phenomenal rate of growth.

If there was any hint of the company's future difficulty during the good times, besides the shortage of management controls, it could be found in an attitude of arrogance that seemed to infuse the company. "It was like the company could do no wrong," recalls John Thibault, a Wang marketing man. "Anything we touched turned to gold. There was not a hell of a lot of regard for the customers. We thought, 'Whatever we make they'll buy because we know what's right.'"

That attitude was allowed to grow by the Doctor and Cunningham. As time passed, both men grew less inclined to listen to customers. With their fat cigars and phenomenal success, they fought, but did not entirely resist, the temptation to succumb to a smug overconfidence. It was that smugness that allowed the seeds of undisciplined overspending to take root in Wang soil.

"The biggest change occurred when the first tower was built," says Dale Jelley. "Up until then everybody walked by everybody everyday. Suddenly things were stacked vertically, hierarchically. People worked there and never saw Doctor Wang, never saw Fred. They came and went in their limousines into the garage and went by elevator to the penthouse."

"It was an environment," says Fred Wang, "where you almost couldn't do something wrong as long as you kept moving. A lot of people thought the industry was going to grow 20 percent a year forever."

In his book about IBM, the company he took over from his father, Thomas Watson, Jr., says that one of the most difficult tasks in a growing company is managing rapid growth: "The hardest task of all, was . . . riding the runaway horse."

At Wang Laboratories, they were hanging on to the reins for dear life.

EIGHT

Fred Wang

O N THE SURFACE, October 4, 1983, was one of the most successful days in the history of Wang Laboratories. On that day, journalists from major newspapers, including the *New York Times,* influential computer industry analysts from throughout the country, reporters from the leading trade publications, and every major executive at the company — five hundred people in all — gathered at the Westin Hotel in Boston's Copley Place development to hear the company announce fourteen new products.

The announcement was made, the *Financial Times* noted, "amid much razzamatazz." To signal the significance of the event, the entire management team turned out, including Doctor Wang, John Cunningham, and Harry Chou. Members of the board of directors were there as well. This was Wang, with some of the finest equipment in the world of technology, trumpeting what a company statement called "the most important products in the company's history." More important than the 2200 small business computer? More important than the extremely successful VS minicomputer? More important even than the breakthrough Wang Word Processing System? It hardly seemed possible. These would have to be extraordinary products.

There was no mistaking that this was Fred Wang's day, his debut in the crucial position as head of research and development. It was Fred's chance to place his personal stamp on the company's products. These were his machines; this was his show. This would be the day when Fred Wang drove his claim stake to the company deep into the ground.

"We tied all the products to a grand theme," says Fred Wang. "We laid out where all this technology was going. It all had to be designed into an office system. We were the first ones to state it as such. It was a vision."

A sense of triumph, even euphoria, swept the towers as it became clear that this announcement gala was a smashing success, the best product-development event the company had ever staged.

It all looked so good at the time. So solid. While other computer companies such as Data General and Digital were having trouble, Wang was racking up its thirty-second successive quarter in which earnings climbed more than 30 percent. However, the glitz of Copley Place masked some unpleasant, even alarming problems. Peter McElroy was the marketing man responsible for organizing the day's activities. "It was the finest product announcement Wang had ever had, bar none," says McElroy.

But there was a problem, he says, and not a small problem. A truly terrible problem. "The problem," says McElroy, "was that all of what we announced that day was vapor."

Among the well-to-do Chinese who had settled in the Greater Boston area, it was common each Saturday morning to take their children to classes in Chinese language and culture. Many of An and Lorraine Wang's contemporaries were determined to pass the lessons of their heritage along to their offspring. But for An Wang there was a difficulty with these classes. They were held in the town of Brookline, a Boston suburb that happened to be in the opposite direction from Wang Laboratories, where the Doctor spent his Saturdays. So he struck a deal with his son.

"My father and I had an understanding," Fred recalls with amusement. "When I was about eight or ten years old, Dad asked if I wanted to go to Chinese school and I said, 'No.' It was my time to watch cartoons. He said, 'Good. Brookline is in the opposite direction of where I need to go Saturday morning, which is work.'"

Thanks to his father, Fred not only escaped Chinese school on Saturday mornings, but he also escaped church on Sunday mornings. Though Lorraine Wang liked taking her children to Sunday services, her husband was not the least bit religious. Fred clearly took his cues from his father, even at an early age. When Fred was about twelve years old, he told his mother: "If he's not going, I'm not going." And that was that.

Though both Fred's parents were Chinese, he says they never discussed China at home, at least not in front of him. Many of his mother's relatives had fled the country for Hawaii before the Communist takeover, and, in 1960, when Fred was ten years old, his mother's father was permitted to emigrate to Lincoln to live with the Wangs. He was eighty years old and in declining health, but he would take long walks in the area, returning home having bought little toys for Fred. He was in the United States for just six months before he died.

"Dad didn't talk about China because he was so busy at work and because they feared reprisals from the Communist government if they found out who they were," says Fred. "My mother had a very, very strong anti-Communist attitude. They said that after the Communists they would go back to China."

Most of the conversation around the house when Fred was growing up revolved around the one topic central to the family's life: Wang Laboratories.

Fred was in the first grade at the Shady Hill School, an exclusive private institution, when the family moved to Lincoln, and, though it was Mrs. Wang's intention to send him to the town's public schools, Fred says his parents left the decision up to him. He chose to remain at Shady Hill, where his friends were.

From the somewhat protective, carefree environment of Shady Hill, Fred went on to one of the best secondary schools in the United States — St. Paul's School in Concord, New Hampshire. Set on a campus of extraordinary beauty — a place that exudes the charm of the New England countryside with its woods, ponds, and centuries-old wood-frame homes — St. Paul's epitomizes the traditional New England prep school.

Though he did well at St. Paul's, Fred did not much like the place. He was not the sort of boy who slipped easily into the in-crowd at school. Fred was small, barely five and a half feet tall, and he lacked the sort of outgoing personality that would ingratiate him with new groups. He found the school far too cliquish for his taste and was disappointed to find some teachers "as narrow-minded as some of the students." A group of students from the New York area, many of them athletes and many from very well-to-do families, particularly rankled Fred. "They derided other people," he recalls. "There were smatterings of anti-Semitic jokes. There was a smattering of the wealthy against the nonwealthy. If not encouraged, this was certainly not discouraged by some teachers. They would make fun of people's clothes. There was an underlying sarcasm."

Fred's response was to try and ignore the condescension and the snobbery, to avoid joining any particular group, and, he says, "to grin and bear it."

Fred and his classmate and friend from Lincoln, Robert Niles, were certainly not part of this clique nor did they strive to be. Nonetheless, says Niles, "I'm sure we would have appreciated the friendship of some of those individuals."

Though Fred did not like St. Paul's, he masked his feelings so effectively that more than twenty years later, one of his St. Paul's roommates is surprised to learn of Fred's dislike of the place. "I thought he was happy there," says Bob Peake, Fred's roommate in the ninth grade. "He seemed to have a lot of friends, to enjoy himself."

In retrospect, Peake sees how Fred might have felt left out. Peake himself felt very much the outcast. He was a scholarship student from humble origins, in sharp contrast to most of the students. "Fred didn't fit the norm, either," says Peake. "He was nouveau riche, not old money. And he is Asian."

Fred did enjoy some of the St. Paul's experience, particularly his classes in science and math. He studied advanced-placement physics and scored well enough on the test to be permitted to skip college freshman physics, recalls John Beust, Fred's physics teacher at St. Paul's. Beust remembers Fred as "personable, likable, a hard worker."

Fred's math ability was "amongst the best of a very select lot," says his math teacher, Bill Faulkner. Fred took all of the most challenging math courses the school had to offer, including, in his senior year, both calculus and the single most advanced math class at St. Paul's, "concepts of mathematics." As he'd done in physics, Fred scored well enough on the advanced-placement math test to bypass college freshman math.

"Fred was not the cool man on campus, but he was very bright," says his friend Niles. "He wasn't the brightest kid. We had a lot of guys in our class [1968] who were brilliant."

Though he was strong in math and science, he was not particularly adept at the humanities and languages. Fred's own assessment is that he was "an okay student, not a great student. In the middle of the pack."

Faulkner also recalls Fred as a rather shy young man. "He was quick to understand; he was less quick to verbalize," says Faulkner. "I never had any doubt about his understanding. He showed by his perceptive questions that he was above most people in his group, but he wasn't always the first one to volunteer that type of thing. He might wait until after class and ask a question or make a comment to me. He would tend to sit back and analyze rather than participate in the flow."

Fred was involved in a number of activities outside the classroom, including the math and science societies and the missionary society, the largest organization on campus. The Mish, as it was known, organized students to do volunteer work in the community. Fred volunteered at a medical hospital in Concord, New Hampshire, and at the state mental hospital, where he helped out at the coffee shop. "It was very, very eye-opening to see what awful conditions these people had to survive in," he says. Fred was also an acolyte, which involved volunteering at campus church services. Sports were a requirement, and Fred tried basketball and hockey, which he quickly decided were not for him. But he enjoyed tennis and was passionate about soccer. And at a school that played high-quality soccer, Fred was good enough to make the varsity.

Inevitably, Fred was perhaps best known for being the son of the founder of Wang Laboratories. It was during Fred's third year at St. Paul's that the company went public and the Wang family became fabulously wealthy. The talk around the school, Peake recalls, was that in his own right Fred was worth $14 million. Whether that was even remotely accurate, it was clear that the family was well-off by the unusual way in which Fred was ferried to and from school. For weekends and vacations, Fred was sometimes dropped off and picked up by a chauffeur in a Mercedes-Benz. That Fred was not picked up and dropped off by his parents was somewhat unusual. But clearly the company was commanding the great bulk of An Wang's time, for Bob Peake, who lived with Fred all of soph-omore year, did not meet Fred's father until he came to take his son home for summer vacation. Doug Hodsdon, who was Fred's roommate senior year, does not recall meeting An Wang prior to graduation.

Fred did not talk a great deal about Wang Labs, but it was something in which he was obviously interested, says Peake. And it was also clear that he took great pride in his father. One day during freshman year, Fred told Peake that a division of Singer had come out with a faster, better machine than the Wang calculator (LOCI). Fred, exaggerating as proud sons are wont to do, told Peake "that his father locked himself away in a lab for two weeks and came up with a machine that was better and could be produced more cheaply." (He probably meant the 300 calculator.)

"Fred had a very good attitude about his father," says Peake. "I think he liked his father very much."

Bob Peake says he envied Fred, but even back then the danger of living under a great father was evident. "He was being groomed for the company, and I envied that he had his life mapped out for him," Peake says. But Peake says that he "always thought that the toughest problem Fred would face in life was living up to his father's image. I thought, 'This is going to be a long row to hoe.'"

During the summers before and after his senior year at St. Paul's, Fred worked at Wang Laboratories. Each day, Fred and his friend Robert Niles climbed into the Doctor's big shiny car and were driven to Wang Labs by the cigar-smoking CEO. There, the two boys went off to the manufacturing facility, where they soldered power supplies into desktop calculators. When he worked on the line, Fred found the people friendly and the atmosphere relaxed.

And he says he held up his end on the line. "I got as much work done as probably anyone else there," he recalls. Occasionally, however, Fred would be called away from the assembly line to some other part of the building. Niles says Fred never mentioned anything about intending to work at the company in the future, but it was clear to Niles that the Doctor was exposing his son to different aspects of the business.

As advantageous as it was to be An Wang's boy, there was a downside, as well. "He was the boss's son," says Niles. "And when he would walk into a room, people would stop talking. Sometimes I would be talking to somebody and would sense when Fred walked up that they weren't as comfortable because he was the boss's son."

During their second summer at Wang Labs, Fred's absences from the assembly line were more frequent and more prolonged. Niles's best recollection is that during that summer Fred was gone from the line about half the time. Says Niles: "I looked at it as him being groomed by his father."

It was clear that Fred Wang was the product of a strong-willed father, but it was also true, though less obvious, that he was the son of a strong-willed mother. Lorraine Wang was a charming, intelligent woman who dressed so elegantly and moved so gracefully that she gave off an air of royalty. She was a petite woman who, unlike her husband, was politically conservative. While An Wang held liberal views on political and social questions, Lorraine Wang had supported Barry Goldwater for president. Fred's parents were dramatically different in another, important respect. While the Doctor was an inveterate optimist, Mrs. Wang was, says Fred, "the eternal pessimist. If something is going to go wrong, her view is that it will not be a little bit wrong, but a lot wrong." She was also different in that she kept to a nocturnal schedule. She would sleep through much of the day and remain up throughout the night, spending great amounts of time playing mah-jongg with Chinese friends.

She was even more of a cultural traditionalist than her husband. Fred describes her as "very Chinese." "She holds to the Chinese belief that the eldest member of the family has absolute final say on anything," he says.

And the fact that her three very independent children were not the least bit hesitant to defy her — that all three married Caucasians when she wanted them to marry Chinese — caused some tension within the family.

She was most comfortable socializing with a large group of Shanghai Chinese who had also migrated to the Boston area. Among that group were numerous impressive intellects, many with ties to Harvard University. To the educated Chinese community in Greater Boston, Harvard was *the* symbol of intellectual excellence in the United States, and the Wangs wanted their eldest son to go there. This was a subject about which Mrs. Wang was passionate. It simply would not do for Fred to go anywhere else, but, much to his mother's disappointment, he was not admitted. It was little solace to her that Fred got into Brown, where he went in the fall of 1968.

Still, she had not given up hope of seeing her eldest son in Cambridge. Even after it was clear that he was happy and comfortable at Brown, far happier than he had ever been at St. Paul's, his mother wouldn't forget Harvard. Fred had been at Brown for only a couple of months when he found in his mail one day an application to transfer to Harvard, courtesy of his mother. Only grudgingly did she finally accept Fred's declaration that he very much liked where he was and didn't want to go anywhere else. "She tried to get Dad to pressure me, but he wouldn't," says Fred. "Dad was always very supportive. He would say, 'If that's what you really want to do, do it the best you can and enjoy it.'"

Though Fred generally got along well with both his parents, he and his mother had a rocky time of it during his high school and college years. He liked not at all her pressuring him to go to Harvard and the implication in her prodding that there was something inferior about Brown, a school to which Fred grew deeply attached.

"She was always harping on my studies," recalls Fred. "I was not a stellar performer. I didn't work hard. I had fun with my friends playing soccer. Mom always wanted the A's. The last year or two I was in high school, she told me, 'You've got to get good grades so you can get into Harvard,' and the last year I was at Brown, 'You've got to get good grades to get into Harvard graduate school.' Mom was more concerned about image — that you get a Ph.D. from Harvard — than what are you going to do with it. Mom is very image conscious."

"I liked Brown right away," says Fred. "There were a lot of people there who were very, very bright, and most of them were curious about other people."

Fred changed his major eight or nine times before settling on a five-year joint B.A./B.S. program in applied math and psychology. He dutifully followed that academic path until October of his senior year, when he was informed by the dean that new curriculum rules would not permit him to take such a course of study. He would have to pick a single major and graduate in four years. He chose applied math.

So little ambition and drive did Fred Wang possess that he had given no thought to what he would do after college. When, after graduation, he finally considered his future, he had no ideas. With no options that attracted him, Fred turned to the easiest route available: the family business. He says he thought of the company as a "fallback." Certainly, he says, he harbored no grand plan of one day ascending to the top of the company. So he went to his father to talk about a job in the family business.

In June 1972, Doctor Wang led his eldest son down to the office of Harold Koplow. "Dad took me to Harold's office and introduced me to Harold," recalls Fred. "Dad said to Harold, 'I'd like you to interview him, then hire him.'" The Doctor left the two men alone, and "Harold didn't know what to say. We sat there after my father walked out, and nobody said anything. I was much more shy and reticent. He asked me a little about Brown and what I knew about programming."

In fact, Fred knew a good deal about programming, for he had had a fair amount of experience at Brown. Koplow did as the Doctor had instructed and offered Fred a job as a programmer. Fred accepted. He went to work as one of five members of a Koplow-led team that was programming a machine that, six years later, would emerge as the Wang VS.

Fred began his career at Wang Labs working part-time. In the fall of 1972, he enrolled at Harvard as a special student and worked at the company about twenty-five or thirty hours a week. He took a course in compilers — devices that translate computer language into instructions a machine can follow — but found it "exceedingly uninteresting. I'm not a theorist. I didn't have the right mental attitude for graduate school." The truth was that he had no interest in graduate school and had enrolled purely because his mother — as a sign of status, in Fred's view — wanted him to go to Harvard.

After abandoning school in January 1973, he went to Wang Labs full-time. And he did well. For two more years he continued working as a programmer until 1974, when Koplow was made head of marketing and he promoted Fred to a position as marketing specialist in charge of tele-communications programs.

A year later, Fred took a new, ill-defined position, what he describes as a "general ombudsman" for his father. The position allowed him to work directly with An Wang, and it was designed to give Fred exposure to various parts of the company. For one month, for example, the Doctor sent his son to Florida to work out of the Tampa sales office — "to get a taste of the field," says Fred. In addition, the job called for Fred to "generally get involved in marketing issues, new product announcements," he says. He adds: "It wasn't a very structured time. I spent most of it in the word processing area trying to figure out what was going on and what needed attention. It wasn't an exceptional year."

John Cunningham says that Fred was "a pain in the ass" during this period. "He was a gofer with a lot of clout. I thought he would be better in any organizational job, where he could understand how managers manage, learn the business."

At the time, the word processing area at Wang Labs meant the ill-fated 1200. With his experience working on that system, Fred was made marketing manager of the Wang Word Processing System in late 1976, six months after it had debuted in New York. He performed competently in that position, recalls Cunningham. He was intelligent and diligent and worked well with other people.

There was a problem with that appointment, however. A marketing executive had hired someone else to run marketing for the Wang Word Processing System. Then, suddenly, the Doctor placed his son in that position. When the fellow who had been hired arrived a few months later, he was assigned to work for Fred. He was twice Fred's age and had thirty years of business experience. But Fred fired him within a few months.

"My father felt it was necessary for me to get more management background," says Fred. "Wang Labs was notorious for not training anybody. We were growing too fast to be able to afford the time."

John Cunningham had suggested to Doctor Wang that he urge Fred to get an MBA, but the Doctor had an irrational scorn for MBAs.

Instead, in the winter of 1978, Wang suggested that his son apply to the Program for Management Development, a thirteen-week crash course for executives at the Harvard Business School.

Between the time Fred applied to the Harvard program in March and his beginning it in September, a momentous event occurred, although it was so private that nobody outside of the Wang family knew anything about it. In a meeting between An Wang and Fred, the father told his son of his vision for the future. It was their first such conversation. Never before had An Wang mentioned anything to Fred about the possibility that Fred would one day take over Wang Labs. But now, on the eve of Fred's twenty-eighth birthday, his father raised the subject.

An Wang told Fred that he wanted his son to have an opportunity to run the company, and that he wanted Courtney, who was seven years Fred's junior and who had joined the company as a salesman upon his graduation from Tufts in 1975, to succeed Fred.

This was An Wang's dream. It was why he cared so passionately about controlling his company. This man, who had been taught the lessons of the Confucian relationship between father and son, looked forward to the day when the empire he was building would be ruled by other men named Wang. He was driven not by money or power, but by a desire to pass along his empire to his sons. He was driven by the need to create a legacy.

As precious as the future of his son and his company were to him, however, An Wang never had lengthy, rambling chats with Fred. It was not in the father's nature to hold such conversations. The Doctor did not need to ruminate about Fred's role in the company or his responsibility as the heir to the Wang dynasty.

Back when Fred had first got out of college and was working at the company, he had lived at home for a summer. He and his father fell into a routine of playing tennis each evening after work. So much did both men enjoy playing together that when the summer was over they contracted for a court near the company and played together one evening a week for the next fifteen years.

Theirs was not always an easy relationship, however. Around 1980, Fred became worried that his father drank too much. "He would have two or three big scotches a night," says Fred. "And there were some events where it was clear he had had too much to drink." Cunningham recalls several luncheons where Wang would have three scotches. Fred confronted his father about what he and others in the company and the family perceived as the Doctor's drinking problem. The Doctor pooh-poohed it, dismissing the suggestion that he had any sort of difficulty with alcohol. But although he never acknowledged a problem, he seemed to cut back somewhat after that.

The tense showdown over drinking notwithstanding, Fred and his father got on well. They were similar in many ways — both stoic and reserved, neither emotional or demonstrative. And both men were filled with a sense of optimism, convinced that their future would be full of sunshine.

Fred liked the prospect of rising within the company, but he did not intend to make Wang Labs his life. By the time he was thirty years old, he harbored ambitions for a second career in public service. In fact, he and his father discussed the possibility of Fred running for public office — the position of governor of Massachusetts interested him — and his father agreed that a second career might be worthwhile. This ambition was an indication of what some considered Fred's inflated view of himself. He had had so much handed to him at the company, had achieved important positions with such ease, that it seemed that Fred had come to believe he had some of the magic of his father. When Fred thought of politics, he did not think of running for alderman or state representative, entry-level political positions; he thought instead of governor. The question in Fred's mind wasn't whether he would get involved in public life, but when. His early forties seemed like the right time to him.

Fred enjoyed his months at Harvard. "The idea is to cram a two-year MBA program into thirteen weeks," says Fred. "The value of the experience is more the associations in the dorm." Students from various industries were mixed together, and Fred found himself in a dorm with people who worked in banking, oil, pharmaceuticals, and manufacturing.

A banker who went through the program with Fred was impressed with his technical know-how. "Fred seemed to be almost an extension of the computer that was there," recalls Bernie Fulp, who worked at the Bank of New England. Fulp found Fred "warm and outgoing. He had a very easy manner and an easy way with people."

A month after Fred returned to work from Harvard, his father split the marketing organization and gave half — product planning and development, the inside marketing job — to Fred, and the other half — marketing support, promotion and advertising, the external marketing — to Carl Masi.

"It was a very exciting time," recalls Fred. "People wanted to work at

Wang Laboratories. It was a very unregimented environment. The perception of the company was so positive," particularly as it related to word processing. The saying in the computer world had long been that "You never go wrong choosing IBM." When it came to word processing, the maxim became "You never go wrong choosing Wang."

Fred was considered a nice, quiet, pleasant fellow during these heady days. Though he was shy, and dealing with people was not his strength, he tried to be outgoing and approachable, and it did not go unnoticed. Other employees appreciated his efforts to put them at ease by kidding around. During one sales meeting, Fred went so far as to participate in a humorous skit in which he dressed as Superman. It was not something that could have been easy for Fred.

His reputation around this time, says John Cunningham, was that "he was doing okay." Cunningham told Doctor Wang that "Fred was probably doing fine, that he was working very hard. 'I think he carries the burden of the Wang name, and he is careful not to push people around. He's trying to become part of the team.'"

Doctor Wang replied: "The Wang name could be a burden, but if he didn't have the Wang name he'd never have that job."

Outside of work Fred was as normal as a fabulously wealthy son of An Wang could be. Like other young men his age, he enjoyed having a drink and talking sports. He played for the company soccer and softball teams and was known to be extremely competitive. Unlike other young men his age, he bought a sprawling seaside mansion — called Avalon — in an exclusive suburb north of Boston. It was a massive structure. At twenty-two thousand square feet, the interior of the house covered more than half an acre. It was graced with a tennis court, English gardens, and a saltwater pool. Fred initially decorated this cavernous space in fraternity-house style with an array of eclectic furniture, pinball machines, and stereo equipment. But by the middle of the 1980s, he had had the home redone by a professional decorator, transforming it into a gracious English country estate.

As Fred approached his thirtieth birthday, duty beckoned. If he was to one day lead the company, he would soon have to become a major player with serious responsibilities. But even as he rose within the corporation, there was no way for Fred to fight his way out from under the shadow of his father. For the ultimate reality was that Fred Wang was destined to live in that shadow for all of his days at Wang. Fred was an intelligent man, but he was no genius. He was not his father.

An Wang was revered as a towering figure in American industry. He was a scientific genius, a visionary — all of those things and more — but the truth was that, for his elder son, he was not an effective tutor. "He was not a real good teacher, at least not for me," Fred says of his father. "He would assume people could just pick it up."

The lifeblood of the company had been its machines — its break-through desktop calculators, the workhorse 2200 computer, the Wang Word Processing System, the sleek, speedy VS computer. And for the company's first twenty-nine years, An Wang had been its R&D guru. A number of immensely gifted designers had played central roles in the creation of Wang machines — men such as Harold Koplow, David Moros, Bob Siegel, and Bob Kolk. But there had never been any doubt that the guiding technical genius had always been the Doctor.

In 1980, An Wang decreed that his son would take over no less vaunted a position than head of research and development, the very heart of Wang Laboratories.

Fred's debut — the product announcement soiree in October 1983 — was a smash hit. It could hardly have been a more successful event In the days following the announcement, Wang stock climbed to $36 a share on two-day gains of almost $3.50. "Wall Street loves Wang again," read the lead to the *Financial Times* story one week after the event. It was the magic of imaging technology in the form of the Wang Professional Image Computer, known as PIC, that stole the show. The *New York Times* thought the event worthy of a story and emphasized the introduction of PIC. The *Financial Times* described PIC as "a significant and innovative development in the office equipment market and a further attractive enhancement of its Wang PC line."

Few observers or analysts had followed the company as closely or as long as John Adams of Adams, Harkness & Hill in Boston. And in the wake of the product announcement, no one was more bullish on Wang Labs. The day after the product announcement, Adams's report carried the headline "Still the Pioneer." He wrote: "The last two years have been great ones for Wang. The company has become established as the leader in office automation; sales have grown vigorously; management has been strengthened at all levels; and the balance sheet has undergone dramatic improvement. However, even though there was progress on all fronts, something seemed lacking." What was lacking, in Adams's view, was the kind of innovation that had been Wang's hallmark in earlier years, when it had produced the 2200, the word processing system, and the VS, one right after the other.

"For those who may have felt that Wang was settling too comfortably into the establishment, yesterday was an abrupt awakening," Adams observed.

Adams liked a lot of those new offerings, but more than anything else, he liked PIC. "By any standard," he wrote, PIC "represents a major advance in the capability of the work station. . . . PIC is eloquent evidence, otherwise lacking in recent months, that the IBM PC is not the sole cure for the ills of mankind.

"PIC and the . . . other new products should serve to strengthen investors' confidence that Wang will continue to play the role of pioneer."

PIC was the first office system that included the use of "imaging" technology, a cutting-edge application that allowed computers to show and store drawings, photographs, handwritten notes, and more. Imaging worked by feeding the image desired — a photograph, for example — through a camera that translated the picture into digits. This groundbreaking innovation made it possible to work on a computer not just with words, but with maps, pictures, memos, or any kind of document. PIC allowed users to merge pictures and text, to send the image or the text or both to another computer location instantaneously, or to store the material for later use.

"Most large companies produce a variety of documents which require input from many different sources," Fred said at the product announcement press conference. "With PIC, they have the ability to create, modify, and transmit documents with images quickly and efficiently."

Imaging technology, *Computerworld* reported, "gained new respectability this month when Wang Laboratories, Inc., announced its Professional Image Computer (PIC) as part of its Professional Computer line, putting those digitized images on the screen and ultimately on a network for transmission and manipulation. . . . Wang's announcement was the first major commitment by an office vendor to this technology. . . ."

It was crucial that PIC sell well, for the truth was that Wang Labs had not had a new hit product, not a big hit, anyway, in five years, and in the computer industry five years is an eternity. But it looked very much as though PIC would be their next hit, that it would take its place alongside the 2200, the word processing system, and the VS in the Wang hall of fame.

PIC was the sexiest new product announced that day, but not the only one. The new offerings were tied together in what the company said were the six technologies needed in any office: word processing, data processing, image processing, audio processing (telephone voice mail), networking (moving words, data, voice, and images from one place to another), and what the company described as "human factors," the physiology of the office.

The integration of technology — the company called its systems approach the Wang Office — put Wang ahead of many of its competitors in recognizing where the future lay. The notion was that Wang would sell its customers total office solutions — technology that would tie together all office functions — rather than simply selling a customer the latest mini or hottest printer. This strategic approach was fundamentally sound.

Fred took charge of R&D at a time of upheaval in the computer industry. During the late 1970s there were the initial ripples of the personal computer tidal wave that was headed Wang's way. And around 1980, Digital and IBM mounted serious campaigns to compete for the billions of dollars at stake in the office market where Wang was so firmly entrenched. It was clear to Fred when he took over R&D that the company could continue living off its three extremely successful products for a while longer, but that some innovation was needed if the company was to grow.

"It was obvious at the time that people didn't want single box solutions," says Fred. "All three products were headed toward the same solution. We came up with Wang Office, a software product that allowed the different machines to communicate."

Though PIC was the star of that day's show, the company had a cast of thirteen other new products, most of which were modifications of previous offerings.

One was a software package offering the Wang Word Processing System magic to users of other types of computers. It was a significant shift in corporate strategy, and one for which Fred was given credit. Previously, the Doctor had jealously guarded Wang's software, refusing to adapt to standards that would allow the material to be used on other companies' equipment. There was, within the company, a miniversion of the struggle going on in the industry. Wang Labs' products, like those of most computer companies, worked exclusively with other Wang products. Wang word processing needed a Wang printer, for example. The 2200 and VS computers could communicate well with each other, but less effectively with an IBM or Honeywell machine. While these proprietary systems, as they are called, were great for the companies' profits, they severely restricted users' options. Many users saw the ideal computer world as one in which they could mix and match different brands, a world where all computers, using the same standards, would be compatible with one another. The analogy often cited was that of stereo equipment. A consumer can choose one brand of compact disc player, a different brand of receiver, and a third brand of speakers with confidence that all will work together. The move toward standards envisioned a similar situation with computers.

But Doctor Wang had seen his company grow on the enormous profits derived from proprietary systems, and he resisted standards. It was clear that standards would bring increased competition within each market and reduce the traditionally hefty profit margins that Wang had long enjoyed. But Fred and other senior managers within the company insisted — correctly, as it has turned out — that standards were the wave of the future. Reluctantly, the Doctor agreed that Wang Labs had to move toward standards in some of its products.

Fred, it seemed, had risen to the occasion. The question on many minds when he took over R&D from his father was whether he had the ability to continue Wang's tradition of technical innovation. Just two months after the product announcement, an industry publication, *Data Communications,* reflected on that question and observed that "the pace of innovation at Wang seems to have accelerated."

On the surface, Wang Laboratories appeared to be a healthy, vibrant, growing company with a glorious future. But John Cunningham was concerned. He was terribly worried, in fact, that the products would turn out to be not very good or that they would be delivered late, or both.

From Cunningham's perspective, the problem was Fred. A crucial element in Wang's success had been the Doctor's skillful management of the R&D group. When the Doctor placed Fred in that position, Cunningham had been alarmed enough to express his concern to An Wang.

"I can see it working if you work together," Cunningham said. "You teach him. You jointly decide what to do."

The Doctor promised he would watch closely over the development operation, but it had soon become clear that Fred didn't want his father looking over his shoulder. Fred wanted to run his own show and the Doctor permitted him to do that.

Cunningham was worried not only about the company but about his stake in it. His financial interest in Wang Laboratories consisted of more than just his salary and bonus. Cunningham earned about $550,000 in 1983, a great deal of money, but not the fortune he could earn through stock. He had accumulated a position of more than 375,000 shares (worth nearly $10 million at a share price in the high twenties) during the fifteen years he had been at Wang. Now, as he looked ahead, Cunningham saw that the net effect of Fred running R&D would be a decline over time in the stock value. He knew that the outside perception of the company was that it was extremely strong. Cunningham believed Wang's peak had been reached two years earlier. He believed that Fred running development was a flaw so great that it could be fatal to the company. And he believed very strongly that he owed it to himself and his family to get his money out of the company while it still had great value.

In the spring of 1983 John Cunningham made the remarkable decision to sell his Wang stock — *all* of it. Or all that he could sell, which amounted to about 140,000 shares. When he went to Doctor Wang and told him he wanted to sell the stock, the Doctor tried to talk him out of it. Cunningham explained that he was building a house in the exclusive Boston suburb of Weston that was turning out to be more expensive than he had anticipated. Doctor Wang offered to loan him the money. Cunningham said he would talk it over with his wife that night and get back to the Doctor in the morning. But he said that only to be polite. He had no intention of reconsidering his decision. The next morning, Cunningham sold the stock and then informed the Doctor what he had done.

It was, in its way, an extraordinary event. One of the top executives of what was perceived to be one of the best companies in the world was dumping all of the shares that he could legally sell. It should have been a signal to the outside world. But only two outside analysts questioned him. And he told both he was building a house and had some taxes to pay. "Gee," said one analyst, "must be a nice house."

At the price of $41.50, the shares he sold were worth $8.3 million. Cunningham's prescience was eerie. He sold his shares at a mere ten cents shy of the peak Wang Laboratories reached before beginning its epic decline.

Cunningham was right. The company *was* in trouble. The simple almost unbelievable truth was that, without exception, every product announced that day in October 1983 was delivered late. Some were months late. Others were years late.

And there were people within the company who knew that what had looked so good on the surface masked a grim reality. To these officials, to those who *knew* that many if not most of the products were not ready to be announced, the event was madness. Some of the products were so far from being ready for the marketplace that they were actually little more than concepts in someone's mind.

Just three weeks before the announcement, Peter McElroy, who was in charge of organizing the events of the product announcement, went to a meeting in Fred's office. McElroy was astounded to see an engineer go to the blackboard and draw his concept of the Wang Office, an electronic mail and message system. McElroy could not believe what he was seeing. A project like this took years to develop and here they were with nothing more than chalk dust for a product that was to be announced to the world in just three weeks. This was insane!

"There was no product," says John Thibault. "It was two years before it came out and two and a half before it worked."

Jake Jacobson, who was then vice-president of international marketing and who also saw what McElroy had witnessed, was so alarmed that he went to Fred privately and said he thought that if they were late in delivering products customers would be very unhappy, and it would present a huge problem for the salespeople. "Fred said, 'That's how we get products out the door. Put a hard date on the ground and rally the development troops to have it out.'"

It was true that such an approach made sense under certain circumstances. Wang had missed delivery dates in the past — with the 700 and the word processing system, among others — yet their products had been so good that customers tolerated the delays. But the world had changed in the years since those products were introduced. In the old days, the computer business, particularly for high-flying companies such as Wang, was a seller's market. Wang had products customers simply couldn't get anywhere else; they had no choice but to wait. In the early 1980s, all that changed. The computer business was growing more competitive by the week, and customers were finding that they had alternatives. If they couldn't get a product from Wang, they could get it, or something comparable, somewhere else. It was turning into a buyer's market. And the level of customer tolerance for screw-ups was plummeting.

There was another difference: when a smallish, $50 million company doesn't deliver its products on time, nobody much notices or cares. When a $2 billion world computer power fails to deliver on time, that's a far more serious matter. "If you announce five products and deliver three on time that's one thing," says McElroy. "But this was zero for fourteen!"

The products were rushed, says McElroy, because "Fred was new at R&D, and he wanted to show that he could produce products like his father."

But it had the opposite effect. It hurt Fred's credibility badly.

Announcing products before they were ready for market was bad, but what the announcement revealed about the company was far worse. The announcement of "vaporware" products stemmed from a growing arrogance within Wang Laboratories. Wang had been so successful for so long that the we-can-do-anything spirit had grown into a poisonous belief in the company's infallibility. John Cunningham walked into a meeting one day and heard someone say that the word processing market belonged to Wang, that it was Wang's market in the first place. So many employees were new that few recalled the failures of the 1200 system, the battles with IBM. Cunningham got angry. "There's a big difference in the way people act when they believe a market is theirs," he said. "We don't own that marketplace. That's IBM's. We took it from them, and they desperately want it back!"

As early as April 1983, there had been scattered doubts within the industry about Wang. A *Datamation* piece that month was headlined "Trouble in Paradise?" The article reported that some industry insiders believed that "Wang's remaining days in the sun are numbered." Amy Wohl, a respected industry analyst, told *Datamation* that Wang had met little competition in the office market, but she predicted "that will change dramatically this year. The competition is massing. Giants like IBM and AT&T are positioning themselves. . . ." The *Datamation* reporter observed: "This is the time when any comparison between [Fred] Wang and his father will be unfair, for the elder Wang has come to symbolize a passing era. Now that he's stepped aside from day-to-day operations, the Doctor leaves behind his legend — but maybe the golden days have gone with him."

Cunningham sensed around the end of 1983, the beginning of 1984, that the Doctor was also concerned. Wang never said anything explicit to him — and Cunningham believes Wang would never have admitted it — but he is sure An Wang had some doubts about the company's course.

A task force was set up to look at acquisitions, but Cunningham didn't believe Wang Labs should be shopping for other companies unless its own house was in order, and it wasn't. The Doctor, however, was determined.

"At the time, there was a takeover mania," recalls Fred. "Dad's view was we have a unique asset with family control, and that perhaps we should leverage that to gain size, to see if synergies could be gained. He'd read Valueline, Barrons. He thought size would be important in the computer industry."

Wang was so serious about it that they hired the Merrill Lynch mergers and acquisitions team, led by its ace Ken Miller, and Miller brought in Joe Flom, a star at the law firm of Skadden, Arps. These heavy hitters traveled to Lowell and gave the Wang executives a basic course in acquisitions. One of the possibilities Wang looked at was Southern New England Telephone. Doctor Wang went so far as to express an interest to that company's chairman, but Wang was told New England Tel wasn't interested.

Around this time, a deal that might have dramatically changed the course of the company's history began percolating. Exxon, the oil giant, was looking to get rid of its Exxon Systems subsidiary in early 1984. Back in the 1970s Exxon had made an ill-fated attempt to break into the computer office market by setting up Exxon Systems. The operation had not gone well. Exxon came to Wang and proposed that Wang Labs buy Exxon Systems and that Exxon buy a 25 percent interest in Wang for between $1.6 and $2 billion in cash.

This was an astounding offer. It would have given Wang, then valued at $8 billion, the assets of Exxon Systems, but, far more important, it would have given Wang a staggering amount of cash, cash that could be used to cushion almost any blow for years to come. It would be particularly useful to a company like Wang, which had borrowed so much money to finance its rapid expansion. For all Wang Labs' growth and success, it still had one of the heaviest debt loads in the computer industry. Wang's debt-equity ratio was a frighteningly high 50 percent in 1981 and 1982. In 1983, it declined to 30 percent, but that was still much higher than Digital's, which was only 3 percent. The infusion of Exxon cash would wipe out that debt, thus immeasurably strengthening Wang's position should something go wrong with the business.

The offer represented a good deal for Exxon, as well. They were looking to unload responsibility for Exxon Office Systems, a business in which their executives were far from expert. If Wang accepted the offer, Exxon Office Systems would be getting top-flight management by people who obviously understood the computer office market. Exxon would be buying management. It didn't hurt Wang's reputation at all that *Dun's Business Monthly* selected Wang Labs as one of the five best-managed companies of 1984, even after cracks began to appear in 1983.

Appearing in the spring of 1984, the *Dun's* article stated:

> Wang has achieved one of the most impressive growth records in all of industry. The company has rung up ten years of successive quarterly earnings increases, scoring a 39% compounded annual growth rate over

the past five years. And its revenues have doubled in just the past two years, a considerable achievement in the highly competitive office automation arena. In fiscal 1984 (ended June 30) earnings shot up 31% to $1.52 a share on a 42% rise in revenues to $2.2 billion. . . .

. . . Beyond its finely tuned strategy and technological prowess, Wang's heady growth has been fueled by the entrepreneurial style of An Wang [who] . . . has imbued management with an audacious, risk-taking willingness to challenge competitors many times Wang's size — particularly, of course, giant IBM. "We have proved that it is possible to move against companies like IBM and succeed, even when they control 80% to 90% of a market," An Wang maintains. "IBM is not that formidable, and we are not afraid of competing head-on in markets."

The streak continued when An Wang and John Cunningham were named co-executives of the year in 1984 by Barrons.

The Exxon offer was an attractive deal that Cunningham very much wanted to do. But the family held a separate meeting over a weekend and the deal, which the family believed would inevitably lead to Exxon's controlling Wang Labs, was nixed.

Just months later, another deal was in the works. In the summer of 1984, ITT, the giant conglomerate, was in some trouble. They were the target of a possible hostile takeover, and Rand V. Aroskog, the ITT chairman, wanted no part of it. Aroskog saw that the best way to avoid a takeover was to preempt it with a merger, and he liked Wang Labs very much. Aroskog called Cunningham, whom he knew, and raised the subject. Serious discussion began right away, and it was immediately clear that a joining of the two companies would immunize the new entity from raiders. The protection lay in the different classes of Wang stock, which allowed the family to control the company through its shares, which held ten times the voting power of nonfamily shares. If Wang and ITT were to merge, the Wang family would be able to halt any hostile takeover by voting its powerful shares. Wang seemed an ideal place for ITT to seek refuge from unwanted attack. As discussions progressed through the summer, there seemed to be no serious obstacles to a merger. Talks went so far as to raise the issues of what Aroskog's and Cunningham's respective titles would be in the new company. They had even agreed that half the board meetings would be held in New York and half in Boston.

Everything seemed set. It was a good deal for Wang, Cunningham believed, because it would supply Wang with ready access to cash. In

November, Wang chief counsel, Ed Grayson, flew to New York City with
Aroskog in Aroskog's private jet (with his initials on the tail fin) to work
out the final details. Aroskog told Grayson the financial structure would
have to be cleaned up. They'd have to get rid of the C stock. Grayson
was alarmed. He told Aroskog the C stock was sacrosanct; it was what
permitted Doctor Wang to control the company. Even though it was the
C stock that would be ITT's ultimate protection from a hostile takeover,
Aroskog said that if that stock continued to exist, Doctor Wang would
exercise control over not just Wang Labs but also over the newly merged
company combining Wang and ITT. That's right, Grayson told him.

The deal died right there.

By the end of 1984, the full scope of the disaster from the landmark October 1983 product announcement was clear. George F. Colony was a
young computer industry analyst whose company, Forrester Research in
Cambridge, conducted research on high-tech companies and advised a
variety of businesses on which computer companies to buy equipment
from, and advised computer companies of customer needs. Colony was
not shy about expressing his opinions, and in a report he wrote in late
1984 he dealt a blow to the company in general and Fred's leadership at
R&D in particular.

"Wang Business Badly Hurt by Late Products," said the front page of
the Forrester report. Inside, in a special report on Wang, Colony noted
that every major product announced in October 1983 was late. He noted
that the late deliveries created "a crisis of confidence on the part of Wang
users and a growing inability for Wang to compete with IBM," Digital,
and Data General in the Fortune 1000 market. Colony wrote:

> While the exact reasons for Wang's declining growth have been hotly
> debated, Forrester believes that three factors are important:
>
>   1) Key Wang products have not been delivered to customers on
> time;
>
>   2) Wang has had its traditional high ground (end-user computing)
> stolen out from under it by the IBM PC . . . ;
>
>   3) IBM's Office Systems Family (the PC, S/36, Mainframe), Data
> General's CEO, and Digital's All-In-1 system have created viable alter-
> natives to Wang's solutions.

The most damaging aspect of the late deliveries, Colony wrote, was
that while annoyed customers waited for Wang equipment, "they began
to examine alternatives from Data General and Digital. Wang's inability

to deliver came at a particularly poor time, coinciding with a competitive resurgence, and a generally slow period in the business."

To right itself, Colony wrote, "Wang's first priority must be re-generating an internal culture of excellent products — a goal which has been lost in the last two years' hurry to get prematurely developed systems out into the market."

The Colony report struck at the heart of the matter. For the truth was that Wang Laboratories would never quite recover from the disaster of the 1983 product announcement.

NINE

"You Shoot Him or I'll Shoot Him"

J OHN RAFFO was a Fred Wang loyalist. Ted Leonsis was a John Cunningham loyalist. In December 1981, Leonsis, who worked in Wang's public relations department, was summoned to Raffo's office. Raffo, Fred's top lieutenant, told Leonsis that he didn't like the way Leonsis hustled publicity for Cunningham. Leonsis argued that positive stories about Cunningham were to the benefit of the company. Raffo said he wanted more good PR for Fred. Leonsis said he wanted that, too.

Raffo went to the window in his office and looked outside at an adjacent Wang office tower framed against an inky night sky.

"Look up," Raffo said to Leonsis. "What do you see?"

Leonsis thought this quite peculiar. "I see the dark sky, John. It's night," he replied.

"No," Raffo said, "the sign." He gestured toward the huge blue Wang logos mounted atop each of the towers.

"It says Wang," Leonsis said.

"Exactly," said Raffo, pointedly. "It *doesn't* say Cunningham."

"It was a highly political environment that started at the top," says Bob Siegel, the designer of the VS computer. "There were armed camps, backstabbing. People have only a certain amount of psychic energy, and it was directed too much to turf wars."

By 1982, or 1983 at the latest, "you had to start picking sides," recalls John Thibault, who had clearly thrown his lot in with Fred. "Either you were on Fred's team or you were on Cunningham's team. If you were going to survive, you had to belong to one of those camps."

The conflict with Fred gnawed at Cunningham. As early as 1982, Cunningham had expressed serious concern about his own future at the company. Louis Cabot recalls that not long after he joined the Wang board of directors in June 1982, "John told me he didn't think he would stay very long because of the conflict with Fred."

No matter what he did, no matter how successful his strategies, no matter how productive his sales force, Cunningham could not get away from the Fred problem. In May 1982, Cunningham was in Europe for a series of meetings with his field people. His last stop was Frankfurt for sessions with his good friend Dick Connaughton, Wang Labs' top man in Germany. Normally, an evening out for these two men, both so skilled at spending the company's money, would have been an occasion to remember. But when Cunningham arrived in Frankfurt, Connaughton found his friend "disturbed. He was trying to figure out where Doctor Wang's head was."

Connaughton says Cunningham was "starting to see that this was finite," that Fred might be destined to take over the company, and, if that was the case, that Cunningham's career at Wang would not only be limited, but it might end far sooner than he could have anticipated.

Connaughton did not want to sting his friend, but he wanted him to have no illusions. He spoke bluntly to Cunningham. "The major reason you're there is to give this kid some street smarts," Connaughton said. "I think the old man's pitting you against him to make him tougher."

If that was true, then the conclusion was inescapable: When Fred was sufficiently toughened, Cunningham would be dispensable.

Cunningham was upset and angry. He had started life with little, earned two degrees, and worked his way up through the ranks of a company to which he had proven himself an invaluable asset. He had deserved his promotions. The Doctor had relied on him, counted on him to be the company's public face, to run the sales force, and to set strategy. There was never any doubt that the man Doctor Wang relied upon more than anyone else was John Cunningham. He had *proven* his worth.

Fred, in Cunningham's mind, had proven nothing. He had been anything but a hard worker. The reality, in Cunningham's view, was that Fred had his job not because of experience or vision or brains or anything having to do with merit. "He had his job," says Cunningham, "because of his name."

Of that, there was absolutely no question.

Cunningham believed that while he had been driving a fabulously successful sales and marketing operation, Fred had been, in Cunningham's words, fucking up research and development. Didn't the Doctor see that? It was so terribly, embarrassingly obvious that Fred wasn't cut out for that crucial role. It was clear he was unable to deal with the company's three development stars — Harold Koplow, Bob Siegel, and Bob Kolk.

While Fred's reputation was as the boss's kid who had screwed up R&D, Cunningham was seen within the company and by financial and industry analysts in glowing terms. The contrast between the two men escaped no one's notice. Fred knew that Cunningham was viewed, in Fred's words, as "a person who had worked his way up through the organization from sales rep to head of worldwide sales and marketing. And there was me who sort of jumped from department to department. I certainly had opportunities others did not have. There was a conflict in our backgrounds and styles."

Both were bright, though Cunningham had an MBA while Fred did not. Where Cunningham was outgoing and charismatic, Fred was quiet and easily lost in a crowd. Where Cunningham was a mesmerizing public speaker — an entertainer, really — Fred's public performances tended to be rather ordinary. Most important, Cunningham was a natural leader, a man behind whom the troops rallied. Fred, on the other hand, had a reputation around the company for being somewhat immature, and even the Doctor felt Fred had a tendency to appear arrogant. Still, his father was rotating Fred through a series of assignments throughout the company so that by the mid-1980s Fred would have experience in marketing, development, manufacturing, finance, and sales.

This was the father's plan. This was what the father wanted. This was what Fred would do.

There was a sense among some senior managers that Fred particularly resented Cunningham's relationship with An Wang. "John was treated by Doctor and Mrs. Wang almost as if he was a member of the family," says consultant George Rich. "Young Fred was jealous of the notoriety and success of his rival." When Mrs. Wang referred to Cunningham as "our American son," Wang observers say, it must have been a stinging moment for Fred. In retrospect, Fred calls his mother's remark "momentary insanity." He adds dryly: "I never considered him my American brother."

Cunningham's view of Fred was harsh. Though not uncritical, Fred's view of Cunningham was less negative. Fred believed that Cunningham deserved some credit for the company's success, but he saw Cunningham taking too much credit. It was true, Fred conceded, that Cunningham did build the sales force, but how hard was it to sell products for which customers were clamoring?

Fred conceded Cunningham's superiority in some areas. "John Cunningham is a brilliant man and a very engaging sales type," says Fred. "John has a certain style that matches his personality. People are comfortable with him, with his glibness and irreverence. He can be quite entertaining. He did a tremendous job developing the sales network for the company.

"John had a very strong following," Fred continues. "John is very bright, charming. It is very enjoyable to sit down over a beer to hear him tell stories. John has great stories."

But there was another side to Cunningham, Fred confided to intimates. Fred felt he had a different value system from Cunningham, whom Fred viewed as extremely materialistic and concerned about being seen with the "right" people. There was a nouveau riche air about Cunningham that Fred disliked. And Cunningham's sharp tongue put Fred off, as well. Cunningham sometimes talks "negatively about people behind their back," says Fred. "I didn't realize that about him at first."

Fred says that for several years he learned by watching Cunningham in action, but by about 1981 Fred says he had learned all he could from Cunningham.

"It's really important to me that you and Fred get along," the Doctor told Cunningham over Chivas Regal before lunch one day in 1983. They were at the Doctor's customary spot, the Lanam Club in North Andover. "It's one of the biggest problems I have." Wang conveyed to Cunningham how seriously he took the rift between Cunningham and Fred. The conflict was hurting the company, the Doctor said, and he wanted both men to make an effort to get along. It was crucial that they reach some sort of accommodation. "The company was driven by two major engines," says Fred, "sales and development. John had one and I had the other."

That lunch was repeated several times through 1984. The color of the Doctor's crisply knotted bow tie would change, but the other details — from the Doctor's prelunch drinks to the message — remained the same.

Wang had similar sessions with his son, during which he told Fred that it was crucial that he and Cunningham get along.

In the spring of 1984, Cunningham promised the Doctor that he would sit down with Fred for a candid discussion. And so they settled in at the conference table in Fred's large, well-appointed corner office. Cunningham had thought carefully about the meeting in advance and he prepared what he considered an honest assessment of Fred and himself. Cunning-ham leaned forward over his handwritten notes and plunged in. Both he and Fred agree that the following is an accurate portrayal of that meeting.

"I had lunch with your father, and he wants to make sure that we basically have a good working relationship," Cunningham began. "I tried to put together some things that I'm worried about to see if we can set sort of a baseline so that we both understand where one another is com-ing from because whatever my long term role might be in this situation, I think I can be useful in the short term. I think that the two of us — despite the fact that we might not have worked well together in the past — if we are going to make this thing through the next two or three years, which are going to be tough, have to figure out better how we can interact with one another. You have to have a better understanding of where I'm coming from on certain things, and I need to understand more where you're coming from. I think we've gotten into trouble in the past because neither one of us has understood where the other one was com-ing from. I tried to scribble through some notes that we can use as a format to try to get some of the issues out on the table."

Fred sat silently, listening intently.

"I started out putting together some of the things that concern me about myself. From where I came, my background, I've reached a lot of the financial objectives and position objectives that I've wanted in life. I've talked to your father about the fact that I've been concerned about my own self-motivation, whether or not I have sufficient self-motivation behind me to really keep going at the kind of pace I've gone at the past ten years. I worry about that. The same thing with the personal goals and objectives. I set very specific financial and monetary position goals, and I've met most of those. And your father has said, 'Well, you ought to set as a goal that we want to become half the size of IBM.' I can't work to a goal like that. I need something that's more tangible, more specific. I've been concerned over the past year, year and a half, about my own per-sonal goals and objectives.

"I basically have some real concerns about this issue of you and me not getting along that well together or not having a good businesslike trust in one another. It's not a new issue. It's been identified as an issue for three or four years; everyone's been talking about it for three or four years, but we haven't made that much progress in three or four years. That doesn't mean that we can't, but I'm just saying I really have some real concerns about whether or not we can build a good businesslike type of relationship.

The original site of Wang Laboratories, Inc.

An Wang as a graduate
student at Harvard

Contemplating a question

Working on the circuit board
of a calculator

Dr. G. Y. Chu went to high school and college with An Wang. He later worked at Wang Labs and served on the company's board of directors.

Harold Koplow, leader of the team that built the Wang Word Processing System

Bob Kolk led the teams that built the 2200 computer and the Wang PC

Bob Siegel headed the group that built the Wang VS minicomputer

courtesy of Wang Laboratories, Inc.

courtesy of Wang Laboratories, Inc.

John Cunningham drove the
company's sales force and,
with Dr. Wang, created
the marketing strategy
throughout the glory years

Ted Dully, *Boston Globe*

In the summer of 1980, John Cunningham, Dr. Wang, and Fred Wang pose with the Wang
Word Processing System

Ground-breaking for a new
Wang facility in Boston
attracts (from left)
Massachusetts Senate
president William M. Bulger,
Lieutenant Governor John F.
Kerry (later U.S. senator),
the Doctor, and Boston
mayor Kevin H. White

The Doctor with Prince
Charles during a visit to the
towers. Note Courtney Wang
to the prince's left.

The towers

Fred and his father

An and Lorraine Wang

The Doctor and Mrs. Wang with Fred and Courtney at the dedication of the Wang
Ambulatory Care Center at Massachusetts General Hospital

Louis Cabot (right) and
Peter Brooke, both members
of the board of directors,
played key roles during the
company's crisis period in
1989

An Wang gave Richard W. Miller what the Doctor had jealously guarded for decades — control of Wang Laboratories

Miller masterminded the deal that brought Wang into an alliance with longtime rival IBM

"I worry at times whether I am more of a brat than I should be. I mean I like being a brat. I probably have always been a brat, but basically I worry about that. I want people to pay attention to me. I want people to pay attention to me *now*. I want my way. I don't want it to stand in the way of being able to get the job done. I have concerns about playing favorites within my own organization. My own judgments on some of my own people aren't as crisp and cold as they should be. I've always had concerns that I've left people in positions too long. I think once I'm unhappy with the people I move on them, but I probably have lost opportunity by letting different people stay in slots too long."

This was something Cunningham knew Fred believed. Cunningham did live for too long with marginal performers. But he believed that, given the company's growth, hanging on to someone certainly wouldn't break the Wang Labs bank, and it might well spare the individual's ego and his income.

"I have concerns about mouthing off," said Cunningham, referring to a couple of instances in the previous year or so during which he had shouted and sworn at people. There was one particular instance in which Cunningham blew up at a couple of Fred's people and called one an "asshole." And although he had done it on purpose and for effect, he suspected that Fred thought his actions indicated a level of emotional instability.

"I have concerns about that, and I have concerns about avoiding conflict and controversy, about staying away from unpleasant issues. So those are some of the concerns I have about myself.

"On the other hand, despite all those concerns about myself, I think that I have some pluses, I have something to add. First of all, I think I have very good interpersonal skills. I think I've done a very good job representing the company both internally and externally to the Wall Street group. I have good verbal communications skills, and I'm a good motivator. I've put together a highly motivated group of average people that became a good organization. And I'm a good quasi-tech."

This was a sore spot with Cunningham. Unlike many executives on the sales and marketing side of computer companies, Cunningham was quite comfortable with and knowledgeable about the technical side of the business. He was, after all, a B.S. in math and physics, who, as a young high-school student, had gone out of his way to take all the IBM computer courses he could find outside of school. Fred, in Cunningham's view, never respected Cunningham's technical ability. "I can deal with the meanings and understand the technical issues. I look at myself as really a good marketing strategist, and I think I have a reasonably good balance of general management skills. I understand what's going on in development. I understand the issues in manufacturing. I've picked up a good understanding of the financial operations and sales and support and distribution. I think I'm a good leader and a good compromiser and I'm a good listener. So there are some pluses to go along with all these difficult things."

And then he turned to his criticisms of Fred. The tension in the conversation rose several notches when he did so. He glanced from his notes at Fred, who said nothing.

"On the other hand I have some concerns, some real concerns, about some of the things going on within the company, particularly within development," Cunningham said. "I'm concerned about whether or not we have the right technology, the right products, whether or not the decision-making process really works right. I've seen us do products that in retrospect didn't make any sense to do. So I'm really worried about that process. I have real concerns about the schedule. We announced all this stuff back in the fall of '83. If we don't get it delivered, we're going to be in trouble. I have concerns about morale within development, about the turnover within development, about the motivation levels within development. And I have concerns about how quickly we're moving in building a strong technical management team. We lost some of the senior technical leaders, and we haven't done anything about really replacing them.

"When you went into development I thought that your father and you would basically co-manage development, and it hasn't worked out that way. You either wanted to run it yourself the way you wanted to run it, or he's just letting you do it the way you want to do it. In any case I don't think that's working as well as it probably should and that sort of bothers me.

"I have personal concerns about you and me. As strange as it may seem and as dumb as it may be, I really have concerns that you feel you want me to fail. We had this situation at Equitable where Equitable was a $25 million potential account and they wanted to do things that were reasonable, and you just didn't want to do them."

(Wang had sold Equitable some $25 million of equipment — the cutting edge of the office future — and it was crucial that the new technology Wang had installed work well. Wang Labs could parlay their success into sales at other large companies and billions of dollars of business.

Cunningham believed that Fred should have gone all out to service Equitable and, in Cunningham's view, Fred had not done so.)

"Or at least I felt that you didn't want to do them and I had the passing thought that, 'Shit, maybe one of the reasons you don't want to do them is because you don't care about Equitable and you don't care if Equitable screws up because maybe that will make me fail.' That's probably more of an indication as to how poor our relationship is more than anything else because I'm sure you don't want to do that. But I actually had that feeling. There are times actually that I really thought that you wanted me to fail despite the fact that I'm in a very responsible position in the family business.

"I also have real concerns that you don't like me for whatever reason. You just don't like me. You don't understand what I did; you don't respect what I did. You just don't like me, and I probably can't recover from something like that. And as a result of that I really have concerns that you see no future role for me in the company. And I have this concern that you either might take action or inaction like not doing something that's reasonable for Equitable to make me fail. Right or wrong, those are concerns that I have.

"I also have some personal concerns about you, so better to lay them out on the table rather than having them and letting you think that I don't have feelings about it. I think you're isolated from the customers in the marketplace. I just don't think you spend the amount of time talking to customers that you should. I think you stay away from them. I think your own capability to listen to multiple sources and to compromise is probably not as good as it should be. I have concerns about your own capability to lead the organization because I don't think the organization currently is a highly motivated organization. I think you have a capability or a tendency to want to decide everything yourself. I mean you just run it very differently than your father did. If we're going to build any relationship I can't be doing all of it and you can't be doing all of it, and you don't have a tendency to want to go halfway in building a relationship. I think you really have a tendency not to learn when I think you are in a learning position and I think your not wanting to co-manage it with your father assumes basically that you're not in a learning position. I think we're all in learning positions. I'm still learning stuff; you're still learning stuff. Yet I think you have a tendency to think you've already learned it. You don't think you're in a learning position. You should be learning like crazy but you want to tell people what to do.

"I think you've lost some key people, and I think you have a tendency to rationalize. I think you have a real tendency to have weak people around you. I have a lot of concerns about whether we're making the right technology products. I think we've lost a sense of urgency over the last couple of years.

"I have real concerns about how much progress we've made in building a senior-level management technical team. I really have concerns about the morale and the turnover and the motivation levels in development.

"That's sort of my laundry list of my worries. They're all perceptions. They all really are things that we're going to have to deal with. I don't know whether this has helped to at least clear the air as to whether or not you understand sort of where I'm coming from."

Cunningham told Fred much, but not all, of what he felt. He did not tell Fred that he thought Fred was a weirdo. "Fred would stare at me all the time," says Cunningham. "It was weird. With anybody else I'd say, 'What the fuck are you staring at me for?' Ellen would say at dinner parties, 'Why does Fred stare at you?'"

Cunningham did not tell Fred that he deeply resented Fred's lack of understanding of his role in the company's history. "I knew Fred was telling the father, 'Cunningham is no good; his people are no good.' I wasn't going to sit down and tell Fred what I had done for that company from 1967 to 1983. If Fred Wang couldn't figure out that I was useful to him, that's his problem. And it's going to cost him a lot of money."

Fred had very little reaction to all of this.

"I didn't think John had to be my friend to be a fellow-employee," says Fred. "I actually thought John and I had a good friendship, but not much of a working relationship."

"He didn't really react," says Cunningham. "He didn't disagree, he didn't fully agree, he just sort of listened."

The meeting proved to be fruitless. The relationship changed not at all. Cunningham had been making an effort to get along with Fred — at least he believed he had been making an effort — but after the meeting he saw that it was hopeless. "I said, 'Hey, what the fuck,'" says Cunningham. "It wasn't important to my life that Fred Wang like me."

The situation had deteriorated beyond the point of repair. Perhaps if An Wang had been as intensely involved with the company as he had been until about 1982 he might have seen how destructive the relationship between Cunningham and Fred really was. Though the Doctor remained the unquestioned leader of the company, he had withdrawn from his intense operational role after turning the reins of R&D over to Fred. Until the early 1980s, An Wang knew the intimate details of the company's finances, manufacturing, distribution, sales, and, of course, product development. With the Doctor even marginally removed from the scene, the destructive conflict between Fred and Cunningham only grew.

"Fred had no respect for me," says Cunningham, "and I had no respect for Fred. After a while, I didn't want the relationship to work. No matter how hard Wang tried, I countered it. I believed Fred was the wrong person to run R&D."

It told Cunningham something that no matter how critical he was of Fred in the Doctor's presence — and he was sometimes brutally so — he was never rebuked. Cunningham thought for a while that perhaps he could win a battle of attrition with Fred.

"I thought that over a period of time, as Fred handled different things, that he would basically strangle himself," says Cunningham, "that the more exposure people had to Fred that he would end up having a role in the company but it would be subordinate to me. I believed that as more people were exposed to him, his weaknesses would become apparent."

Cunningham thought perhaps that he could beat Fred on the merits — he truly believed he was vastly more valuable to the company than Fred, and he thought the Doctor recognized that. But he also believed he could beat Fred up politically. And he set about doing so. "Over a three- to five-year period when Fred screwed up, I made sure people knew it. I made sure he got nicked." Cunningham shrugs at the recollection and adds: "You subtly kick the shit out of anybody you think is going to get in your way."

It was all so crazy, so unnecessary, thought Louis Cabot, a member of the Wang board of directors. "I think Fred is going to be one of the richest and most powerful men presiding over one of the greatest companies in the world," Cabot told Doctor Wang when the problems between Fred and Cunningham became obvious to Cabot. "The way to do it is not to kid yourself that he worked his way up. Be concerned with getting the best, most effective people he can find. This is a tough industry, and he should think about how to get the best possible people and not worry about running R&D or manufacturing."

Cabot repeated this advice on a number of occasions in the early 1980s. He said it to Fred as well as to the Doctor. For Fred to aim at becoming the operational head of the company made no sense to Cabot. "Preside over a giant success story," he told Fred, "but don't try to run it. Get the best damn people in there."

And the best operational person might have been Cunningham. "I thought Cunningham was a winner and probably understood the business as well as anybody except the Doctor and maybe as well as anybody including the Doctor," says Cabot. "Cunningham was aware that things would have to change, that the world was changing, earlier than the family did. The family was so optimistic about everything. John Cunningham put together a sales force that could handle 50-percent-a-year growth. He was sensational at that."

It was not the last time Cabot would express concerns about Fred leading the company. Nor was it the last time that Cabot would be ignored by the Wangs.

Peter McElroy, a Harvard Business School–educated Boston Irishman, had been so delighted with the immediate success of the October 1983 product announcement that he refused to believe at the time that the company had any serious problems. But by the summer of 1984, he had grown worried. As was his wont, McElroy had been doing some doodling with numbers and what he saw concerned him. His analysis showed a company that was shifting in a dangerous direction. As he read them, the numbers indicated that Wang's revenues from maintenance and add-ons to existing systems were rising as a percentage of the company's total revenues. It was great to have those revenues, but they masked a disturbing trend: Customers were not interested in Wang's new products. Plenty were buying additions to systems already installed, and, of course, they were paying for maintenance, but there had been a dip in revenues from new products. For a company that soared on the strength of its innovative new ideas, this was an alarming turn of events.

McElroy talked with Cunningham about it. A similar phenomenon had occurred at Honeywell, Cunningham said, and, in fact, the phenomenon of a company living off of its customer base without expanding was known as the Honeywell Syndrome. "We had no new product, no new creativity," says McElroy. "We were becoming another Honeywell."

The problem was in R&D, the company's engine. The difficult but brilliant design team leaders — Harold Koplow, Bob Siegel, and Bob Kolk — were all still there, but something had changed. These men, who had created such fine products that had together yielded billions of dollars for Wang Laboratories — these men without whom "you'd have never heard of Wang," as one engineer put it — were not producing as they once had. The problem, in the minds of many, was not them, but the management of R&D.

Koplow, Siegel, and Kolk had never gotten along terribly well, in part, at least, because the Doctor had always pitted them against each other in competition for the greater glory of Wang Laboratories. As Kolk puts it: "We were made to be natural rivals."

But theirs was a cold war in which the Doctor rarely permitted open hostilities. He kept them apart — each team leader presiding over his own project. And he had just the right touch — he knew when to push or cajole, when to lay off. Fred's style was different. "If I had a problem with Siegel and Kolk, Doctor Wang would work it out," says Koplow. "He kept all of us happy. With Fred, we all had to agree or he wouldn't approve anything."

When Fred took over, he tried to adopt a more cooperative style. He believed that the combined brains of these men would be needed in the newly competitive environment within the industry. Instead of fighting with each other, Fred said, "Let's worry about IBM, DEC, Prime, and Data General."

In theory, at least, it was a terrific idea.

Fred wanted to integrate the family of Wang products. He wanted to make everything the company manufactured work with everything else made by Wang. The future of computing, he quite correctly believed, was in systems — solutions to total office computing problems — rather than in individual machines.

Koplow, Siegel, and Kolk all agreed. They too believed that Wang should integrate its systems. "For a while it was exciting," says Kolk. "We were talking back and forth about where we were going next." But there was a rub. The company had to pick the computer architecture upon which to base its standard. Would its products be standardized on the architecture of Siegel's VS? That would mean changing Kolk's 2200 and Koplow's word processing system. Would the standard be word processing? That would mean changing the VS and the 2200. It was not an easy decision. Whatever the choice, two of the three men would be disappointed.

Though there was agreement on the overall goal, there was sharp disagreement on how to reach that goal. "I was trying to overcome what was not a logical problem," says Fred. "Each of them was saying we totally agree with you — use my hardware base."

Siegel says the problem was that Fred "had a low tolerance for conflict and didn't have his father's basic good judgment."

The flirtation with consensus was brief. It was not long before each development team leader was fighting to make his machine the company standard. "It was a very frustrating time because it was almost as if none of them would accept a company view of things," says Fred. "They were more tied to their babies."

It was frustrating for the development team leaders, as well. "If you're working with creative types, you have to have an understanding of personalities and create an environment that allows them to be productive," says Siegel. "You can't ask them to gain consensus. If they're really doing something advanced, you can't then say, 'Okay, let's hold this up to the light and see if anybody sees it the same.' You also have to recognize you're taking risks. Doctor Wang knew you weren't going to win every time. If you don't take risks you get left behind because the world is changing so quickly. Under the Doctor, Wang could reach and stretch and push."

But that was not the case when Fred took over, according to Siegel. "Fred would say, 'Get together, agree, come back to me. I want something everybody likes.' It was the lowest common denominator approach to doing things."

"Creative people," says Ed Lesnick, referring to Koplow, Siegel, and Kolk, "are different. They can be difficult. You have to understand that. The Doctor understood. Fred didn't."

As time passed, it became clear, even to Fred's allies within the company, that Fred simply wasn't up to the job. He had nothing close to the level of respect his father had enjoyed.

Koplow started out as a staunch supporter of Fred's. He went so far as to recommend to Doctor Wang that Fred be put in charge of R&D, but "I never thought he would leave Fred alone," says Koplow. Things soon soured between Koplow and Fred.

Fred's job was complicated by the fact that he was younger than any of these three men, and, in Koplow's case, by the fact that Fred had worked for Harold for a number of years. Harold had been Fred's first boss at the company and the two men, says Koplow, "got along very well, and became very good friends." Koplow also respected Fred's intellect. "He didn't have the intuitiveness his father had, but he was very bright," Koplow says.

Fred was now Koplow's superior, however, and Koplow says that Fred's style of management changed after he was given development. "He had to have consensus. He would take forever to make a decision." So their relationship changed too. Koplow began to believe Fred simply didn't have what it took to get the job done. He was chagrined that the Doctor was not sufficiently involved in development. "I never thought he'd leave Fred out there to dry," says Koplow.

According to Fred: "If they could communicate, I was confident they'd make the right decisions. I never got them to trust each other enough to communicate. We'd sit down in a room, and they'd be yelling, shouting, screaming. Insults would be thrown back and forth."

It got so bad with Fred and his three stars that it became clear he had to retreat from trying to gain consensus and go back to the Doctor's method of dealing with them individually.

"My father said, 'I don't want you to have these three people together again without me,'" says Fred, who did as he was instructed.

At the core of the development problem was the Doctor as deity. When Doctor Wang became larger than life — when he was transformed from the man in charge of day-to-day operations at Wang Labs into a gray eminence and philanthropist — the company lost its finest development mind ever. And it removed Wang from a position in which he had tried to listen very carefully to the needs of customers.

Fred was removed from customers as well, says Bob Doretti, whose view was that "Fred couldn't see a customer with binoculars. . . . Listening stopped when Fred took over."

Jake Jacobson agrees. "When Fred took over the development organization, Wang the company, Wang the man, Wang the son just stopped listening."

Harold Koplow had demonstrated through the years that he could be abrasive, sometimes very abrasive. He had never been one to hide his emotions, and in 1982 his emotions were running high. He was growing progressively angrier with Fred Wang. He was, in fact, fed up with Fred. Part of his anger stemmed from Fred's inability to manage the development groups, but much of it was directed at Fred's handling of Koplow's new project. As envisioned by Koplow, the system would assemble a group of the latest, most powerful microprocessors to create a versatile workstation that would be able to do anything, from word processing to Macintosh-like graphics.

There was a good deal of excitement within the company for the idea, but when Fred assigned the jobs of implementing various parts of the product to three different design groups, Koplow complained that it would never work. The way to get products done was to let a single team see the development through — the course that had always been followed at Wang.

Koplow was furious. Who the hell did Fred think he was, anyway? Koplow was so mad he decided to quit. The place had changed too much from the days when Doctor Wang had run development. Besides, Koplow wanted to move to Florida, where he had found another job, and an attractive one at that. When Koplow told the Doctor of his plans, they held a tearful goodbye. They had been through a lot together, had worked in the lab alongside each other since 1967, back when Wang was known as the calculator company. They had worked on the 700 calculator together, had celebrated the fabulous success of the word processing system together. It was clear they had a genuine fondness for one another and a deep mutual respect. An Wang, who was far from effusive, once compared Koplow to Thomas Edison.

Cunningham told Koplow he had a responsibility to the company before leaving to tell the Doctor what the problems were in development and what could be done to solve them. Koplow agreed. As part of his goodbye in the fall of 1982, he told Doctor Wang exactly what he thought was wrong with R&D. Soon thereafter, Doctor Wang asked Koplow whether he would be willing to go to a meeting of the R&D group and "tell everybody what I thought of R&D," Koplow recalls. "I said, 'Sure!'"

He had a great deal to say.

The meeting at which Harold Koplow eviscerated Fred Wang was attended by about sixteen people, including Fred's dozen or so lieutenants, Cunningham, and Fred's father.

When Koplow began his talk, his face flushed with anger, he turned to Fred Wang: "Fred, you have screwed up. You're the wrong person. You've made so many bad decisions. You don't have any idea what you're doing."

"I went through and blasted everybody with a shotgun," recalls Koplow. "I said, 'Fred, you blew it.' I told Fred, 'You don't have the background to run it. You could run it if there were good people under you, but you don't.' No one said anything. They hung their heads.

"I laid them out for an hour and a half. It was all true."

Koplow stood at the front of the room, enraged, letting it all out, hiding none of his anger. And the longer he spoke the more furious he grew. Smiling his sarcastic smile, nearly in a frenzy, he was "shaking and loud and angry," says Sam Gagliano, vice-president of product planning, who reported to Fred. "He said, 'Look, this could be very, very dangerous if you don't listen to what I have to say.' He thought everybody was asleep at the wheel. He basically said we were muddling around. There were a lot of new things he felt we should be doing that were passing us by. He said we've got to stop trying to squeeze more life out of old products. Everybody walked away amazed that the guy had the nerve to say it."

Cunningham says, "There were a couple of small arrows back from Fred's people, and Harold would deliver large spears in return."

Fred, characteristically, is dispassionate in his recollection of the meeting. "Harold doesn't debate very well so it quickly became personal. He attacked my management ability and that sort of thing. I was surprised. People told me Harold was just hot-headed, and he'll get over it."

Fred claims that the assault had no effect on him.

And the truth was that Harold went too far.

"His method of delivery was questionable," says Sam Gagliano. "He was screaming at Fred."

"It was insane," says Cunningham. "It was wild. He had a loaded gun. He was shooting at guys' heads, balls, hearts. He was like a lone wolf against the bad guys. He shot Fred" and attacked John Thibault and criticized Joop Spanjaard, a senior marketing vice-president. "He had one bullet left and he was going to shoot Kolk, but this was going to be like a trick shot," says Cunningham. "He was hyperventilating. He reached around behind his head to trick-shoot Kolk, but he shot himself in the head! He went too far. He didn't know when to stop."

Though Koplow's diatribe had been excessive, it contained a rational message, and the message was that the R&D operation, under Fred, had not worked. It had not delivered the products the company needed to continue to grow. For the Doctor to tolerate such an enraged performance was an indication to Cunningham and others that he wanted that message delivered. Why would he have tolerated such a scene if he had not agreed with at least the essentials of the message?

That, to Cunningham, was the most astonishing part of it all. That Wang himself had called the meeting and given Harold the forum in which to attack Fred. It was a clear signal, Cunningham believed, of the father's misgivings. And Doctor Wang had merely used Koplow to deliver his message.

Joop Spanjaard agreed with Cunningham's assessment. Says Spanjaard: "Koplow walked in, put a gun on the table, and said to the Doctor, 'You shoot him or I'll shoot him.'"

*   *   *

Koplow, Siegel, and Kolk had all had their ups and downs at the company, but never before had all three been so miserable.

Siegel was as brash as he was brilliant, and Fred's taking over development had sent him into a private rage. He went so far as to leave R&D to take refuge working for Cunningham. ("I work well only for people I respect.") By 1984, he had had it with Wang Laboratories. Fred's influence had simply worn him down. Siegel quit and went to a small, dynamic computer outfit not two miles from Wang Labs.

Kolk hung in longer. He would take the criticisms of colleagues — Siegel had been particularly brutal on him during meetings — and walk stoically down the hallway, his head lowered, shuffling along with one hand in his pants pocket. But by 1985 he, too, was gone. He took a senior position at NEC, a major computer firm.

Though Koplow had said his goodbyes, the Doctor could not deal with the thought of him leaving. Not long after the bloody show at the development meeting, the Doctor called Koplow in and said that if he would stay with the company, the Doctor would arrange for him to buy a home in Florida and build him a facility in which to work. Koplow agreed. He found a $1.2 million, two-acre house lot in Boca Raton with 300-foot ocean frontage and 300-foot frontage on the Intercoastal Waterway. He also found a spot for a Wang research facility on Interstate 90 directly across the street from IBM. But the arrangement was not to be. While plans for the house were being drafted, Koplow had another run-in with Fred. He told Fred: "It's all over. I can't report to you. I'm leaving."

And so, the three men who had worked so well with the Doctor, the men who had created the products that had yielded literally billions of dollars of revenues for the company, were all gone — worn out by Fred Wang.

TEN

The Personal Computer Revolution

THE REVOLUTION had begun in the garages, basements, and workshops of California computer hackers, but it took shape under a veil of secrecy in, of all places, Boca Raton, Florida. And the unlikely force behind this upheaval was none other than the largest computer company on earth.

Originally, the computer freaks who fiddled with small machines did so as a hobby, more for the fun of it than anything else. These untidy collections of wires and electronic gadgetry — known as "home computers" when they first sprouted up in the mid-1970s — were made possible by tiny, ever-cheaper microprocessors, the fingernail-sized chips that performed most computer functions. With a few microprocessors, a printed circuit board to store and guide information in the form of electronic impulses through the system, a TV screen, and a keyboard, hackers had a home computer. These contraptions were rudimentary, to be sure, but one measure of the extraordinary technological progress in the industry was the fact that they were far more powerful than any *mainframe* computer in existence as recently as 1960. For a thousand dollars, you could buy something in the late 1970s that would have made the original UNIVAC look like an abacus.

In the mid-1970s, the few small companies that made these machines did so for hobbyists. But Steven Jobs saw the future, and in 1976 he co-founded Apple Computer. Jobs was not the only one who believed in the potential of these little machines. There was a small group of technical people at Wang Laboratories who believed it as well. In 1979, Sam Gagliano, vice-president for product planning and management, put a proposal together suggesting that the company build a personal computer. Fred Wang liked the idea very much and took it to his father.

But in the first indication that his once nearly flawless vision had become impaired, An Wang didn't like the idea. He was worried about spreading his R&D resources too thin. He did not want a PC project undertaken at Wang Laboratories.

Fred disagreed. Fred believed that it was only a matter of time before the use of PCs would be widespread. He could see the trend in his own company. The Wang 2200, the workhorse small-business computer, had become smaller and smaller through the years, so that, by around 1980, the entire 2200 could be placed in a box not unlike a PC.

Fred did not quit easily on this one. Six months after he had initially been turned down by his father, he broached the subject again. But, again, his father said no. It was a crucial moment in the history of Wang Laboratories. Unfortunately for the company, Gagliano says, the Doctor "thought it was the stupidest thing he had ever heard of."

In fairness to An Wang, he was not alone in his failure to see the approaching PC revolution. Two giants of the computer industry, Digital chairman Kenneth Olsen and Data General founder Edson deCastro, also missed the PC in its early stages.

Other companies saw it clearly, however. Commodore, Atari, Tandy, Apple, and IBM all were ready for it. And so the PC race was on, but Wang Laboratories wasn't even at the starting line.

In 1980, IBM quietly assembled a team in Boca Raton with the charge of building, from scratch, a personal computer. Project Acorn, as it was dubbed within the company, was an effort by IBM to bring out a high-quality machine very quickly and to surprise the market. Just one year after beginning the project — a remarkably short time for such things — IBM was manufacturing personal computers.

By 1983, IBM had taken the market by storm. It had gone from not having a PC at all to producing the best-selling PC in the world, a machine so popular that the company could not make them fast enough to keep pace with demand. The IBM PC was a landmark in the history of computing.

It was also a serious blow to Wang Laboratories, for it threatened to supplant two of the three products the company had ridden to superstardom — the 2200 and the word processing system. The PC could be used for small-business computing purposes, thus replacing the 2200. It could also run word processing software and thereby replace Wang word processing. It could perform many functions well, and just a few years down the road PCs would be able to team up with a file server in a Local Area Network, thereby competing with the VS. Then the PC would be competing with *all* of Wang's key products. The beauty of the PC was that it could do whatever its software told it to do, and the possibilities for software applications seemed endless.

Suddenly, the Wang Word Processing System, which just a few years earlier had been the hottest machine in the business, seemed a bit of a clunker. While the IBM PC could perform whatever tasks its thousands of software disks directed, the Wang Word Processing System could do nothing but word processing.

George Colony, an astute follower of Wang Labs, likened the Wang Word Processing System to "a tractor that would only bale hay." The PC, on the other hand, was a tractor that could bale hay, plow a field, haul timber, and do dozens of other chores as well.

Bob Kolk, the father of the Wang 2200, saw right away that the IBM PC "would replace our 2200 and would become the standard" that others in the industry would copy. "It was like the 2200 in a lot of ways, but it was totally programmable. We quickly concluded that we had to follow that standard."

Wang had no choice but to respond to the threat with its own PC. And Kolk gives Fred Wang credit for pushing hard to build one. Within a few weeks after the announcement of the IBM PC, Fred had permission from his father to develop a Wang PC, and he shifted Kolk and his team over to start it.

Kolk's team produced a machine that was reliable, powerful, and three times faster than the IBM. But the Wang PC had one problem: It was not IBM compatible. It could run none of the software created for the IBM machine, and the vast majority of independent software companies were writing programs for that machine.

It had been a difficult decision for the Wang people — whether to create a PC based on an open system, one that would be compatible with other makes of computers and software made for other machines, or to build a computer based on a proprietary system, a machine that would work only with Wang machines. Initially, it was not entirely clear that IBM would set the standard for PCs, although this was certainly one of

IBM's goals. They went so far — and, for IBM, this was unheard of — as to publish the technical information other companies would need to make their machinery work in concert with the IBM PC. Nonetheless, there was some thought early on that another machine might become the standard and Wang did not want to make a mistake in choosing IBM compatibility only to see some other company capture the bulk of the market. But the primary reason Wang chose to make a machine that ran on a proprietary system — that is, a PC that would work only with other Wang equipment — was because proprietary systems were much more lucrative than open systems.

Fred was happy to leave the compatibility decision up to his development team, but his father was not willing to do so. The Doctor wanted a proprietary system because Wang had always made proprietary systems and profited hugely from them through the years.

The Wang PC was a Cadillac, Cunningham said. It was a well-designed machine that worked beautifully as a workstation for the VS, but very few pieces of software were written for it. Kolk recalls that by the mid-1980s something like ten thousand programs had been written for the IBM PC, including the likes of Lotus 1-2-3. The Wang machine could run none of them. "It became very important to be 100 percent compatible with IBM," says Kolk.

By about 1983 it was obvious Kolk was correct, that IBM had set the standard and that very few PCs that were not IBM compatible would survive. After a pitched battle within the company — one of Fred Wang's finer moments, in fact — Wang altered its machine to make it IBM compatible.

But Wang had yet another problem, for its machine was more costly than most of the competition. It was so expensive to manufacture that the company could not make any money selling PCs through retail distribution channels. IBM's price had quickly become the de facto ceiling on what could be charged for a PC, but Wang couldn't manufacture a PC cheap enough to make any money at that price. Thus, neither Cunningham nor Wang saw any point in competing in the retail PC market. Historically, Wang Labs had been unable to design products that could be built for a low price in high volume. The Doctor did not believe his company should compete in the low-end market, anyway, where profit margins were far thinner than those to which Wang Labs was accustomed. Besides, the Doctor argued, the Wang Word Processing System would keep the company in the PC competition. "He said sixty to seventy percent of PCs were only being used for word processing anyway," recalls Bob Doretti, who was head of U.S. sales.

"The low-end, high-volume stuff was anathema to the Doctor," says analyst George Colony. "PCs probably reminded him of calculators."

Cunningham didn't like the idea of getting into a business where Wang would have to compete on price, either. One Wang executive recalls that, during the debate over whether to get into the PC market, Cunningham told him a story. He said there was a prostitute who went out one night and returned later and gave her money to a pimp. She handed over a total of $50.25, and the pimp asked, "Who's the cheap bastard who gave you 25 cents?" She replied: "All of them."

To Cunningham, that was the PC market. Wang and Cunningham feared that PCs would become commodities, as calculators had, and the PC war would be won by companies equipped to compete in such a battle. Such a company was surely not Wang Labs.

"I wasn't going to sell anything that didn't make any money," says Cunningham, who was convinced Wang Labs could not do a cost effective design.

Wang did explore the possibility of teaming up with Apple and putting Wang word processing software on the Macintosh. The discussions got serious enough to include talks in Lowell with Steven Jobs and John Sculley from Apple. But Cunningham didn't like the idea. "I thought if we do that, it says we cannot do easy-to-use workstations, and that's what Wang did.

"We could never get a design that you could see you could make some money off of," says Cunningham. "You need a high volume, low-cost design."

The shame of it was that Wang Labs could have gotten there first. Wang had a history of innovation in ease-of-use technology. All its big machines — calculators, word processing, the 2200, and the VS — set the standard for user-friendly machinery. And the Wang Word Processing System was but a half-step shy of being a personal computer. Wang Labs was perched on the edge of the PC breakthrough.

"Wang plays a big part in the history of computers," says George Colony. "Wang's legacy is the IBM PC. Wang word processing was a huge breakthrough. Wang defined that market, laid the groundwork for the PC. It was the next logical step for Wang."

But the company did not take that step.

*   *   *

Top managers within the company knew that Wang had screwed up. When the *New York Times* spelled it out on October 14, 1984, the rest of the world knew it, too:

> When personal computers started replacing word processors, Wang Laboratories Inc. knew it had to make a move. The word processors that had made Wang famous and became the darlings of the secretarial pool were being outdistanced by the more technologically advanced personal computers — and Wang's future growth was at stake.
>
> Its solution? Move out of the steno pool and into the executive suite with a new offering: state of the art office-automation systems for managers that would feature computers, text editors, electronic mail systems and graphics devices, all linked in a network enabling managers to summon and dispatch vast quantities of information with a single keystroke.
>
> So far, however, this vision has not yet materialized, and Wang, which has bet its future on it, now faces the most serious threat in its 33-year history. . . .
>
> . . . "The next six months could be critical for Wang," said Patricia B. Seybold, a Boston-based office-automation expert and a former consultant for Wang. "They will definitely have to work harder for sales."
>
> . . . "They blew it," said Mrs. Seybold. "They allowed IBM PC's to proliferate in accounts that Wang already had control of."

There were other indications of trouble. One of the company's worst mistakes ever was a product called the Wang Office Assistant, which was born amid much fanfare. In October 1984, when this small, stand-alone word processor — with a price of $2,400 — was introduced, analyst John Adams was effusive about the product's potential. "For not a great deal more money than an electronic typewriter, the buyer gets a full blown word processor with some data processing capabilities thrown in," wrote Adams. "Initial reaction from the trade has bordered on the overwhelming. Management believes it may sell $100 million worth of office assistants in the first year."

The idea was to put the wildly popular Wang word processing package on to a low-cost PC, which would be able to run a few other applications but would essentially be a small word processor.

"This was Fred's personal project," recalls Bob Kolk. "This was going to make his mark."

It was designed as a slick piece of machinery with some attractive features and plenty of horsepower. But a number of key development people within the company thought the machine was not only not a good idea, but a truly terrible idea. It had one gigantic and, as it turned out, fatal flaw: Amidst a PC revolution in which competitors were turning out machines that could run thousands of programs, the office assistant could do essentially one thing — word processing. The Wang Office Assistant was limited in precisely the same ways that the Wang Word Processing System was limited. Both were easy targets for PCs.

Sam Gagliano was among those who believed the project was folly. "I told the Doctor and Fred that I didn't think the product was viable," says Gagliano. "The Doctor really got irritated with me."

Toward the end, Bob Kolk was asked to go in and try to breathe some life into the Wang Office Assistant, and he tried. He argued that it was crazy to manufacture a product capable of only one application and that the machine could easily be made into an IBM-compatible PC for no more than about $25 per machine. Kolk said he thought that was the only way the machine could be salvaged.

But at this stage the idea of becoming IBM compatible still greatly angered the Doctor. When Kolk made his suggestion, Doctor Wang "got furious," says Kolk, and "pounded his fist on the table."

Sam Gagliano believed it was a disaster waiting to happen. It was bad enough that the machine could perform only word processing and a few other applications. But the machine was even worse than that, says Gagliano: "It could only use a Wang printer, which was very slow, looked like a robot, and it wasn't reliable!"

But Doctor Wang's outbursts made it amply clear that he wanted the machine to proceed, and proceed it did. Tens of thousands of Wang Office Assistants were manufactured, perhaps as many as forty thousand of them. And the great majority — perhaps as many as thirty thousand — wound up collecting dust in a Wang warehouse. It was a loss to the company of more than $30 million.

The PC revealed something disturbing about the company — that the arrogance of the glory years still lingered. It had infected the company culture, got into the fabric of the place. It had taken particularly deep root within the Doctor himself. For so long, he had made so many good calls, remarkable judgments, that he had come to believe in his own infallibility.

"Wang was arrogant," observes Bob Siegel, "too successful."

"It was believing your own bullshit," says Gagliano. "He stopped listening to what the customers really wanted. I think he lost touch in the early '80s, and there wasn't anybody in the company who was going to stop him from doing that."

Says Peter Brooke: "In the early '80s, they developed a we-know-everything attitude. They insulated themselves from any outside advice. [Wang] bought its own story. You have closed architecture because you've got a closed mind. When you've bought your own act, you're in trouble. Everybody needs help."

In the early 1980s the computer business was undergoing fundamental change. No longer did customers line up clamoring for every bit of gadgetry that tumbled off the line. Customers were becoming choosier, more interested in getting the maximum mileage out of the machines they already had than in buying the latest magic box. Demand for computer equipment, which had for years been insatiable, began slowing, and even as it did the industry was beset with several technological tremors.

The PC revolution alone would have been enough to rattle the industry, but with it came the upheaval caused by the issue of standards. All computer companies found themselves wrestling with the question of whether to standardize their machines, whether to make equipment that would work with the hardware produced by other companies.

While these issues were percolating, between about 1979 and 1983, Wang Laboratories was growing faster than anyone around. But even as the company rocketed ahead, John Cunningham worried about its future. He worried that the company's sloppy operations had been masked by fantastic growth. He worried that if Wang Labs continued to operate the way it always had, it would wilt in the face of the tougher, leaner days that lay ahead. He worried about the direction of the company. In this more competitive industry, decisions about where to take the company were crucial and not at all obvious.

Cunningham thought it would help to take a time-out of sorts, to step back from the fray and to study the company and its problems. But he also wanted that report to be independent of him. He believed that if he coordinated the study, Fred would automatically dismiss its findings. So he assigned the task to a group of smart senior executives from every area of the business, people such as Bob Siegel, Joop Spanjaard, Ray Cullen, Peter McElroy, and Bob Ano. Their job was to examine the company and the marketplace, to identify the company's strengths and weaknesses, to make recommendations for improvements and for strategic direction. He called the group the White Paper Task Force. "It was a chance to take a fresh look at Wang, its future, and its problems," says Bob Siegel.

To lead the group in its work, Cunningham chose a man he considered the most impressive business mind he had ever encountered. Chev Haskell had been vice-president of corporate planning at IBM; he had been vice-president of marketing at IBM Europe, and he had been on the corporate management committee at IBM.

Haskell's clarity of vision and his ability to distill concepts and articulate them was striking. Cunningham's initial impulse was to hire Haskell as vice-president of long-range planning, but the Doctor, who, Cunningham says, "knew Haskell thought Fred was a jerk," blocked that move. The Doctor would permit Cunningham to use Haskell only as a consultant.

The group would convene each morning in Cunningham's conference room and, under Haskell's guidance, explore issues crucial to the company's future. To help with its work, the group invited in a variety of experts and consultants. They visited MIT and talked with leading thinkers there. This intensive work went on for two months.

The group's product was a presentation to the company's executive operations committee by Haskell in March 1983.

The report found profound problems within the company. The task force believed that Wang would have to change its ways to be a healthy company in the coming years and that change would be difficult, even traumatic, for some people.

One problem that was obvious to all was the company's cumbersome decision-making process, which required agreement from the Doctor, Cunningham, Harry Chou, and Fred. That Cunningham and Fred could not work well together slowed down the process significantly, stripping it of the crispness that had once been its hallmark.

The White Paper Task Force report concluded that Wang was overreliant on the Doctor, that internal communication was poor, that there was a lack of teamwork, and that quality was lacking. It found that the company's leaders were not united about the company's mission, its strategy, or its goals — something akin to building a house on a cracked foundation.

The report was sharply critical of Fred's development operation, charging that there was an "unclear development direction and focus" and that the development environment did not allow the Koplows, Siegels, and Kolks of the world to flourish.

The task force further found that the company's focus on customers had diminished and that the company had not trained its employees well. The report urged the company to recruit management talent from the outside, the sort of talent the company had been too busy to develop internally.

The task force proposed the establishment of a planning operation — which Cunningham wanted run by Chev Haskell.

"You have to understand you're an alcoholic before you can fix yourself" was how John Cunningham explained it. He believed that the top people in the company had to face up to the fact that there were serious problems. It was not easy to do amidst all of the extraordinary growth and success with which the company was blessed, but Cunningham hoped the White Paper Task Force — coming from such widely respected people from all parts of the company — would do the job. "The task force was designed to be a change agent," says Cunningham. "It was designed to say, 'The current ways will not work.'"

But the report and its ideas were destined for obscurity.

"Chev came in at a time when we were growing quickly," says Fred. "He was asking people to plan the next five years and they were saying, 'Hey, I'm doing all I can to plan ahead to next *month*.' The concept he was pushing was not wrong. I tried it years later with similar results. Dad was not at all interested in long-range planning. He felt it was a waste of time."

When the results of the group's work were presented to the Doctor, he had little reaction. He didn't say he opposed or disagreed with the analysis. He didn't say he supported and agreed with it. The result was that there was no momentum for making the report a blueprint or, at least, a guideline for the company's future direction. The report was placed on a shelf, where it was soon covered with dust.

On and off for several years, Harold Koplow had been working on a device that would switch data from almost anything hooked up to a computer network — voice, data, text — to telephone transmission lines at a very low cost. After he left Wang, Koplow wasn't sure what, if anything, to do with the idea. He was working in Florida as senior vice-president of development at a company called MODCOMP at the time, and Dave Moros was consulting to MODCOMP. During one of Moros's trips south, Koplow laid out the idea and asked Moros what he thought. Moros thought it had potential. Still, they didn't know what to do with the device. Moros suggested that he ask John Cunningham's thoughts when he returned to Boston.

On a gorgeous summer day in 1984, Moros and Cunningham had a drink at the Sheraton in Lexington, just off Route 128. Moros explained the idea and Cunningham immediately liked it so much he asked Moros whether he, as an individual, could invest in the product's development. Cunningham then told the Doctor about it, and the Doctor was intrigued.

"John called and said, 'The old man is interested,'" Moros recalls. "'Are you interested in working with the old man?'"

Moros said they'd be interested in discussing it. A couple of months later, a meeting was finally arranged. The Wang people were intent on keeping secret the fact that the Doctor was talking with two of his old development aces — without the knowledge of his son. The first meeting took place at the Marriott Hotel in Burlington, on Route 128. Soon thereafter, the Doctor invited Koplow and Moros to his home for further talks. At that meeting, it was obvious the Doctor was seriously interested in the project. While Cunningham and Wang chief counsel Ed Grayson sat and listened, the three technical wizards sat enthusiastically talking away about this idea. The electrical engineering and computer jargon flew around the room.

To Cunningham, Wang seemed more excited than he had been in a long while. "This is the happiest I've seen the old man in two or three years," Cunningham said to Grayson. Perhaps it was the fact that he was back with the team that had brought his company the word processing megahit. Perhaps it was simply that he fancied the idea. Or was it Koplow in particular, a man for whom he had always had an extraordinary fondness?

"The Doctor said, 'I fund it,'" Koplow recalls. "'I give you money. You design and build prototype and I give you 5 percent royalty.'"

Within a couple of weeks, lawyers for both sides had worked out an agreement. The day before the contract was to be signed, Cunningham and Grayson got on the phone to Koplow. The deal was off. Koplow was stunned. How could this be? The Doctor had been so enthusiastic, so excited. Everything was set and now, with numbing swiftness, it was not to be.

"Grayson said, 'The deal's off,'" recalls Koplow. "'Fred had a temper tantrum. He doesn't want to have anything to do with you.'"

An Wang told others at the company that Fred said he would lose face if the company did anything with Koplow.

In the end, Doctor Wang asked Cunningham's advice. Cunningham said he did not want to go to war with Fred over this issue — that it wasn't worth a drawn-out battle. Cunningham said he thought Doctor Wang had to pass it by.

ELEVEN

A Rejected Son

THE RELATIONSHIP between John Cunningham and Fred Wang was a failure. The fundamental problem was that Cunningham did not believe Fred Wang was qualified to hold a position of major responsibility within the company. In particular, Cunningham found it absurd that Fred was in charge of a division as crucial as R&D.

Cunningham is normally a reasonable man, but, even years later, the subject makes him very angry. "From '72 to '82 we had a rule," he says. "Whenever I wanted to do something, I had to convince Doctor Wang, then clear it with Harry. Now you had Fred in the equation. Now I had to fuckin' go to Fred and explain it to him and listen to his questions about why it was a bad idea. Fuck me! Life is too short."

Cunningham's face becomes flushed as he talks about it. "I wouldn't do it for $10 million a year. For ten years, when Wang and Chou and I wanted something done, it got done. Doctor Wang, Harry, and I worked as a team. There was trust among us. We didn't worry about the others' turf. If Harry came to me and said there was a problem with accounts receivable on a certain account, I wouldn't argue. I'd get it fixed. We were of one mind. We understood one another. We had tremendous respect and trust for one another. It worked. Then Doctor Wang tried to force Fred into that equation. After I got agreement from Harry and Doctor Wang, Doctor Wang would say, 'Make sure it's okay with Fred.' I found it horribly frustrating trying to explain things to Fred. I didn't want to spend the next five to ten years of my life teaching this kid. I didn't want to share the power with Fred. Let him go get an MBA at Harvard if he wants to learn all this shit."

Cunningham also saw it as contrary to his self-interest to teach Fred. "If I transferred all my knowledge to Fred and he learned it, I destroyed myself. I fought too hard to get where I got to do that."

It was a strange situation. Here was Cunningham, in what amounted to open warfare with the son of the founder of the company, yet he continued to enjoy a uniquely strong relationship with the Doctor. Through his seventeen years at Wang, Cunningham and the Doctor had had thousands of conversations, and not once did they exchange a harsh word. Not once had there been even the slightest bit of nastiness.

But that changed on Friday, October 12, 1984. On that gorgeous, sunny, perfect New England fall afternoon, in the Doctor's huge corner office in the penthouse atop tower two, he and Cunningham met privately. Not far from where they sat, construction workers were racing feverishly to complete the third tower, nearly identical to the first two. Wang, as was his custom, was seated at his conference table flanked by stacks of papers. As usual, the Doctor was dressed formally in a suit, jacket on. Cunningham was in shirtsleeves.

Wang began the meeting by saying that he wanted to make some major changes within the company. "I want to move Fred in to run manufacturing," he told Cunningham. Fred would replace John Kropper, who had been doing an outstanding job in manufacturing. Kropper would go to field engineering.

Cunningham thought the idea made no sense, and he told Wang that. First of all, why take Fred, who knew nothing about manufacturing, and put him into such a sensitive position, especially when the company already had someone in that job with a proven record of excellence? It was crazy. And sending Kropper to field engineering didn't make any sense either because it would take him a full year to figure out what was going on. And it would mean replacing Ray Cullen, who was doing very well in that position.

Cunningham did not like this at all, but he had to be careful. His relationship with the Doctor was not one of peers. Wang was clearly his superior, and Cunningham had always had a somewhat formal relationship with Wang in which it was clear that the Doctor was the superior, Cunningham the subordinate.

Nonetheless, Cunningham was president of the company and he thought the Doctor's idea was terrible. Cunningham looked directly at Doctor Wang. "It's not going to work," he said emphatically, an unintended edge in his voice. But Wang was insistent on his plan, and his voice, too, took on an edge.

Suddenly, there was a palpable level of tension between them, a new and alarming distance. With stunning swiftness, their discussion took on a contentious air. It was, Cunningham believed, a potentially explosive, truly dangerous moment. Cunningham suddenly thought, "'If I say three or four more sentences, this could be all over. I could be fired!' I was scared. I was very frightened."

The thought of being on the street with no income and a lifestyle that burned up $550,000 to $600,000 a year was terrifying to Cunningham. "I backed off," he says. "We sat for fifteen or twenty seconds. We both backed off. Things quieted down."

Cunningham left the meeting in a state of shock. What was happening here? What was Wang doing? He went to his office, quickly gathered his coat and briefcase, and left. He rode the elevator from the penthouse to the garage, where his driver was waiting in his Mercedes limo. During the fifteen-minute ride to an airfield, where a jet was waiting to take him to Nantucket for the weekend, Cunningham realized that something was terribly, terribly wrong. As he thought about it, Cunningham realized there had been a few other recent signs of a change in his relationship with Doctor Wang. The Doctor, for example, had recently said that he had never really liked the achievers' trips. Cunningham had been stung by the comment. The trips were a Cunningham production and had long been considered a stroke of management genius. They were one of the most popular perks at the company, and a very effective motivational tool.

As he rode along Route 3 toward Hanscom Field, Cunningham felt as though he'd been up all night; as though he'd seen a ghost. Reclining in the back of the limousine, he thought about what had just happened. He believed he'd come perilously close to being fired, kicked out, on the street. Incredible. It would mean no limousines, no aircraft. He boarded the small, sleek executive jet looking catatonic.

Ellen, who was already on the plane, took one look at him.

"What *happened?*" she asked.

What had happened was that An Wang had chosen sides.

As president of a fast-growing, high-technology company, Cunningham was constantly under pressure. Executives in positions such as his were paid staggering amounts of money, in part, at least, as compensation for the pressure with which they had to deal day in and day out. Even in the best of times, when an executive's career was on track and when the company he ran was doing well, there was great stress. In tough times, the pressure mounted. Cunningham was facing such a time. There were continuing signs that business wasn't what it had been. The increasingly competitive nature of the industry added to the pressure on him, as did the conflict with the son of the CEO.

Now, on top of it all, there was a problem with the old man. Cunningham felt under siege. The truth was that he had been feeling that way for a while. It had been so bad that Ellen Cunningham urged him to quit earlier that year — to simply get up and walk away from the presidency of Wang Laboratories. He was only forty years old, but Ellen feared for his health.

"He was one miserable person, and he took it out on us," she says, referring to herself and the Cunninghams' two daughters.

His encounter with the Doctor in October left Cunningham reeling. He wanted desperately to work things out, but he knew there was little chance he could coexist with Fred. During the fall and into the holidays, Cunningham grappled with the cooling of his relationship with the Doctor. He concluded that it could only mean that Wang wanted Fred's rise within the company to continue. There was no question what that would mean for Cunningham.

He was so badly frazzled that he woke up in a foul mood on Christmas morning. Ellen and the girls knew he was under pressure, knew he was terribly stressed, but to Erin, who was then twelve years old, this was simply too much. This was Christmas morning! She wanted a happy, cheerful father, not a grump. She went to her mother and cried, "What's *wrong* with him?"

What was wrong was that Cunningham felt the end was drawing near. He had worked so hard to get where he was, and now it looked as if it might all soon be gone. It was clear there wasn't enough room at Wang Laboratories for both him and Fred, clear also that Wang was prodding Fred in what amounted to an inexorable march to the top of the company.

In January 1985, Wang and Cunningham met again. Again, it was private, just the two of them. This time they convened in the Doctor's new office, atop the just completed tower three. The new office was vast — an absolutely staggering three thousand square feet, the size of a large American home. The office was L-shaped with windows on three sides — the only office at the company with a view in three directions. There were two conference tables, one of which was rather formal looking with seats for sixteen, and the other smaller, able to accommodate perhaps six. The Doctor's desk was dwarfed by a room so cavernous that it could have passed for a small gymnasium or a movie theater. Easy chairs and coffee tables were set in various locations around the room. And in a space off to the side, there was a marble fireplace and a whirlpool bath. The size of the room was not so much an indication that the Doctor's conservative lifestyle had changed, but rather a sign of his comfort playing the role of a man of stature, a certified Towering Figure in American business.

Wang began the meeting as he had in October by suggesting a series of administrative changes. This time, the atmosphere was not nearly so tense as it had been three months earlier.

"I was less afraid," says Cunningham. "It was more of a calm and reasoned discussion."

After Wang suggested the changes, Cunningham looked at the Doctor and said: "What's really going on? We're having disagreements for the first time. You've got to tell me what you're really trying to do with the company."

An Wang nodded. "Okay," he said. "I want to position it so that Fred, over time, will be the president and chief operating officer."

Cunningham then asked what was the central question. He thought perhaps that Fred's sorry performance at R&D might have caused An Wang to rethink his long-term plans for his son. But he was wrong.

"For real or as a figurehead?"

"For real," the Doctor replied.

That was bad news, for it meant that Cunningham was doomed at Wang Labs. If Wang had wanted Fred in a figurehead role, as Louis Cabot and other board members had suggested, perhaps something could have been worked out where Cunningham ran the operations. But with Fred in operational control of the company, there would be no room for Cunningham. And it would be, Cunningham fervently believed, a disaster for the company.

Cunningham shook his head. "It has a high probability of not working," he told the Doctor. "And I'm going to stand in the way." Cunningham said he couldn't go along with an arrangement under which Fred had operational control of the company. "I can't do it. It would be tearing down what I've spent ten years building."

But there was nothing John Cunningham could say on this day that would affect An Wang's thinking. The Doctor's mind was made up. He said he wanted Fred to take over manufacturing to help prepare him to become president. He said he wanted Fred to become president in two to three years and serve in that capacity for five or six years. Fred would then leave the company and go into public service, perhaps even run for governor. When Fred left, Wang said, he wanted Courtney to take over. The notion of Courtney, a young man — kid, really — who was more of a gadfly than anything else, seemed preposterous to Cunningham. But, at the moment, he was more interested in his own fate than in Courtney's.

"What happens to me?" Cunningham asked.

"You be vice-chairman and work with major accounts," Wang said. And after Courtney's tenure was up, he said, Cunningham could return to being president. Again, Cunningham shook his head. "This is no longer making any sense to me," he said. "It's not going to work for me. I think it's going to cost you a lot of money and the shareholders a lot of money."

Then the Doctor revealed something that astounded Cunningham. Wang said he was very concerned about the R&D operation and had been for some time. He said that he had known for a year that Fred was not doing a good job there. He had known for a year that Fred was the wrong man for the job.

Cunningham was stunned. He couldn't believe what he was hearing and it took him a moment to recover.

"I'm having real difficulty with you telling me this," Cunningham replied. "With you telling me you've felt for a long time that Fred was not doing the job in development. How can you tell me now Fred is the wrong person for R&D? I have been saying all along that he was the wrong person and all along you agreed with me but you said nothing and gave me no support. Part of the problem between me and Fred is that Fred knows I think he is the wrong person."

"I didn't know what else to do with him," the Doctor said.

Cunningham was growing as angry as he was incredulous.

"I don't know if I can forgive you for that," Cunningham said. "You knew Fred was wrong. You've hurt this company. It's done real damage to the company, and you did it for the family."

"You've had people in jobs too long," said Wang.

"Yes, but once I made the decision that they weren't right I moved on them right away," Cunningham replied.

"You knew Dick Hebert [formerly vice-president of field engineering] was the wrong person to run field service and you let him stay too long," Wang said.

"Once I knew Dick was wrong I moved on him," said Cunningham. "But there's a big difference. Having a bad field service guy is like having a bad foot doctor. Having a bad R&D director is like having a bad heart surgeon."

Wang was adamant. He said that when Fred left R&D, he and Horace Tsaing would take it over. Cunningham didn't like that idea either. "You've lost touch with customers," Cunningham said. He argued that the Doctor had been out of the day-to-day activities in development for so long that he would not now be able to get back into it effectively. And Cunningham considered Horace far short of a visionary.

The conversation lasted for twenty minutes, maybe half an hour. By the time it was over, Cunningham had "mentally crossed the border. I knew I was out of there. I couldn't spend my forties seeing what Fred and Courtney were going to do with the company. I'm too selfish a person to work my ass off until 1987 or so and turn it over to Fred. I wouldn't want him to get the credit for the work I did. That isn't the way the system is supposed to work."

Finally, there was nothing more left to say. Cunningham was quite calm. This was business now, and he wanted to do it right. "I don't want a messy departure," he said. "I don't want to do my termination in the heat of battle. I don't see myself playing a role in this."

When the meeting ended, Cunningham returned to his office, closed the door, and sat down with a pen and a pad of paper and began writing. An hour later he was finished. He took the five pages, photocopied them himself, and walked down to Doctor Wang's office. It was early Friday evening. He handed him the document and said he was headed for Australia and the Far East for three weeks. Cunningham gestured to the document and said they could talk about it when he returned.

But Cunningham felt he owed it to the old man to tell him, candidly, what he truly believed before he left, and that was that Wang wasn't dealing with reality. He was talking about sustaining 25 percent compounded annual growth so that in fifteen years Wang Labs would eclipse IBM. He was convinced the company would become a major, worldwide industrial organization run by his family. He was talking about this even as the company had lost three years in product development. Cunningham conveyed his message with a striking metaphor.

"You're watching a movie, Doctor Wang," Cunningham said. "And you're so engrossed in it you think it's real. But there comes a time when the movie is over, when the lights flicker on and the film piles up on the floor and you have to rewind."

*   *   *

The spring of 1985 was not a good time for Wang Labs. In April, the regional office of the Securities and Exchange Commission began looking into sales of stock by top company officials only weeks before the announcement of a bad quarter, news that triggered a decline in Wang stock value. At the time, Willis Riccio, the administrator of the SEC New England office, said he considered the timing of the sales by company officials to be "extraordinary." Of the eight top executives who sold stock, Cunningham sold the most. On February 11, when Cunningham traded forty thousand Wang shares, the stock price was $28.25. Just a few weeks later, after the poor earnings report was announced, Wang shares had tumbled to barely over $19 a share.

Cunningham and the others selling stock made no effort to hide the sales. All reported their activity to the SEC as required by law. All were aware of strict laws against insider trading. And all complied with company guidelines on when stock could be sold. Though the situation looked very suspicious indeed, the company said the sales were a coincidence, albeit an embarrassing one. After talking with some of the executives involved, the SEC dropped the matter.

On May 24, before Cunningham's formal departure from the company but long after he had disengaged from the business, An and Lorraine Wang stood before a magnificent oil portrait of themselves in the lobby of the brand-new Wang Ambulatory Care Center at the Massachusetts General Hospital. The Wangs had contributed $4 million to help build this impressive new structure, and the hospital had selected artist George Augusta to paint a stunning, life-size portrait. It was a glorious moment for An Wang, representing so much of what was good about his life and his business. Here he was, a Chinese immigrant, a man who had arrived in this country with nothing but his own genius, whose money was doing so much good, being honored by some of the leading medical people in the world.

Sadly, though, as he participated in the impressive ceremony, An Wang knew that his company was in trouble — worse trouble than it had ever faced. In April, the company announced a 66 percent decline in third quarter profits. It was the first quarterly decline in profits in a solid decade of sustained prosperity. The worldwide computer slump had finally caught up to Wang as the office computer market, so robust just a few months earlier, slipped fast.

As had so often been the case, analyst John Adams was among the first to spot the trend at Wang. In January, at the time Wang was telling Cunningham he didn't believe Fred was the right man for the R&D job, Adams had written: "We believe that the gut issue at Wang is R&D productivity or, more specifically, the lack thereof. Yes, competition has become more of a factor; yes, margins are and will continue to be under intense pressure. However, Wang has always coped very successfully when it has a state-of-the-art product line and today it does not."

The company's "one true enemy," he wrote, is "the creeping bureaucracy that tends to accompany growth."

Adams, who had spotted Wang's huge potential years before the company reached superstardom, declared the glory years officially over in February 1985. "By one important yardstick, Wang is the longest running success story in high tech: sales have gone from $134 million in FY1978 to $2,422 million in CY1985 with nary a down quarter."

But that's ending, he wrote, because "Wang has been too late too often."

On April 1, 1985, *Datamation,* the trade magazine, published a very tough piece on Wang:

> After a nine-year joyride during which it became one of the legendary success stories of American industry, high-flying Wang Laboratories Inc. may be coming back to earth with a resounding thud. "They've traveled a long way with their word processing equipment," says one Wang customer near Cleveland, but now that the office automation marketplace is moving away from [word processing to data processing], the company is in a quandary.

Later in the month John Adams hit R&D again, writing that "the root problem at Wang is R&D productivity. Once the company's pride and joy, the R&D function has not been yielding an adequate or timely flow of creative new products."

On April 30, in a *Boston Globe* report on the company's poor showing, Patty Seybold, editor of the *Seybold Report,* an office automation publication, said, "There is no sense of vision at Wang anymore."

A story in *Computer & Communications Decisions* stated that "Wang is now hampered by organizational problems and challenged by aggressive competitors, and many analysts predict that not even a Herculean effort will help Wang regain the health of its heyday."

Wang wasn't the only company in trouble. The entire computer industry was in a slide. "The once unthinkable is becoming irrefutable: The computer business is in a slowdown," announced the *Wall Street Journal* in late May. "And while computer makers blame short-term causes that may fade in coming months, important changes under way in the market pose sticky problems in the long run."

But having company was little solace to those in misery at Wang. The trouble didn't suddenly descend upon Wang Labs in 1985, of course. It had been building for at least a couple of years. "The business was in trouble in '83 and '85," says John Cunningham. "The industry was more competitive in '84, and we were losing market share. Products were not coming out on time. It started to show up in the financial results in '85. PCs were dramatically eroding the word processing business and the 2200 business."

Things were bad. But they were about to get worse.

The rumors started in May. The buzz around the company was that something unheard of at Wang, unthinkable, really, was about to happen: layoffs.

The word hadn't been used at Wang in more than a decade. And the only time the company had ever had to let people go had been during the oil embargo that had so devastated sales of the 700 calculator. In the layoffs back in the early 1970s, a grand total of forty people had lost their jobs, and most of them had been hired back within six months.

In May, managers were asked to rank their employees. By the first week in June, the tension throughout the towers was palpable. On June 5, the ax fell, and it fell hard.

On that morning, managers were informed the layoffs would come that day. They were asked to remain in their departments, while employees were instructed to remain at their desks and not to go to lunch. Employees were told that if they were to be laid off, they would be summoned to their supervisor's office. Wang workers, frozen with fear, remained at their posts.

That morning, Wang Laboratories announced to the world that it was laying off 1,600 of its 32,000 worldwide employees, a total of 5 percent of its work force. One thousand of the 1,600 were laid off in Massachusetts, most of those in Lowell. The news sent Wang stock tumbling to a fifty-two-week low.

Managers were given very brief remarks that they were to deliver to each laid-off employee. "I regret to inform you that due to financial difficulties the company is experiencing, we must terminate your employment" was how one manager recalled it. "Thank you for the time you've spent."

At that point, the employee, usually in tears, was escorted away by a security guard, who watched the person clean out his or her desk and then guided the employee to the building exit.

It was a macabre scene. One man who was led to the door by a security guard walked outside, turned around, and began frantically banging on the door, screaming at the guard, begging to be let back inside. Farther on, in the huge parking lot, a man sat on the ground crying inconsolably. People with as many as six children were thrown out. People who had worked hard, long hours for ten years or more were dismissed.

It was a calamitous day. The hallway near the exit was swollen with a constant flow of people, some with death stares, being guided to the door. And as they were led along they passed directly by the customer center, where officials from some of the large corporations heading Wang's customer list had gathered for meetings and demonstrations of new products. The customers watched this dreadful exodus with horror.

"We just sat there and cried for a week after that," recalls Karen Smith Palmer, who worked as a publications manager and who saw numerous friends laid off. She had revelled in the glory years, worked day and night to be part of the fantastic growth of this incredible company, and now, although she had been spared, she grieved mightily, as did many survivors. "It was never the same again," she says. "We never fully recovered."

"People felt betrayed," says Peter McElroy. "Prior to the layoffs, Cunningham and the Doctor went around and spoke to employees. The first question from everybody was, 'Are there going to be layoffs?' They said, 'If the conditions don't change, there'll be no layoffs.' What employees heard was a flat 'no.' Forty-five days later, there were layoffs." Conditions had changed, says Cunningham. The outlook had turned much grimmer.

Fred Wang says it was a particularly bad day for John Cunningham. "As president, he had gone out and told employees there would be no layoffs, and then we turn around and have them. His credibility got eroded internally."

Many employees, including many who were not laid off, were bitter. There was a widespread belief within the company and the industry that Wang was a fat, bureaucratic organization — that the extraordinary growth of the glory years had swaddled the company in a thick layer of unnecessary management. "There was a feeling that the officers had run the ship on the rocks, but the crew was being executed," says Dale Jelley. "People were shell-shocked."

And it was not the end of the bad news. In July, six thousand production workers were forced to take a two-week unpaid vacation.

Karen Smith Palmer was right. Wang Labs never was the same after those layoffs. "It was a painful experience," says Fred Wang. "It shattered some myths that had developed during the growth years. The myth of 20 percent annual growth forever, that there would never be layoffs. It was very difficult to deal with. Most employees had never had to deal with adversity before."

There had been much talk through the years about Wang being a family, says Dick Connaughton. It was a family company and employees were part of the extended family. "People felt betrayed by the family," he says. "If you're part of a family, you don't get cut off when times are bad."

That night, as Dick Connaughton was leaving for home, terribly dispirited for having to lay off half a dozen of his workers, he saw An Wang leaving also, shuffling toward the exit, his head down.

It had been the darkest day since the founding of the company thirty-four years earlier.

In the document that Cunningham left for Wang to review, he wrote that his job with Wang Labs was "one I enjoy, feel competent in, and is very important to me." But he made clear that he understood that "there are some 4- to 8-year strategies that could very well create conflict with some of the goals of the family, the company, and myself."

These four- to eight-year strategies were a euphemism for the Doctor's plan to move his sons in to head the company.

To avoid doing his separation agreement in the "heat of battle," he had proposed that they agree on it in January. He had received since 1980 Wang stock valued at "only $150,000. I believe this is woefully inadequate given the performance and the current competitive situation in the industry." He requested an option of 150,000 to 200,000 shares — the stock was then selling at $28, making those shares worth about $4.5 to $5.5 million.

"I am particularly concerned," Cunningham wrote, "that an activity or event will occur that will precipitate a situation where my abrupt departure will be in the best interest of the company, the family, the employees, stockholders, and myself. I would wish that there are proper incentives in place to make sure this is done properly, professionally, and maturely. This should be structured to be fair to the individual yet provide flexibility to the company if changes occur in the future."

He requested that, upon his separation from Wang, he begin a four-year consulting deal with the company under which he would be paid $400,000 a year for 250 hours of consulting — roughly the equivalent of six weeks of full-time work. He also asked to receive payment for an office and a secretary for a year.

"I would be committed during this agreement to publicly and privately support the company, its strategies, and personnel," he wrote.

He also asked that substantial blocks of stock be given to a dozen key executives. "I will be gone to Far East and . . . will return end of next week and would like to reach a resolution on these issues upon my return. Hope I'm not causing major problems."

He signed the memo, "Thanks, J. Cunningham."

When Cunningham returned, he was prepared for the worst. But when the two men sat down, the Doctor said only that he thought one hundred thousand shares of stock were more appropriate than one hundred fifty or two hundred thousand shares. Everything else Cunningham requested was granted. Cunningham said he wanted the deal in writing, but the Doctor said no, he didn't want it to be made public. That worried Cunningham.

"What if you get run over by a truck?" Cunningham asked.

The Doctor said he would make the arrangement known to Mrs. Wang. He also sat down with Cunningham, Harry Chou, and Fred to review the specifics of the deal so that if something happened to the Doctor, they would know his wishes with respect to Cunningham. Says Cunningham, "Fred was probably thinking, 'This is great. Cunningham's not out the door, but he's getting his coat on.'"

To cover all the bases, Cunningham went to the board members individually and, with each one, he reviewed his memo on the deal. By February, Cunningham was ready to unhook from Wang. Though he still held the title of president, the fact was that he did little Wang work. "I traveled the world for six months. I filled the tanks up" on a leased jet, he says, "and traveled around the world to see my friends."

And he began to contemplate life after Wang. He would surely be gone within six months or so, certainly by the end of the summer. He would walk out the door with a great deal of money. He had been earning $550,000 a year in salary and bonuses. And when he left, he would have sold stock through the years worth $12 million. It was a lot of money, but Cunningham remained bothered by one particular statistic: While Doctor Wang owned 48 percent of the stock (although because of the C stock the Doctor controlled 100 percent of the company), Cunningham, at his peak, owned .2 percent. That meant that for every dollar Cunningham earned on the stock, Doctor Wang earned $240.

Nonetheless, when Cunningham left Wang Labs in the summer of 1985, he had taken almost $12 million worth of stock with him. After paying $3 million in taxes, he was left with $9 million in cash. He was building a spectacular home in the exclusive Boston suburb of Weston that he had expected would cost between $2.5 and $3 million, but which ended up running closer to $4.5 million. He put $1.5 million into his vacation home in Nantucket (grand enough to be rented one August by no less a character than Ivan Boesky).

He could have easily afforded to retire but he had no such interest. He was only forty-two years old. Besides, he believed he had never received the credit for Wang's success that he deserved, that he had always been overshadowed by the legendary Doctor Wang.

"He needed something after Wang," says Ellen Cunningham. "He needed to prove himself again. He needed to do it in case history showed that Doctor Wang was the whole story there. He needed to prove himself."

So he began looking for a way to do just that. The flirtation in 1984 with Koplow and Moros and their idea suggested to Cunningham that he might want to team up with them when he left Wang. Cunningham told Moros: "Go out and find a company that's in the shitter and we'll turn it around."

They looked at forty companies and went so far as to sit down and talk with officials at eight or nine of those firms. They were within hours of completing one deal that fell through. Finally, in June, Moros found a company he liked called Computer Consoles Inc. (CCI). CCI made various computer equipment, most of which was tailored for use by large telephone companies. Many directory assistance operations in the United States, in fact, were based on CCI systems. It met nearly every criterion on Cunningham's list. It was large enough, with revenues of $125 million a year, so that it wouldn't involve the struggle of a start-up. It had no block ownership and no entrenched management, so Cunningham and his team could effectively take it over. Although its operations were flung from Irvine, California, to Israel, from Reston, Virginia, to Rochester, New York, it could easily be run out of Boston. It had technology that Moros and Koplow liked. And the whole package was priced right. With most of the remaining money — and $3 million more, which he borrowed — he bought stock in CCI: 600,000 shares on the open market at $7 a share, for a $4.2 million investment. His total position eventually reached 1.2 million shares, a cash investment of $7 million.

Cunningham went to Doctor Wang immediately, told him he thought he had found something, and asked for permission to discuss it with Grayson, the Wang general counsel. It was late on a Saturday afternoon, and Cunningham was about to board a private jet to fly down to his Nantucket home. He offered Grayson a lift to the Cape, where Grayson was vacationing, and said they could chat on the way down.

He said he wanted his departure from Wang to be swift and definitive. "We're going to make this look like a happy event," Cunningham told Grayson. "Pretend I got splattered on a bridge abutment on Route 3."

He left with distinctly mixed emotions. John Cunningham's eighteen years at Wang Laboratories — where he had risen from the very bottom to second in command — had been a once in a lifetime experience. Having the title of president at such a prestigious company, even if he'd never had full authority, had won him widespread respect. He had earned a fortune. He had had some extraordinary days at Wang Labs, none more memorable than a day early the previous December, when he had hosted the opening of a Wang facility in Stirling, Scotland, a depressed mill town where the new Wang Labs complex would put hundreds of people to work. It was a big enough deal to attract Prince Charles; Cunningham was the prince's host for six hours that day.

But it was not ending pleasantly. Cunningham was disappointed in himself. He was not terribly proud of having been so obstinately opposed to making a relationship with Fred work. He believed that hurt the company, and he had never intended to hurt the company.

But he was also disappointed in the Doctor, for whom he still had immense affection. He was hurt by it all. He felt as though he was being pushed out the door like a "rejected son." He was also, in his final months, worried about the Doctor. Cunningham believed An Wang to some extent had lost his grip on reality.

But it was all ending now on a muggy Thursday night, July 13, 1985. Wang had called a special board meeting at his home. Everyone knew what was coming. Cunningham was an unemotional man, at least in professional settings such as this, but when he began reading a prepared statement, he was so choked with emotion that he could not continue. He broke down and cried.

"It was very traumatic for me to leave that company," he says. "It was more than just a job."

"John Cunningham was a very important person in Wang's history," says Bob Siegel. "He was very smart, very astute, a good spokesman, a good salesman. He had a good feel for where the industry was going."

The *Boston Globe* noted, when the announcement of Cunningham's departure was made, that he was "credited with applying his sales and marketing prowess to help propel the company from a sleepy scientific calculator maker into a world leader in word processing and office automation." A nice sendoff.

The week Cunningham left, analyst John Adams's report was headlined "A Sad Day." He wrote: "Everyone who may read this piece is old enough to have experienced good friends getting divorced. That is how we and they must feel about present events: we all wish John well; we all wish Dr. Wang well; and we all grieve that they are no longer together."

Cunningham remained on the board of directors of the Wang Institute through the remainder of 1985 and, at meetings, occasionally saw the Doctor. He ran into Fred at Fenway Park one night, and "Fred tried to tell me I didn't understand the high-tech industry."

When he left Wang, Cunningham told his mother: "For the first time in my life I'm going to do what I want to do, not what someone else wants me to do." His mother was surprised by the comment and replied: "I have known you longer than anyone and you always did exactly what you wanted to do." He could easily have retired to a life of splendor, but that wasn't what he wanted. He would not take his hard-earned $9 million after-tax proceeds from sale of Wang stock, tuck it away someplace safe, and put his feet up. No. Instead, he would risk it. Not some of it, or most of it, but *all* of it. Every nickel he had and more.

In just six months' time, Wang Laboratories had suffered a significant financial loss (when it lost $109 million for the last quarter), endured large layoffs, and lost its president.

Analyst John Adams observed in August that Wang had grown from being a $250 million company to being a $2 billion company "without a hiccup." But the company was in trouble and continued to be dogged by the product announcement of October 1983. "It will take a good deal of future punctuality before the national accounts forgive and forget," wrote Adams. "Yes, the worst trauma of the personnel cuts and management changes is over, but a virgin, once deflowered, is never quite the same.

"For all our doubts, we have an abiding faith in Dr. Wang and the organization he has built."

It was, of course, the Doctor who shifted into action amid the trouble. "It was clear when John left that it was a challenge for Doctor Wang," says Paul Guzzi. "People were in disarray with John leaving. They wondered what would happen to the company. Doctor Wang knew at that point that he had to become much more visible."

Cunningham's control of the company's day-to-day operations had permitted Wang to lie back a bit, to concentrate on whatever projects caught his fancy. Now he could not afford that. There was only one person at the company who could replace Cunningham, and that was An Wang.

He promised to visit every field office in the United States and many around the world, not an easy thing to do for a man who disliked traveling as much as the Doctor did. Although he traveled as luxuriously as is humanly possible — on a large, elegantly appointed, awesomely powerful private jet — these trips were a strain for a sixty-five-year-old man who had been out of the daily rough and tumble of business for a while and who was afraid of flying.

An Wang was so frightened of flying that between 1967 and 1978 he didn't set foot once on an airplane. And he flew in 1978 only when forced to. He had taken a trip to the West Coast through the Panama Canal, then traveled up the coast to Canada by limousine. He had intended to return home by train as well, but a blizzard shut down the Canadian rail system, leaving him with no alternative but to remain out West or fly home. Now, from the summer of 1985 until the summer of 1986, he flew off on no fewer than twenty-three trips — to Dallas, San Francisco, Chicago, Atlanta, Detroit, Chattanooga, Vancouver, New York, London, Stockholm, Bonn, and other destinations. Doctor Wang disliked it thoroughly. The trips required him to engage in the kind of customer and employee stroking that he neither enjoyed nor excelled at. But he never complained, for he knew he had no choice but to go out and tell employees and customers that though the company had hit some turbulence, smooth air lay ahead.

Even as Wang was traveling the country and the world with the message that all would be well, however, he was contradicted by press reports. "After a decade of spectacular growth, Wang seemingly has lost the magic," stated an article in the *Boston Globe* in the summer of '85.

That fall, another critical article appeared in the magazine *New England Business,* which cited familiar problems such as increased competition for the office market, late deliveries of products announced back in October 1983, and the threat of the IBM PC, particularly to Wang word processing.

The article also stated:

When the industry suddenly went into a slump, analysts say, it not only
hurt Wang, but also brought to light some basic management problems
within the company — problems that took root during 10 years of
unbridled growth.

"Their infrastructure and management style was very weak because
of years of 30% growth," says John C. McCarthy, an analyst at Forrester
Research Inc. in Cambridge. "They didn't have the lean management
in place to get the decisions made to react to the marketplace. When all
of a sudden everyone else took aim at them, the company just couldn't
react fast enough."

Out of all the bad press, there was one piece that particularly hurt. It
came from industry analyst Frederick Cohen at L. F. Rothschild, Unter-
berg, Towbin. After a meeting for analysts in New York at which An
Wang gave his pitch, Cohen wrote bluntly: "While we have a very high
regard for Dr. Wang and his past accomplishments, he is clearly past his
prime."

TWELVE

"He Is My Son and He Can Do It"

WHEN AN WANG stepped forward on Liberty Island in New York Harbor on July 3, 1986, to accept the Presidential Medal of Liberty from Ronald Reagan, it was surely the public pinnacle of his life. Wang was one of a dozen naturalized American citizens chosen for the award, which was inaugurated at the rededication ceremony of the Statue of Liberty. Wang found himself in heady company. Among the others chosen to receive the award by a committee headed by Chrysler Chairman Lee Iacocca were Henry Kissinger, the former secretary of state, composer Irving Berlin, Bob Hope, architect I. M. Pei, Itzhak Perlman, the violinist, *New York Times* columnist James Reston, and Elie Wiesel, chairman of the U.S. Holocaust Memorial Council.

"This is all very interesting and pleasing to me," Wang told a reporter. "It is a wonderful thing to show the opportunities that immigrants such as myself have received."

Fred Wang says he was told that his father was not selected on the first pass by Iacocca's selection committee. There were no minorities included in the initial group selected, says Fred. Subsequently, Wang and I. M. Pei were chosen to give the group ethnic diversity.

The Doctor greatly enjoyed the weekend in New York. He stayed at the Waldorf-Astoria Hotel and played mah-jongg during the day with friends such as Harry Chou and attended various official parties in the evening.

When his name was called out for the award, he bounded up to the stage and shook the president's hand.

"He was obviously very proud," says Fred. "To him it was a real achievement."

Another achievement with which Iacocca was involved that the Doctor found admirable was Iacocca's publication of a best-selling book. Its success prompted more than a few successful business people to search out a ghostwriter and tell their own life stories. Doctor Wang liked Iacocca's book so much that he told Fred and Paul Guzzi, one of his top staff members, that he was interested in writing a book. Coincidentally, Addison-Wesley, a Massachusetts-based publishing company, approached Wang and suggested that he write his autobiography. Wang agreed. The Doctor and Eugene Linden, his ghostwriter, would meet, often along with Guzzi and Fred, in his Lincoln study or at his office conference table, where they would listen to him answer questions about his life. It was a fascinating experience for Fred, who heard many of his father's recollections, particularly about his life in China, for the first time.

Lessons, as the book was called, was published in 1986, and An Wang was "very, very happy" with it, says Fred. Though the book is distinctly impersonal — and can fairly be described as aloof and even smug in its tone — Fred says the Doctor believed it captured his experiences. "It was very impersonal, but *he* was very impersonal," says Fred. "He was very much the engineer."

While the book pleased its subject, it impressed few reviewers and displeased many of those who had been players at Wang Laboratories through the years.

A *Los Angeles Times* review said the book lacked "the critical depth, reflection, and insight that one might hope to find from one of the greatest innovators and businessmen of this century." A *Datamation* review asked: "What lessons has An Wang learned that might enable him to revitalize his company? Unhappily, the answer is not to be found in this book." In the *Washington Post,* James K. Glassman noted that Wang's story "needs seasoning . . . and probably needs to be told by someone other than Wang himself." Glassman wrote that Wang "seems more concerned about self-image than someone of his achievements should be."

"*Lessons* was not that close to reality," says John Cunningham. "It's very ego-centered. It's missing important things and how they happened. I made big contributions to the company, and I'm almost not mentioned in the book. It could have been retitled *I.*"

Dale Jelley, who worked at the company for many years, complained that "a lot of his recollection of events and his role in them is inaccurate. He took credit for things he had very little to do with. He's a genius, but he has a terrible tendency to believe that everything that was right and good was his doing, and nobody else deserves any credit. He's glorified himself at the expense of people who really did the work."

Peter Brooke was angry about the way in which Wang dismissed a deal from the 1950s in which Brooke had been instrumental. In its early days, when Wang Labs had been strapped for cash and searching for a financial partner, Brooke had found Warner & Swasey, a Cleveland machine tool company, and worked out an arrangement for Warner & Swasey to buy a 25 percent interest in Wang Labs.

"Wang had a selective view of history," says Brooke. "Jim Hodge and Myron Curtis, the director of research at Warner & Swasey, convinced Wang to manufacture his own products. In the pivotal years of the early '60s, the Warner & Swasey guys had an important influence. Warner & Swasey gave him an equity base to expand and gave him guidance."

But in the book, Wang trashed the Warner & Swasey deal.

Frank Trantanella, an engineer who worked at the company in the early days, was also angered by the book. "My own view of him changed after reading the book," says Trantanella. "It was sad. The book shreds facts to create a fairy tale to suit his own purposes." Trantanella says a particularly egregious omission is the significant role played in the company during the 1960s by Wang's old friend from China, Dr. Ge Yao Chu. Chu had worked extremely hard during the early years, says Trantanella, and he produced much of the fine work done by the company back then. Chu was a major player at the company and the book, says Trantanella, does not convey that. Indeed, Chu is mentioned only once.

Another serious slight by Wang involved the case of PHI, the software company Wang Laboratories acquired in 1968. Within a year after the purchase of PHI, the Doctor writes in *Lessons,* "a large number" of the people "whose expertise was PHI's principle asset — had left the company. . . . The defections were irritating at the time, and it taught me the lesson that if you enter into a relationship with a company whose principal asset is people, you should do so in a way that does not remove all incentives for those people to continue working."

PHI founder Phil Hankins says it is his recollection that only one of the major players at PHI left after about a year, and Hankins himself left after about a year and a half. But the crucial point that Doctor Wang does not acknowledge was that, in taking over PHI, Wang Labs embraced three engineers whose products earned many *billions* of dollars for Wang. No less a group than David Moros, Bob Siegel, and Bob Kolk came to Wang through PHI. Not only is it contrary to the historical record to discount the PHI deal, there are those who believe that without the brain-power that PHI brought to the company, Wang Laboratories might never have been anything more than a small maker of scientific calculators.

If *Lessons* disclosed little about the Doctor's emotions, about the inner workings of the man, one thing it did reveal was Wang's expectation that his sons would follow him into the business. It was the first time he had ever made that declaration publicly.

"I want my children to have the opportunity to demonstrate their skills at management," Wang wrote. "In fact, I consider it their obligation — rather than their privilege — to do so."

This attitude contrasted sharply with the practice of fellow Lincoln resident Kenneth Olsen, president of Digital Equipment Corporation. In *The Ultimate Entrepreneur,* their book about Olsen and Digital, Glenn Rifkin and George Harrar write that Olsen "came to believe strongly that nepotism was as bad in business as in politics. . . . Digital was his, not the family's, business."

Olsen's brother Stan worked at the company for a number of years, but after Stan took a year's leave of absence, his brother did not urge him to return to work. And

> no other family members, be it his youngest brother David, his sons Glenn and James, or his daughter Ava, were invited to join the business. He was adamant that, as a public company, DEC owed its allegiance to the stockholders and not members of the Olsen clan. Unlike corpo-rate neighbor An Wang, who groomed his son Fred to take over Wang Laboratories, . . . Ken has no interest in passing along his legacy to an Olsen.

Though Fred says he "never did anything just to please Dad," a senior company executive close to both Fred and his father says that "Fred was following his father's plan. Fred was *obediently* following his father's plan, sublimating, to a certain degree, himself as part of this very, very strong-willed great man."

Life in the Cunningham period suited the Doctor well. During those years An Wang had been able to remove himself from the day-to-day affairs of the company, to leave most operational matters to his president, freeing himself to dabble in whatever R&D, financial, philanthropic, political, or educational projects caught his eye. But with Cunningham's departure came the Doctor's return to the responsibilities of the company's top operational role, and his rapid reimmersion in the details of the business. While that was welcomed by many customers and some company executives as a sign of stability, it was not long before senior managers grew weary of a system under which almost all control was centralized in the hands of one man. With Doctor Wang back in charge, management could be chaotic. Important decisions were delayed until the Doctor could be made to focus on them, while other decisions were put off by executives fearful of being second-guessed by their leader. It was clear that the Doctor's management style was ill-suited for the $3 billion company that Wang Laboratories had become.

George Colony, president of Forrester Research, suggested that Doctor Wang was "far more effective on a pedestal, as a motivator in the company" than as day-to-day manager of operations.

But if managers within the company wanted new leadership, there was one alternative and one alternative only. It was a given, a fact of life at Wang, that there would be no international search for the smartest, most experienced manager available to fill the Doctor's shoes. The job was taken before it became vacant. If anyone other than An Wang was to lead the company, it was to be Fred Wang. That the company would be run by a man named Wang was as certain as the rising of the sun. And though there was no great groundswell of support for Fred Wang, there was a growing feeling in 1986 among senior managers that Fred would be better than the Doctor. Fred, it was believed, would share the power, establish clear lines of authority, apply modern management techniques to the running of the company.

"A group of senior VPs was starting to feel alienated or out of the decision-making process," recalls Fred. "Dad's style was to make decisions himself or in small groups, and that left out the senior VPs."

Toward the end of 1986, Fred's time had come. In November he and his father sat down to talk about the company's leadership. His father raised the subject of the presidency. "That's a role I would like to play," Fred said.

The following Monday, November 19, before Fred left on a business trip to Pennsylvania, he and his father talked again.

"Congratulations," said the Doctor. Fred Wang, at the age of thirty-six, was president of Wang Laboratories.

The *Boston Globe* noted that, in the early years, Fred had "rankled some older executives who disliked his immaturity." The *Globe* quoted Patty Seybold as saying that "Fred was a petty, arrogant snot who at times wouldn't listen. He often was arbitrary and acting somewhat spoiled, the rich kid throwing his weight around. But he has matured, and he still knows he has to measure up for the job."

The most interesting comment — one that John Cunningham surely must have viewed with amusement that morning — came from Fred himself, who said that his rise to the top of the company, in his view, was "never a sure thing."

Fred's ascendence was not marked by any kind of celebration. When Cunningham had made president, the news was announced before a dinner gathering of a thousand people at Anthony's Pier 4 restaurant in Boston. After the dinner, Cunningham had gone out with a group of friends and Wang executives and, amidst congratulations and many slurred, sentimental speeches, drank until closing time, singing Irish songs at the Black Rose, a Boston bar. But Fred held no party, no celebration, because the truth was that his appointment came as a surprise to no one. And it was not something for which he had toiled for years. It was something that was destined to be his by virtue of his birth.

Fred Wang took over a company with one of the greatest growth records ever in the modern industrial world. Wang Laboratories, with its breakthrough products, had a massive installed base with tens of thousands of exceptionally loyal customers throughout the world. And around the time Fred took over there was renewed optimism within the computer industry that the slowdown that had hurt nearly every major computer player was about to end.

Fred was lucky to become president just as the industry began coming out of a difficult period. During the early 1980s, most minicomputer companies in the northeast struggled through slumping demand in a recessionary economy. But from 1981 through 1984, when companies such as Digital and Data General were having problems, Wang was riding the crest of its hot product wave. The company's financial performance was the envy of the industry.

While it was a good time to take over in one sense, it was also a difficult time. Competition within the industry was stiffening fast, and it quickly became clear that the days of 30-plus percent annual growth were ancient history. Fred took over a company that still suffered from the void left by Cunningham's departure, whose sales force was not nearly as sophisticated as those at other computer companies, a company that did not have the home-run products it once relied upon.

Ironically, however, Fred's most daunting problem was his father.

Since its birth in 1951, Wang Laboratories had been An Wang's company. Of that there had never been even the slightest doubt. But in recent years, particularly since Cunningham's departure, overreliance on the Doctor had grown to a dangerous level.

Among senior management, Fred says, "there was a feeling I would use the organization more. . . . Dad had a few areas he was very interested in and others he just let go. No one was willing to make decisions in those areas for fear of being countermanded."

It would not be easy to follow in his father's footsteps, but Fred would have his chance to show what he could do.

When Fred became president, Paul Guzzi became Fred's chief-of-staff. Other than that, little about Fred's routine within the company changed after his promotion. His hours remained as they had been — about 8:00 A.M. to 6:00 P.M. And he kept the same office. It was an enormous space in a corner of the penthouse with a spectacular view toward the southeast. Across from his desk was a small, informal arrangement of two comfortable sofas and four easy chairs. The office was carpeted in white, and there was a white throw rug with a large blue Wang logo. On the other side of the office was a large conference table seating twelve, and yet another conference table stood in a room adjacent to the office.

Though there were few outward changes, Fred went to work immediately to alter the way Wang Labs operated. In an effort to wean the company from its unhealthy dependence upon his father, Fred moved to decentralize decision making. He demanded more accountability from his managers, and he shifted the company to vertical markets so that the sales force, rather than working within a given geographical territory, would work within one of four industries the company had targeted: manufacturing, legal, government, and financial services (including banks and insurance companies).

Wang Labs had always tended toward vertical markets. While companies such as Digital and Data General were known for selling the flashiest and most powerful computer iron, Wang was known for its applications. The company had worked a vertical market when it tailored its 700 calculator for automobile dealers, for example. But Fred pushed Wang toward the next level of vertical marketing. It was, in part at least, a recognition by Fred that the company needed a sales force that understood not only Wang Labs' products, but also its customers' needs. Law firms required more than just powerful computers. They needed computer companies that understood their business enough to guide them through the maze of technology to the right solution. Under Fred, Wang Labs would seek to change its orientation so that its salespeople could specialize.

With the passing of the high-flying days of 40 percent annual growth — when Wang Labs' products had been so hot that the salespeople had been branded "order takers" — Fred moved to train a more sophisticated sales group that could compete in the ever-tougher computer industry. This was a big change. In the old days, former venetian blind salesmen and secretaries had come to Wang and sold word processing systems without the slightest problem. Part of the company's early success with word processing, in fact, came from selling the machines not to sophisticated technical experts — the MIS (management information systems) people — but to office managers. MIS people in general had an IBM bias, and even those who didn't were generally technically savvy and demanded a similar sophistication from the salespeople with whom they dealt. Since Wang had never done well in the MIS environment, they could get away without the most polished sales force. No longer.

Wang was going head-to-head with IBM on its core computer business. IBM had made its name with mainframe computers, big, muscular computing workhorses. With the advent of the minicomputer — small, powerful machines that could perform many of the tasks formerly accomplished only by mainframes and at a much lower cost — IBM had leaped to the aggressive defense of its territory. But it had been hurt. Companies such as Digital and Data General convinced customers to supplement mainframes with their minicomputers. And the latest threat came from personal computers. Not those that stood alone, individual outposts on a desk, but those hooked together in so-called Local Area Networks. These connected stations gained power from one another and replaced minicomputers altogether in some instances.

In the spring of 1987, after Fred had been on the job barely six months, Wang employees were suddenly barraged with a new, somewhat bewildering series of numbers that, they were told, represented Fred's overall goals for the company. It was known as the "1-3-5-10-20" mission. And it was so significant in Fred's mind that he had a flag made up with those numbers emblazoned on it. Fred talked the program up in his monthly newsletter and in whatever other opportunities he had to communicate with large numbers of employees.

Number one meant that Fred wanted Wang Labs to be first in customer satisfaction among computer companies. "We were constantly picked at by our customers" over sloppy or unreliable service, says Fred. "There wasn't consistency in field service." This was an effort, in part, "to get over the stigma" of the '83 product announcement.

Number three meant the company wanted to be among the top three computer companies in technical innovation.

Five meant achieving $5 billion in revenues.

Ten meant reaching an after-tax profit of 10 percent.

And twenty meant that Fred wanted the company to grow 20 percent per year so that it would double in size every five years.

"There was a big to-do about this program," says Fred, who was its main booster. He pushed it hard among the employees, but it was not easily grasped. Only half jokingly, Fred says that it took a full nine months "for everybody in the company to remember the numbers."

Only a few months into Fred's tenure, there was bad news. During the first week of January 1987, Wang Laboratories announced that business had slowed to the point where it had to lay off 1,000 employees, cutting its worldwide work force to 30,000. The company also announced it would reduce all wages by 6 percent, and that it would soon disclose a substantial quarterly loss. Two weeks later, when the loss was announced, gloom deepened around the company.

But Wang's new president was nothing if not optimistic. The characteristic that Fred had inherited from his father above all others was optimism. For what stood out amidst all of the clutter surrounding the announcement was one comment by Fred: "The worst is behind us."

He believed it. The loss, he explained, was due in part to his new head of U.S. sales throwing questionable orders out of the sales backlog. Trimming down that backlog made the loss larger on paper, but it also served to get expectations closer to reality. Fred was optimistic because the industry slump that had begun back in 1984 showed signs of easing. There was a feeling among the company's sales force that there were good times ahead and there was renewed hope in the industry.

Besides, Fred believed that with imaging technology — the original imaging product had been PIC, the professional image computer — the company had developed yet another home-run product, something to rival the epic successes of word processing and the VS. The company had made marked improvements to imaging since PIC. It allowed paper-intensive industries such as insurance or the legal profession to store their paper files on easily accessible electronic files. The future of imaging looked very good indeed. And if the technology were to catch on in the way, say, that word processing had, Wang Labs would be out front, for it was one of few companies in the world offering imaging products.

But if the worst was truly past, that did not mean Wang wasn't still fair game for a few more hits from the press. In the spring, a *Business Week* cover story on executive pay ranked executives according to their performance for shareholders. Among those giving shareholders the least performance for their pay was the Doctor. (Among executives giving the most was Digital's Ken Olsen.) And when the New York publication *Financial World* chose the worst-managed public companies in the United States according to stock performance, management errors, and earnings, Wang Labs was on the list.

These embarrassments did not bother the Doctor, says Fred. "He would say, 'How big a time frame do you want to look at? If you go back and compare it starting in '67, I give a bigger return than anyone'" on the *Business Week* list.

Perhaps one of the most painful setbacks for the Doctor was the realization that the Wang Institute, the school he had founded and nurtured himself, was not going to make it on its own. The place had become a serious financial drain on which the Doctor had spent a literal fortune — between $25 million and $30 million — and 90 percent of those funds came out of the Doctor's pocket. He also found that he was subsidizing the education of numerous software engineers from other companies, particularly Digital. And the notion of paying for talented engineers to enrich themselves intellectually only to return to help Digital compete with Wang Laboratories struck the Doctor as counterproductive. There was little choice other than to merge it with a larger, established institution of higher learning. The obvious choices were MIT and Harvard, but neither university was interested. That hurt. Finally, Boston University agreed to take it over.

In early 1987, Wang suddenly had a run of good business. That April, the company surprised analysts when it announced a quarterly profit. Coming as it did after six months' worth of losses, it was a relief. The news was so good, in fact, that Wang began some selective hiring, nothing like the old days, of course, when hundreds of new people poured into the towers every Monday morning, but it was certainly better than the now almost routine announcement of layoffs.

Observers of the company saw Ian Diery, a swashbuckling young Australian, as a key player in this newly found good fortune. Fred had been so impressed with Diery's success as head of Wang's European operations that he brought him in to run sales and marketing for the United States, which then accounted for 60 percent of the company's worldwide revenues. With his charismatic style, Diery revved up the salespeople and instilled in them a new confidence that paid off fast, for in July 1987 Wang completed its most profitable quarter in three years with record sales of $824 million.

Analysts were delighted with the news and suggested that the company was in the midst of a steady comeback. In September, a *Computerworld* article stated that "although short-term skepticism still abounds, the long-term prospects for the company seem bright." The story quoted a New York analyst as saying that Wang Labs had "indeed turned the corner."

In the early fall came another healthy quarter and, with that, a *Boston Globe* story suggesting that Wang was "continuing its recovery." Diery spoke of the company's "ongoing and accelerating turnaround." And Bob Ano, senior vice-president for marketing, declared: "Make no mistake about it. Wang is back."

Even analyst John Adams was impressed and said it was clear that Wang management was "running the business very well."

And with that heady sentiment came something unusual — praise for Fred Wang. When, in addition to being president, he added the title of chief operating officer in November 1987, a *Globe* article read in part: "Though Wall Street at first greeted his appointment with skepticism, he is now credited with a key role in reversing a string of losses."

In the article analyst John McCarthy of Forrester Research commented: "Fred deserves a lot of credit for the turnaround. A lot of us had to eat our words."

As Fred Wang basked in the glory of his company's success, John Cunningham struggled to avoid financial ruin.

Cunningham and a small team of former Wang people, including Harold Koplow, Dave Moros, and Jake Jacobson, were fighting mightily for the survival of Computer Consoles, the company they had taken over. When they had moved into CCI in a friendly deal, Cunningham had known the company was in trouble. But he had seen it as a company with the kinds of difficulties that his team had the expertise to solve. So confident had he been that they could revive CCI that Cunningham had invested a massive amount of his personal wealth in the firm.

But not long after he took over, Cunningham found CCI to be in far worse shape than he had imagined. By the middle of 1987, it appeared that CCI would collapse. For Cunningham, this would be a catastrophe of the first order. "The hardest part would be that people would look at my success at Wang and say, 'I knew it was luck.' It would have been personally very embarrassing to have CCI not make it. People would have a completely different view of me. My whole reputation as a manager and strategist of technology companies was at stake."

By October 1987, when Fred's resurgence was in full throttle, the CCI stock had fallen from an earlier high of $7 when Cunningham took over to $2.63 a share. At that point, Cunningham was down $3.5 million cash. If CCI should go into bankruptcy, and that looked increasingly likely, he would lose $7 million as well as his homes.

John Cunningham, who had done such remarkable work at Wang Laboratories, who had made himself a millionaire many times over by the age of thirty-five, was on the edge of financial ruin.

He had borrowed $2 million to finish off his house in Weston. He had borrowed to fix the Nantucket house. He had borrowed to buy the CCI stock. The cost of all this debt — not including his living expenses — approached $750,000 a year! Cunningham had been seduced by the ethic of the '80s. Like other Masters of the Universe, he was leveraged way over his head. When he tried to borrow more money to keep his head above water, and when he offered CCI stock as collateral, Citibank — to whom he already owed $2 million — flatly refused him.

Cunningham had come a long way since his childhood days in West Roxbury, where he had hustled odd jobs here and there to make money. He had lived as high as one could live in Paris and Monte Carlo, traveled the world in a private jet, been chauffeured around in a Mercedes-Benz limousine. But here he was on his own, without the shelter of Wang Laboratories after eighteen years, and he was on the precipice of disaster. So precarious was his personal financial situation that he had to delay payments on routine monthly bills — household expenses and credit cards. He searched frantically for a loan to get by for a while, to pay for basic necessities. Finally, the Summit Credit Union in Rochester, New York, agreed to loan him $40,000 that enabled him to limp along as he tried desperately to salvage CCI. The task and the prospect of failure — of the fiery crash and explosion of John Cunningham — left him "panic-stricken," he says. "If you come from nothing and never have anything, that's one thing. But if you come from nothing and then you've got something and then lose it, that would be very difficult."

The irony was rich. For even as it appeared that John Cunningham was headed for a humiliating crash, it looked as though Fred Wang would gain glory and vindication as head of a revived Wang Laboratories.

Wang's good fortune during 1987 did not comfort Peter Brooke, a thin, impeccably tailored Yankee whose roundish face was prone to squinting in an owlish fashion behind his horn-rimmed glasses. And Brooke's discomfort was a sign of trouble, for Brooke knew the company well. Back in 1958, when Wang employed a grand total of six people and was tucked away in a grimy building on Hurley Street in Cambridge, Brooke had gone looking for Wang's business. He was then a young cub in the credit department at the First National Bank of Boston. Though he was green, he was also smart and determined. He worked hard and he had vision. He saw that the technology companies sprouting out of garages around MIT would one day grow into formidable enterprises. So he stalked those streets, banging on garage doors and looking to loan money to the young technical geniuses creating products of the future.

He had little trouble seeing the principals in these tiny operations, but Wang Labs was different. The mysterious Chinese owner would not talk with him. When Brooke visited, he was turned away by the Doctor's secretary. Brooke was persistent, for he had studied Wang's business, talked with Wang's customers, knew the firm's work was first-rate, and believed in Wang Labs' future. One day in 1958, as Brooke dropped by to try, once again, to win an audience with Doctor Wang, a knot of people surrounded the hole in a wall that the company used as its loading dock. Brooke, dressed in his banker's uniform of a suit and tie, saw that they were moving a large piece of equipment and had summoned all hands to help lower it onto a truck. He quickly jumped in. It did not escape the Doctor's notice that this gray-suited stranger had pitched in with the grunt work. Brooke won an audience, and he told the Doctor he wanted to be Wang Labs' banker. But the Doctor, committing to nothing, told Brooke to see his lawyer, Chuck Goodhue.

At the time, Wang had a relationship with the Merchants Bank of Boston, but Brooke told Goodhue he would give the company a much better deal than Merchants offered. He told Goodhue that he would double the company's credit line to $50,000 and that he would take Wang's name off the note so that the Doctor would not bear any personal liability for the loan. On top of that, he offered a prime rate. Goodhue couldn't resist. Wang Labs was in business with Peter Brooke and the First National Bank of Boston.

Brooke never played an operational role at Wang, but through the years, as a member of the company's board of directors and an adviser to the Doctor, he had an important impact on the company. It was Brooke who put Doctor Wang together with Jim Hodge of Warner & Swasey. And it was Brooke who got the Doctor together with Phil Hankins, a meeting that led to the acquisition of PHI.

In his own business, Brooke had been extraordinarily successful. At the First National Bank of Boston, fresh out of Harvard Business School, Brooke loaned venture capital to small, very risky start-ups in the Boston-Cambridge area. He researched his companies so thoroughly and invested so wisely that in four years during the late '50s and early '60s, Brooke lent $10 million and lost a mere $15,000 of that.

At Tucker, Anthony in Boston, Brooke founded a venture capital operation that he built into the largest such firm in the United States. He subsequently founded and built Advent International into one of the largest international venture capital firms in the world.

He was a man of formidable intellect and vision, and for several years the course of Wang Laboratories had troubled him. By the early 1980s, when it appeared the company could do no wrong, top management had developed what Brooke describes as "a we-know-everything attitude." This arrogance grew even as the company began having serious problems with production quality. From his venture capital work around the world, Brooke knew a small company that specialized in quality control. He considered the company the best he had ever seen, and they were only a couple of hours away from Wang in western Massachusetts. The firm consisted essentially of two brothers, Armand and Donald Feigenbaum, who had advised dozens of the world's largest corporations. The Feigenbaums were so well known among top managers at major companies that much of their work was done directly with presidents and CEOs.

Brooke thought they could be of immeasurable help to Wang, and he arranged for the Feigenbaum brothers to sit down with Cunningham, Fred Wang, and a few other Wang executives. When he heard after the meeting that during the brothers' presentation a distracted Cunningham had sifted through his mail while Fred Wang had sat back yawning, Brooke was embarrassed and angry.

"The Feigenbaums — brilliant guys — were dealing at absolutely the top level of industrial companies, and they come to Wang and are treated like third-rate consultants," says Brooke, still upset years later.

After the meeting, Fred told Brooke he didn't think the Feigenbaums would fit into the company's culture. The reason, thought Brooke at the time, was that the company had grown too insular. So successful had Wang Labs been that the company's top managers — with the possible exception of Cunningham, who tried to bring in Chev Haskell at a senior level — had insulated themselves from any outside advice.

Brooke worried in part about the company's leadership. There was no question in his mind that Fred Wang did not have what it would take to lead a major corporation. It was not that Brooke didn't like or respect Fred. It was simply that Brooke didn't believe Fred had it.

There was no question in Brooke's mind that the company needed tough, seasoned leadership from an experienced player in the industry. "We as a group had severe reservations" about Fred, says Brooke, referring to other outside directors of the company. "We didn't think he could do it without a hell of a lot of help from the old man."

On the surface, the company performed well throughout 1987 with Fred at the helm, but Brooke was worried about the future and he was not alone. A core group of the company's board members — all outside directors — shared his fears. Brooke, Leo Beranek, Richard A. Smith, and Louis Cabot all doubted Fred's leadership abilities. This was not a group of idle complainers thoughtlessly bellyaching. These were some of the most successful and distinguished businessmen in America.

Leo Beranek, who had taught An Wang at Harvard, was co-founder of Bolt Beranek and Newman Inc., a highly successful consulting and research firm specializing in noise and vibration control. Beranek taught at both Harvard and MIT, was the author of numerous books, and served as a Harvard overseer and as president of the American Academy of Arts and Sciences.

Ironically, two of the board's strongest opponents to Fred Wang's operation of the company were Smith and Cabot, both of whom were heirs to family-run businesses, and both of whom ran those businesses well.

Dick Smith was chairman of General Cinema Corporation, a billion-dollar-plus company that owned the nation's largest chain of movie theaters and had a controlling interest in Neiman Marcus. Together with his sister, Smith owned a stake in General Cinema estimated at nearly $300 million. Through the years, he had built a reputation as a savvy, tough-minded businessman.

Cabot was born into one of the most distinguished Boston families. ("The Lowells speak only to Cabots," went the expression, "and the Cabots speak only to God.") Like Peter Brooke, he graduated from Harvard and Harvard Business School. After graduation he moved into the family business, Cabot Corporation, a billion-dollar-plus chemical manufacturing company. In 1986, Cabot left the company to become chairman of the Brookings Institution, the prestigious Washington think-tank.

Before departing Cabot Corporation, however, Cabot had driven his relatives from the company. "I dealt very harshly with nepotism at our company," he says. "It's very hard, but it's important to do to keep the company healthy."

Cabot was under the impression that Doctor Wang admired what he had done, but it soon became clear that what truly mattered to Wang was family control of the business.

Brooke, Cabot, Smith, and Beranek felt they could not remain silent. During a series of lunches with An Wang at Boston's exclusive Union Club, they argued that Wang Laboratories needed to bring in a top executive from the outside. They first made their case in January 1987 just two months after Fred became president. The setting was perfect. These pillars of the establishment settled in comfortably among the old wood, the worn, elegant chintz, the heavy crystal.

"The pitch was that we should open the management of the company to the best professional managers we could locate in the industry," says Brooke. "We thought there should be a senior industry man brought into the business, make him CEO, and groom Fred. Fred would be an apprentice to him and learn the business. He would expand his skills and, at a later date, become CEO."

They conveyed to Doctor Wang their belief that Fred did not then have the experience, the brains, or the savvy to run the company.

"Fred screwed up research so much, who the hell would think he could do it?" says Brooke.

They did not succeed in January, so they met again with the Doctor at the same place in March and made the same pitch. Again, he did not agree. In August, they returned to the Union Club for another lunch and another pass at convincing An Wang to bring in an industry professional. They tried again in September. And, finally, they tried a fifth and final time in October.

The Doctor would not make a change. Smith had had it. In October 1987, he resigned from the board of directors of Wang Laboratories. The talk later was that Louis Cabot wanted to do the same, but believed it would look very bad for the company if he and Smith bailed out at the same time. Board member Martin Kirkpatrick says there's no doubt why

Smith left. "He quit because the Doctor was not listening," says Kirkpatrick.

The Union Club lunches were futile, says Louis Cabot. Wang simply would not budge. Cabot says that in response to the board members' pleas to bring in a professional, An Wang simply said: "He is my son and he can do it."

THIRTEEN

Never-never Land

T HE FINAL MONTHS of 1988 were among the happiest of Fred Wang's life, for it was at the end of that year that a child was due to be born to Fred and his wife, Laurie. Fred had met Laurel O'Connor in the summer of 1984 at a company outing at Avalon, Fred's North Shore estate. At twenty-eight, Laurie was six years younger than Fred. She was tall, with dark hair and a lovely smile. When she and Fred met, Laurie was working as a product manager at Wang Labs. She had joined the company in 1980 when Wang was in the midst of one of its frenzied drives for new employees, and she had immediately got caught up in the excitement of the company's growth. She was slowly working her way up to the middle-management ranks.

Laurie was not entirely comfortable with the idea of dating the boss, so she and Fred were careful to keep their budding relationship quiet. When Laurie took a leave of absence from the company to get her MBA at the Simmons Graduate School of Management in Boston, they continued their private courtship. She and Fred were quite different in several respects. Though Laurie had grown up in Weston, an affluent Boston suburb, her middle-class existence was far from the extraordinary privilege that had marked Fred's upbringing. Where Fred was introverted and shy, she was outgoing and affable. Where he was cool and unemotional, she was fiery and passionate. With Fred, it was often difficult to tell how he felt. He rarely expressed anger. Laurie, in contrast, made no pretense about hiding her emotions. When she was angry — and she often was during the turbulent years during which Fred was so often criticized —

she made herself heard. She was opinionated and rarely shrank from expressing her views.

Although it was clear to Fred that his mother fervently hoped he would marry an Asian woman, he told her he intended to marry Laurie. He had not often heeded his mother's wishes in the past and he was not about to start doing so at the age of thirty-five. Fred and Laurie were married in October 1985 at Avalon.

Laurie returned to Wang Labs after their marriage and focused her energies on identifying women at the company with potential for upper management. To her dismay, she found that she was feared and avoided by some employees while others groveled before her. It was impossible to do her job as she had before she became Fred's wife, the Doctor's daughter-in-law.

In 1988 Laurie's attention turned from work to home when, on the last day of November, she gave birth to a baby girl. She was An Wang's first grandchild, and, in his honor, she was named Andrea. But the glow of the moment was to be the last bit of sustained happiness in Fred Wang's life for some time. Immediately after Andrea's birth, a protracted war began between the company and its bankers.

Fred was not terribly keen on banks, an aversion he had inherited from his father. An Wang neither liked nor trusted banks, and he came to feel deeply embittered at the end of his life by the way the banks — the Bank of Boston, in particular — had treated his company. Many years before the company was in trouble, An Wang told his son: "Be very careful with bankers. When you don't need money they're all over you. But when you do they're nowhere in sight."

What would grow into an ugly confrontation between Wang Labs and its consortium of eight large banks began innocently enough with concerns among the banks about the slumping computer industry. Their worries were legitimate, for the highest of the industry's high-flying days were clearly past. The dizzying growth of earlier years could not be sustained, and the industry appeared headed for the kind of shakeout that had occurred decades before in the auto industry, which had shrunk from dozens of companies to only the big three.

In the face of this, many bankers were scouting for industries with greater growth potential. Wang not only happened to be in an industry from which some banks were looking to escape, but the company also showed more signs of trouble than some of its competitors. Wang's weak performance in a flattening industry stirred little enthusiasm among the consortium, which was led by the Bank of Boston and included Chase, First Chicago, Bank of America, Chemical, Harris, Mellon, and Baybanks.

Big American commercial banks were also having their own problems. The boom of the 1980s, particularly in real estate, had made many banks, especially those in the northeastern United States, very rich indeed. But by early 1988 the banks were getting an inkling of the painful contractions that lay ahead in the real estate market.

Industry problems aside, however, there was every reason for the Wang people to expect support from its lead bank with which it had such a long and mutually beneficial history. For thirty years, ever since Peter Brooke landed the Wang account for the First National Bank of Boston, which later dropped the words *First National* from its name, the bank and Wang Labs had been linked. Doctor Wang had included Brooke on his board of directors. He had also asked Ernest F. Stockwell, Jr., senior vice-president of the bank, to join his board. Outside of Wang Labs itself, no company had such strong representation on the Wang board. The relationship between the Doctor and the bank grew so close, in fact, that the Doctor was asked to serve on the Bank of Boston board of directors, which he did from 1972 until 1983. He became an honorary member of the board in 1984.

However, while it was true that there was a long and warm history between the two institutions, it was also true that the bank was, beneath that veneer of warmth, still a bank.

To Wang Labs, a good relationship with its banks was essential. High-technology businesses in general have large appetites for cash, and Wang Labs' appetite was voracious. Wang especially needed cash to support its massive manufacturing and sales networks. Wang was unlike some other computer companies such as Apple or Compaq, which subcontracted out the manufacture of their products and sold through retail outlets. Though Wang's revenues fluctuated, sometimes wildly, from quarter to quarter or even week to week — customers didn't purchase computer equipment at a steady, predictable pace — the company had a constant stream of obligations. Wang's 30,000-plus employees needed to get paid every week, not just when the company's revenues happened to be up.

Wang Labs had traditionally been more debt-laden than other computer companies largely as a result of the Doctor's fanatical concern for control. While many other companies raised capital by selling stock,

Wang had preferred to borrow on the commercial paper markets and from banks, sources of capital that would not dilute the family's stake in the company.

When the company and its banks began renegotiation of Wang Labs' revolving credit agreement, the tone of the talks was quite civil. The agreement, under which Wang had $600 million available to it from the consortium, was due to expire in the fall of 1989. The company and the banks began an unhurried negotiation of those terms a year earlier. There was no great urgency to working out the deal, particularly since the company had very rarely actually used the credit line. In the nearly twenty years the line had been in place, the company had borrowed from it only once, and that had come during a difficult, but brief, period in the early 1970s. The company had always preferred the cheaper routes of borrowing on the commercial paper markets in both the United States and Europe.

When company officials and bankers met in late October, the consensus was that they would have a new arrangement worked out by Christmas 1988. And they did. Or so it seemed. The company reached agreement with the Bank of Boston on a term sheet setting out the terms of the deal. The agreement pulled all Wang loans into one deal and called for a modest increase in the fees the banks would receive. But when the term sheet was circulated to the other banks in the consortium, one bank, Chase, would not sign.

Company officials believed the issue was the size of the fee. During the 1980s, commercial banks such as Chase watched in awe as small, private investment banks raked in huge fees on leveraged buyouts and other daring financial maneuvers. Commercial bankers responded by creating services for which they, too, could charge high fees. Though banks made good money from fees paid by companies like Wang, the truth was there was no comparison between the money made on unused lines of credit (as was the case with Wang) and fees charged on an LBO.

Whatever the reason, Chase wouldn't sign the agreement. Chase officials said they wanted to wait and see the financial results of the next quarter of the company's fiscal year. These results, for the quarter ending in December, would be available by the end of January. Chase would sign the agreement only if the numbers looked good then.

While this was happening, John Cunningham was in the final stages of a deal to avert financial catastrophe. The idea had been to fix CCI within five years and sell it, but Cunningham had found the task of fixing it far more difficult than he had anticipated. When Cunningham took over CCI, the company employed 1,760 people. He had to slash expenses so deeply that he fired 530 of them, including sixteen of the company's top seventeen managers. Even after such massive cuts, the company sagged under its huge debt.

Cunningham started work at CCI in the summer of 1985. By 1987 the situation looked so grim that he believed for a while that the company was going to go down that year and he along with it. It was at this point that he sought out an old pal who had managed Wang's aircraft. He told the man that he wanted to buy a small jet but only one that could be financed at more than 100 percent. "I figured, shit, if I'm going to go down I may as well go down in style," says Cunningham. And so he bought a $600,000 Citation Executive — a "poor man's jet," he called it — with room for seven passengers plus a pilot and co-pilot, and he financed the deal at a few points over 100 percent. He used the plane for business trips as well as the short weekend hop to his home on Nantucket.

By the spring of 1988 Cunningham was working desperately to refinance CCI. Most of all, in order to be able to borrow enough money to put CCI on firm financial footing and give him the time to turn the company around, Cunningham needed to sell the directory assistance system leases. The truth was that CCI would fail unless Cunningham could refinance the company by selling leases at a decent price on the directory assistance computer systems that were the company's main strength. Finding a buyer was not a problem — he had General Electric Credit Corporation all lined up, ready to buy. The problem was getting permission to sell the leases from CCI's largest customer, Southwestern Bell, which paid CCI tens of millions of dollars annually to supply directory assistance computer systems. At the time Cunningham was attempting to sell the leases, the deal between CCI and Southwestern Bell was up for renewal. Southwestern Bell held nearly all the cards in the negotiation of a new contract. CCI, financially weak and urgently in need of cash, was at Southwestern Bell's mercy.

Initial indications were that the phone company negotiators were fully aware of the strength of their position and intended to pressure CCI into offering a very low price, one so low that it would jeopardize the lease sale and cause the collapse of CCI and John Cunningham. As he considered his options, Cunningham decided to bypass the phone company negotiators and go directly to the president of Southwestern Bell. He did not know this man, but he believed he had no choice but to appeal to him personally.

Cunningham flew to St. Louis on his jet to plead his case before the phone company president. He argued that he had fixed CCI's operations and that he needed to sell the leases in order to fix the balance sheet. If the lease sales went through at a certain price, Southwestern Bell would have, in CCI, a reliable supplier for years to come. If the sale did not go through at that price, Cunningham said he wasn't sure what the future would bring.

The situation reminded him of a similar problem in the early '80s at Wang. A couple of brothers in Chicago had built a 400,000-square-foot office building for which they had signed Wang up as a minor tenant. Later, they signed up IBM as the anchor tenant. But when IBM discovered Wang was in the same building, IBM threatened to pull out, as was their right under the terms of their lease. The brothers, who had their futures invested in the building, needed IBM as a tenant to make the deal work. They went to the Wang people in Chicago and asked to be let out of the contract. The Wang people wouldn't do it. The brothers flew to Lowell and appealed, hats in hand, to Cunningham. They told him their story and said their project would go down without IBM.

Cunningham told them he was glad they had come. No problem, he said, Wang would move. The brothers were ecstatic.

The chairman of Southwestern Bell had the same reaction to Cunningham that Cunningham had had to the two brothers. He told Cunningham there would be no problem. They would approve the sale of the leases at a price that would permit CCI to refinance.

That one decision allowed Cunningham to get refinancing for CCI, sell the leases to GE Credit Corporation, and nurse the company back to health. In the process, he hired an additional three hundred people.

By the end of 1988, Cunningham had reduced CCI's debt by $100 million. In the fall of 1987, CCI had been worth $35 million. In December 1988, Cunningham sold the company for $217 million to STC Group, the $4 billion British conglomerate.

Just a couple of years earlier, it had seemed that Fred Wang was headed up as Cunningham was going down in flames. But as the new year dawned in 1989, and as John Cunningham walked away from the CCI deal with a cool $17.5 million in his pocket, it was clear that the reality was exactly the reverse of what it had seemed before.

The results of the December 1988 quarter, so eagerly awaited by the banks, were announced on January 18. The news was not good. The company had suffered a shocking 97 percent plunge in earnings compared with the same quarter a year earlier. The results were sharply lower than Wall Street analysts had expected. "It's a surprise and a real disappointment," Jay P. Stevens of Dean Witter Reynolds told the *Boston Globe*.

Fred, however, was undaunted. He said he was "disappointed, but not discouraged. The problem was one of timing. The basic strategy we have in place is taking hold." Fred also said that the company had faced production problems with the new VS, and that the company's older products simply had not sold as well as expected. But there would be no need for layoffs in the current quarter because attrition was cutting the work force enough. "We aren't expecting any Draconian cuts," he said.

In Fred's view the results were no more than a "blip" on the company's screen. But outside the company there was skepticism.

Analyst John Adams, who had long been bullish on Wang, was caustic in his comments a few days after the results of the December quarter were posted. "Wang has suffered through a multi-year period of underachievement," he wrote. "Remarkably, this experience has not affected management's enthusiasm for the business. As a cynic would put it, the company no sooner misses one optimistic forecast than it makes another."

The December results were bad enough to alarm several other banks in addition to Chase. The results of the March quarter, which would be posted in April, would be crucial to a new bank agreement.

That was fine with Fred, who boldly predicted that the company would have a strong second half. Orders looked good, and top people at the company believed that business was about to pick up markedly.

"The sales and marketing people gave optimistic, rosy forecasts" about sales for the coming months, says Frank Kinsey, a consultant who worked at the senior levels of the company from 1987 until the summer of 1989. "The philosophy was, 'We'll grow ourselves out of the problem.' People behaved as though that would happen."

Kinsey, who worked closely with Fred, urgently advised him to make drastic cuts in expenses. But that sort of advice wasn't readily taken at Wang Laboratories. Such was the nature of the optimism that had permeated Wang Labs from its earliest days that even in the face of great difficulty, there was a cheerful outlook. Much too cheerful. For the fact was that the combination of circumstances did not bode well for the company. The computer industry continued to hurt, especially overseas, where the strong dollar dented revenues. And one of the most profitable areas of the company's business, the servicing of equipment it had sold, was in decline. Worst of all, of course, was the massive shift from minicomputers to personal computers. Minicomputers were not only a Wang strength — the VS was one of the finest minis in the world — but the sale of minis generated huge profit margins. PCs, in contrast, were not one of the company's strong suits, and even when it did sell PCs, the profit margins were nothing close to what minis brought in.

All of this, though very bad news, was not fully recognized by Fred and other company managers. But Fred was about to receive news that was far worse than anything having to do with Wang Laboratories' business.

An Wang smoked nearly his entire adult life. As a young man, it had been cigarettes. In the 1960s, Fred Wang recalls that the smell in the family's Lincoln home suddenly changed one day when his father switched to cigars, fat ones that he chomped as he smoked. After a while the Doctor switched yet again, this time to a pipe. But this was short-lived, and he returned in the 1970s to cigarettes. Finally, in 1982, An Wang stubbed out a butt one night and declared it his last. Although he kept his word, it was apparently too late.

In January 1989, around the time the December quarter results were announced, the Doctor's throat began to constrict. It became so tight he had difficulty swallowing even small amounts of food and could eat only soft foods. He delayed having the problem checked until after a series of business trips he had planned. Finally, in March, he visited a throat specialist at the Massachusetts General Hospital.

He broke the news of his diagnosis to his wife, sons, and close associates after a company board meeting during the third week in March 1989. At the meeting in Wang's office were Lorraine, Fred, and Courtney Wang as well as Paul Guzzi, Harry Chou, and Bill Pechilis, a trusted Wang adviser who had been the family's personal lawyer for many years. Though the Doctor's tone was matter-of-fact, his message was stunning: He was suffering from esophageal cancer, a deadly disease.

"We were all shocked," says Fred. "He told us it was a very dangerous situation in a very difficult area. He said most doctors believed there was a 10 percent chance of survival to five years. Some said there was an 80 percent chance, and he looked at the 80 percent and Mom looked at the 10 percent.

"He was very matter-of-fact about it, like it was just one more thing. He wasn't overly emotional about it. He was overly pragmatic if anything. His attitude was that there are service people who fix computers and M.D.s who do this sort of thing, that the best doctors in the world are in Boston, and they'll work on it."

Wang's calm exterior belied the gravity of his illness. Esophageal cancer is among the most savage forms of the disease. Though it is relatively
rare in Americans, afflicting only about ten thousand people every year
(just 1 percent of all new cancers), it is lethal, killing 80 to 90 percent of
all those afflicted.

And, in An Wang, the tumor was located in an especially sensitive area
of the esophagus, a muscle tube about nine inches long that follows a
route from the pharynx, down the neck, through a small space between
the trachea and the spinal column, to the stomach. Cancer in any part of
the esophagus is serious. But Wang's tumor was located at the top of the
esophagus, a spot that surgeons considered particularly hard to get at.

The plan was for the Doctor to undergo a series of tests during the
month of April, then to receive two separate treatments of chemotherapy,
one in May, another in June. The idea was to use the chemo to shrink
the tumor so it would be easier to operate, if that were necessary.

Few people were told the news. It was decided by those assembled
that the board members would have to know, and each was called individually. They were advised that the situation was somewhat unclear.
During the weeks following the news, Wang was subjected to further
tests. The results convinced his physicians that he would have to have
surgery. The operation would come in July, after the two months of
chemotherapy.

While the Doctor suffered from a physical illness, his company suffered
from a financial malady. With the December numbers having been so
disappointing, the results of the third quarter of the fiscal year — which
ran from January through March of 1989 — suddenly loomed as enormously significant. Good news would relieve a great deal of financial pressure. It would mean not only a new bank agreement, but it would also
permit the company to raise about $200 million through the sale of pre-
ferred stock. That $200 million coupled with a new credit line would give
Wang breathing room for years to come.

Fred expected all that to happen. In January, as he looked ahead to the
coming three months, he liked what he saw. He believed, based on orders,
that revenues would increase, and he also believed that some cost-cutting
measures he was implementing — including limited layoffs — would
trim expenses. The net result, he believed, would be a far healthier balance
sheet. But only a month into the quarter, it was obvious to Fred that
something was wrong. Sales projections simply weren't translating into
actual orders. Since the company had geared up for a strong period —

with a large sales force, plenty of support staff, and an expensive marketing effort — fixed costs were high. But revenues fell suddenly, and the
company was soon losing money. A lot of money. The vicious circle was
completed when the company was forced to borrow additional funds to
meet its obligations. At no point in the quarter did orders pick up enough
to offset losses. Sales were nowhere near what had been forecast, and the
new imaging products just weren't catching on in the marketplace.

At the March board meeting, the directors were told that orders were
lagging far behind projections. "I was shocked at how fast things turned,"
says board member Howard Swearer, the former president of Brown
University.

Louis Cabot found the situation extremely distressing. Cabot had long
been mistrustful of projections from the company's senior management
team — projections that had been consistently wrong. But "what was
really scary," recalls Cabot, was that in the first few months of 1989 the
estimates weren't just wrong, "they were being missed by miles. And cash
flow was suddenly wildly in the wrong direction."

While revenues remained low, the company's expenses — at nearly 40
percent of sales — were close to being the highest in the computer industry. To make matters worse, the salespeople, under intense pressure to
push products out the door, were offering customers steep discounts that
drove down profit margins. The combination of high overhead, slow
sales, and thin margins was a prescription for disaster.

And still, remarkably, there was a sense that something would somehow pull the company through. Nobody in the penthouse was quite prepared to believe that Wang Laboratories could post truly bad numbers.
Although every indicator pointed to a tremendous loss, management
refused to believe it. Hadn't the company always gotten by? Hadn't Doctor Wang, in times of trouble, always been able to think of something?
Surely they'd get a break. A sudden order for imaging, a huge contract
worth tens of millions of dollars, would come in. *Something* would happen. Some miracle. They waited, these otherwise rational men, half
expecting a miracle they knew — or should have known — would not
materialize.

Analysts weren't expecting a huge profit for the third quarter, but they
were expecting a profit. Instead, Wang Labs announced a stunning
decline of $63.7 million.

Analysts were thunderstruck.

"It was a disaster," says Louis Cabot. "We found things were much worse than we realized."

The *Wall Street Journal* quoted Marc Schulman on the company's woes: "Wang is a company that needs major surgery," said Schulman, an analyst at UBS Securities, a unit of Union Bank of Switzerland. "Instead, what they do periodically is go to the outpatient clinic."

Incredibly, Fred remained steadfastly positive, saying at the time that the loss would have "no effect on the company's long-term viability." He said the company was doing what it needed to do to be profitable. "We have all the programs we need in place, but we're not moving as quickly as we need to," he told the *Journal*.

But his sentiment did not square with reality. For the effects of the March results were swift, far-reaching, and severe. In the wake of the announcement, Wang lost its ability to borrow on the domestic commercial paper market, was forced immediately to draw on its bank credit line, stepped up efforts to sell assets, began searching for a strategic partner, and lost any possibility of floating an issue of preferred stock.

In the middle of April, Fred began to reduce the work force by at least 2,200 people. He hoped to do it through attrition, but layoffs weren't ruled out. He took a 20 percent cut in his $433,000 salary and the Doctor, who received $511,000 a year, did the same. This was no hardship, of course, since both received substantial amounts of money in dividends — in Fred's case hundreds of thousands of dollars annually, and in his father's case millions of dollars a year.

Fred was also forced to retract his assertion of three months earlier that Wang Labs would finish the fiscal year with a strong rally and do better than it had the previous year. That was obviously unrealistic now. Though the company still looked for a strong fourth quarter, the truth was that costs remained high even as sales fell and profit margins continued to shrink.

Boston Globe columnist Alex Beam had followed the company for a number of years, first as a *Business Week* reporter and then at the *Globe*. Not long after the results were announced, Beam wrote that "the five-year-long meltdown at Wang Laboratories has not been a pretty sight. In 1984, the Lowell-based minicomputer vendor dominated the fast-growing word processing business, pumping out new sales at an annual rate of 40 percent. Now the $3 billion company is teetering on the brink of extinction, pumping out red ink like a frightened squid scuttling across the ocean floor."

Late in the winter of 1988, the company owed about $140 million on the European commercial paper market and about $190 million on the U.S. commercial paper market. The European paper was not at immediate risk. Europeans weren't as ratings conscious as American money managers were. And, besides, in Europe, Wang was a blue chip name, which was largely what European commercial paper sellers based their decisions on. European paper also had longer maturities and wasn't coming due as quickly as the domestic paper.

Though Wang was all right for the moment in Europe, it was in trouble domestically. Because of the March results, the company's bond rating dropped, effectively lowering Wang to junk bond grade, forcing the company to pay off the domestic debt within a matter of days. On the day after the March results were announced — April 19, 1989 — Wang Labs borrowed $190 million from its credit line to pay off its U.S. commercial paper obligation.

Before CFO Gene Bullis exercised the company's right to borrow against the credit line, he checked with two company officials: Doctor Wang and Harry Chou. Both agreed it was the right course of action. He did not check with the president of the company, Fred Wang. The reason was that Fred was not very much involved in the financial side of the company. This was strange. For the truth is that the financial structure of a company — *any* company — is one of the primary responsibilities of its leader. And to have an important, even crucial source of borrowing dry up because of something the company did — that was indeed a major event. Fred, however, didn't realize that.

A week after the results of the March quarter were announced, representatives of all eight banks in the consortium, more than twenty bankers in all, traveled to Lowell to listen to the company's explanation of its problems. Officials from Bank of Boston were among those least concerned about the company's health. They believed the company knew what it needed to do to correct its course. But other banks worried that the company was in deep trouble.

The financial pressure was growing more acute every day. The proposed sale of $200 million in preferred stock was now, in light of the March results, out of the question. The two most promising ways to raise cash and relieve some of the pressure were selling company assets and attracting a strategic partner — an investor who would pay cash for a portion of the company but who would not control Wang's operations.

Fred had long wanted to unload company assets that he didn't believe fit in with Wang Labs' objectives. Asset sales for strategic reasons could proceed at a leisurely pace, but sales for financial reasons took on a new urgency. The need to raise cash through asset sales became so pressing by May that Fred held daily meetings with Gene Bullis and Harry Chou to discuss the sales. Wang put many of its holdings on the block. Leading the list of assets the company was most eager to sell was InteCom, a Texas company that made telephone switches. On the block as well were both of Wang Labs' large leasing companies (one domestic, the other international), the company's modern European headquarters building in Brussels, and a small Wall Street company called Shark, which sold specialized computer services to stockbrokers.

By early spring it was clear that the company's debt was crushing. The company moved to cut costs and pushed harder on the sale of assets, but with news of its woes seeping into the press, potential buyers of Wang assets felt their positions were strengthened. Possible buyers, knowing of the company's troubles, were driving hard bargains. The company needed fast cash, and it was soon obvious that it wasn't going to come from asset sales.

Even in the face of bad times — with the company on the verge of a crisis — Doctor Wang clung desperately to control. He was willing to part with a minority piece of the company in return for cash, but he would not even entertain the suggestions of some board members that the possibility of selling the company at least be considered.

"We were looking around for minority partners," says board member Louis Cabot, but Cabot didn't believe that selling the company should be ruled out. He raised it with Doctor Wang, who replied sharply: "I'll never do it."

The downward spiral fed on itself. The company was subject to a rash of negative stories in the press that hurt the ability of the sales force to close deals. Who wanted to buy a computer from a sick company when there were plenty of healthy competitors out there?

Analyst John Adams issued a report in May headlined "Trouble":

Just three months ago, Wang was forecasting that it would earn $80–85 million in the back half of FY89. Now, it is hoping to lose only $75 million for this period, having already lost $63 million in the quarter ended March.

Wang's management is given to optimism, a trait that we have always admired, but excess optimism does not account for the sea change that has occurred. There has been a fundamental deterioration in the business that, in our opinion, goes beyond weakening domestic demand, start up costs, and other villains that one might appoint.

Memorial Day passed without any sign that the company was coming around. The situation was so serious that during the third week in June the president of the Bank of Boston, Chad Gifford, traveled to Lowell for a private session with the Doctor. Gifford's mission was to convey how serious the bank considered the company's financial problems, and to find out whether the company was taking appropriate steps to remedy them. After meeting privately with the Doctor, Gifford and Mark MacLennan, another bank official, had lunch with the Doctor, Fred, Bullis, and Harry Chou.

"We were trying to make sure everyone understood each other," Fred says of the meeting. "Chad wanted us to understand where the bank's thoughts were. He felt we needed to understand that the rest of the banks were getting reluctant on the terms and the fees."

Bullis says that Gifford also made it clear that the banks wanted security for a line of credit that had always been offered without the company's having to put up any collateral. This was the surest sign of all of the banks' deteriorating confidence in the company.

If Fred didn't get the message, perhaps it was understandable. He was, after all, preoccupied. His father was seriously ill; he had a new baby at home; and his wife, with whom he had once discussed so much about the company, had refocused her attention on their baby. All this while the company was experiencing its worst problems ever. If ever there was a time when Fred needed his father's guidance, this was it. But as tough as the old man was, he took a beating not only from the disease but also from its treatment — the chemotherapy sapped his strength. On top of it all, Fred had little help from senior management. None of them had ever experienced a business crisis anything like this. The company was flying blind.

In the spring of 1989, An Wang was a very sick man. He spent April and May undergoing chemotherapy treatments. Each of the two sets of chemo took four weeks to run through his system. He would begin the chemo by going into the hospital for three to five nights. The chemicals would be introduced into his system but would not begin their cell-killing mission for a few days.

During these two hospital stays, it was difficult to tell he was sick. At one point, Fred, Laurie, and Harry Chou went into the hospital to play bridge with him, and Laurie recalls his being "very upbeat, positive, feeling well."

"We wanted to keep him company," says Fred. "He was not a great conversationalist, and you could only talk about business so much." So they played cards, and the Doctor used his usual rat-a-tat machine-gun style of bidding and playing faster than anyone.

"He liked it when people would say, 'You're a gambler,'" says Fred. "He would always say, 'I take the calculated risk.'"

Though the chemicals made him tire easily, the therapy clearly worked. Only a couple of weeks after the beginning of the first application, the Doctor could swallow more easily. The disease and the treatment did not get him down mentally, either. When he lost his hair as a result of the treatments, he joked to Fred that he really didn't mind because he hadn't had much to begin with.

Though his spirits remained almost unnaturally high even after he emerged from the hospital, the chemo was punishing when it finally kicked in. He would go to work, but the chemicals wore him out so that he would have to leave for home by 3:30 or 4:00 o'clock each afternoon. His loss of weight and hair and early departures caused people at work to speculate that he was ill. And that worried Fred. He was concerned about how people within the company and how analysts outside the company would react to the news. But there was enough speculation so that by late June they had to get the news out. The company announced on June 28 that An Wang was suffering from cancer and was scheduled for surgery in July. This announcement came only days before another announcement predicting "substantial" losses for the fourth quarter and for the fiscal year.

Peter Brooke believed that it was only a matter of time before Fred would be gone and a new leader brought in from the outside.

One evening in May, as he sat contemplating the company from within his elegant Georgian-style home in the historic town of Concord, Massachusetts, Brooke picked up the phone and dialed John Cunningham. At that moment, Cunningham was enjoying the fruits of his CCI labors. He was seated on the terrace of his spectacular Weston estate with a glass of expensive Chardonnay, chatting with friends. Cunningham and his guests enjoyed the balmy spring evening on a meticulously landscaped terrace overlooking the exclusive Weston Country Club golf course. Cunningham loved this location, for his home not only sat on a hill above the course where he played his beloved game of golf, but it had a view of what was easily the loveliest hole on the course. Number seven at Weston is a short par four, a slight dogleg left with a narrow fairway that rises slightly from the tee and descends gradually to a tiny green well guarded by trees, with a bunker on one side and a tranquil little pond on the other. It had once been selected by a golf magazine as one of the most beautiful holes of golf in the United States.

When the call came, Cunningham was more than a little surprised. He had not heard from Brooke since he left Wang four years earlier. Brooke said he wanted to drop by for a confidential conversation, and Cunningham said fine.

Brooke's visit came the following Saturday morning. The two men sat in a large, oak-paneled library at one end of Cunningham's home. The room was in a corner of the house facing dense woodland hard by the golf course. Just outside the room's many windows, trees swayed in a gentle breeze and a brook flowed below. The room was one of the most comfortable in the sprawling home. It contained a desk and sofa; two big easy chairs flanked a fireplace. Along one wall, above a wet bar, bookcases and shelves housed an elaborate sound system. Over coffee, Brooke told Cunningham that the company was in a precarious position, that the bank debt was a massive weight around the company's neck, that the effort to sell assets was going poorly. Brooke made it plain that he was very worried, that the balance sheet was so far out of whack it was scaring him. There was barely enough cash to pay interest on the company's debt, Brooke said.

"He thought the company was in real trouble," Cunningham recalls. "He was worried it would unwind, and fairly quickly."

Then Brooke really stunned Cunningham. He asked whether Cunningham would have any interest in coming back to the company either as a consultant or as CEO.

Cunningham said he would be interested in doing some consulting, but he would definitely not want to come back in a full-time operational role.

"I just didn't want to do it," says Cunningham. "Those jobs are *very* time demanding." Besides, to a certain extent, Cunningham felt as though he had already run the company. And he was having fun, relaxing with friends, playing golf nearly every day. The stress of the CCI near-debacle hadn't entirely worn off yet, either.

No, he told Brooke, he wasn't interested in going back to run the place, but he would be willing to talk about coming in as a consultant to help out. He didn't want to see the company sink. The truth was, he cared a great deal for Wang Laboratories, and the idea of riding back into the towers to save the place appealed to him.

For the first two years of Fred and Laurie's marriage, the company had been, in Laurie's words, "our baby." When she married Fred, Laurie became part owner of a substantial stake in the company, and since both she and Fred worked there, the great bulk of their lives was centered around the company.

That changed with Andrea's birth. Laurie showered her attention on her daughter and spent little time thinking about Wang Laboratories. She knew there were problems, of course, but she was not aware how serious they were. When Fred talked about difficulties at work, she always asked, "Well, what's the worst that can happen?" Usually, his reply was that one glitch or another might hurt but that the company was basically very healthy. In the first five months of 1989 that, too, changed. One evening in June Fred was talking about difficulties with the banks. As usual, Laurie asked, "What's the worst that can happen?" She was thunderstruck by his response.

"The worst that could happen," Fred replied, "is that we could go into bankruptcy."

She wasn't sure she had heard him correctly and asked him what he meant. He said he meant precisely what he had said. The worst thing that could happen was that the company could go under.

Laurie felt as if she might pass out.

For one of the most successful computer companies in the world even to be discussing the possibility seemed almost too much to believe. But Fred was not speaking lightly. In the summer of 1989, Wang Laboratories was teetering on the verge of bankruptcy.

Taking the company into Chapter Eleven "was certainly one of the things we discussed," says Louis Cabot.

It was so seriously considered that Bullis and Grayson worked with the outside counsel from Skadden, Arps to educate themselves and other senior managers about bankruptcy law. They wanted to understand how a Chapter Eleven filing might help and hurt.

"It was seriously discussed," says Howard Swearer, a member of the board of directors. The notion was that bankruptcy would buy the company time to reorganize, and it would protect the company from the carnivorous bankers. "There was a feeling," says Swearer, "that the banks were trying to extract a pound of flesh."

The company's loans with the bank group had always been unsecured — the banks had never required Wang Labs to put up collateral. This was standard practice for healthy companies in healthy times, but now that things had gone sour at Wang, the banks wanted to make sure they would be repaid. Negotiations between the company and the bank group grew particularly intense over the issue of how much collateral the company was willing to put up. The way senior management at the company saw it, the bankers wanted, in effect, to place a lien on the entire operations of the company. Wang was willing to put up collateral — in fact, a great deal of collateral, including the company's inventories, real estate buildings, accounts receivable, and more. But company officials didn't want to give up *everything*.

The banks' position was either give us the collateral we want, or we're going to demand payment for all $575 million you owe us. A demand to pay would have bankrupted the company. Nonetheless, the bankers kept pushing, and the company's senior managers advised Doctor Wang that he essentially had no choice but to accede to whatever demands the bankers made. But Ken Miller, the head of Lodestar, a small New York investment bank, who had worked with the company in earlier years as head of the Merrill Lynch mergers and acquisitions division, offered the Doctor different advice. He said the company's position should be that it had put up all the collateral it could. If the banks didn't like it, too bad. Sit down with them, Miller advised Wang, and tell them, in effect, to take it or leave it.

It was clear to Ken Miller that if the banks got a lien on everything, the company would be unable to borrow any cash to fund operations. When that happened, Wang would go belly up. Ironically, the prospect of bankruptcy was the one card the company still held in these increasingly nasty negotiations. For if Wang Laboratories were to seek the protection of Chapter Eleven, it would put the banks in line with all of the company's other creditors. Bullis likened it to a nuclear deterrent.

The Doctor was angry in the extreme about the pressure the banks were putting on the company. He was furious with the Bank of Boston, in particular. "He was bitter about the bank," says Peter Brooke. "He felt that they had shared only the good times with him and not the bad."

Doctor Wang was so angry with the bankers that he told close associates within the company that if bankruptcy would save his company from destruction at the hands of the bankers then he would declare bankruptcy. And he was very close to doing so. In July, the company began to use the prospect of bankruptcy against the banks.

Most Wang employees were stunned by the news of the Doctor's illness. And many were frightened by it. Frightened for him, of course, because they cared about him, but they were frightened for themselves as well, and for their company. Wang was their livelihood, their identity, the source of their family's security and prosperity. Their company faced hard times, and their leader was sick — maybe even dying — just when they needed him the most.

And it was absurd for anyone to expect that Fred would somehow suddenly be able to fill his father's shoes. Even some of Fred's allies within the company worried that he was simply in over his head, that the crisis was far too much for him to handle. Frank Kinsey, a consultant with whom Fred had worked closely, advised Fred to cut personnel across the board by 15 percent. In preparation, Fred asked those executives who worked directly for him for three lists: one of their best workers, a second of their weakest 15 percent, and a third of everybody else.

Kinsey was amazed when some of Fred's direct reports sent in lists of only a couple of names while others gave Fred no lists at all. So ineffectual was Fred that his subordinates felt they could ignore an order from him with impunity.

On May 25, Peter Brooke met with three other members of the board: Louis Cabot, Howard Swearer, and Paul Tsongas. Tsongas was a Lowell native who had enjoyed an enormously successful political career in Massachusetts from an early age. Not long after he was elected to the United States Senate came talk that perhaps he might one day try for the White House. But his career was cut short by the frightening news that he had cancer. Tsongas decided not to run for a second term, to return home to Massachusetts to battle his illness and spend time with his family. He had responded well to treatment and was practicing law in Boston. After he left the Senate, Doctor Wang invited him to serve on the company's board of directors. His appointment to the board came long before he ran for the Democratic nomination for president in 1991.

The topic of the meeting, in Tsongas's downtown Boston law office —

from which, ironically, the massive Bank of Boston building could be seen looming across the street — was the gravity of the situation the company faced. A few days later, the four men traveled to Lowell to meet with Fred. They discussed the drive to sell assets and the search for a strategic partner. But the directors also wanted to propose that Wang bring in some outside management help, and they wanted to determine whether Fred understood just how precarious the company's position was.

During the meeting, Brooke said he had a particular person in mind who he thought would be an ideal consultant to help the company through the crisis. The man knew the company and the industry well, and had experience in a crisis. His name was John Cunningham.

When Cunningham's name was mentioned, Fred appeared absolutely stunned, says Brooke, as though he had been shot. To Fred, the suggestion was preposterous, out of the question. It was bad enough that Fred opposed hiring someone with obvious ability to help the company, but what was even worse — what appalled the directors — was Fred's attitude.

"There was a crisis," says Brooke. "Was he aware there was a crisis? No. This escaped him completely. The guy was in never-never land."

FOURTEEN

Freefall

I N THE SUMMER of 1989, Fred believed the banks were panicking, that they were mortally afraid they might not get repaid. In their
negotiations over the new loan agreement, Wang Laboratories was
no longer dealing with the friendly relationship officers from the banks —
the affable people the company knew well and with whom company officials were comfortable. Instead, Wang officials now sat down across the
table from grim-faced and much-dreaded workout people. Workout
departments are the goon squads of commercial banking, comprised of
people who go to work on a loan only when it is already in trouble.
Workout people scare a lot of executives, and for good reason   they
have reputations, deserved in many cases, for being heartless money-
grubbers.

Rick Miller is not given to rhetorical excess, yet he describes the mentality of bank workout people this way: "If child abuse were legal, this is
what they would do. But it isn't, so they become workout people."

One workout person who was negotiating the Wang deal, when told
of a troubled company who owed the bank money, was said to have one
response and one response only: "Fuck 'em." The mission of the workout
people was to get the bank's money out of the company as expeditiously
as possible. Says Louis Cabot: "They didn't care about the company
anymore."

The negotiations were tense and difficult. The company and the banks
argued heatedly over issues of collateral, fees, and the cost of money.

The Doctor watched these negotiations with growing dismay. His long relationship with the Bank of Boston now seemed to count for nothing. "He believed the relationship he established with the lead bank wasn't reciprocated," says Fred. "He felt part of Bank of Boston growth in the '70s was due to us. He felt that when we had difficult times, it wouldn't hurt them to go out of their way to be supportive. He didn't feel the support was there."

Fred also says the Bank of Boston told company officials they would work to get more favorable terms for the company from the other banks, but failed to do so.

By July, the workout people were in control of the relationship, and they arrived at meetings with little if any thought to Wang Labs' long-term health. Their "sole goal," says Fred, was "to get their money out as soon as possible. And if they have to break things to do it, they're more than happy to do it."

Board member Howard Swearer says that by July "the outside directors were quite alarmed. Sales projections were far too optimistic, and there was a reluctance to cut back. And the banks were being very difficult. They were asking for the moon in the way of guarantees."

In July, Wang Laboratories defaulted on a $12 million loan. Under the law, such defaults by publicly traded companies must be announced to the public. Some in both the company and the bank group panicked. Customers froze purchases. The competition could now legitimately raise the question of whether Wang was viable.

"The banks were being very unprofessional," says Fred. "They were playing a negotiating strategy and we were not sophisticated at negotiating. Any time we reached agreement, the banks would say, 'We want a little more.' In July we said, 'That's it. Take it or leave it.' They were playing hardball. They were clearly playing hardball and they enjoyed it."

Negotiations grew ominously quiet during the month of July. Recalls Gene Bullis: "Everyone was waiting for the bomb to drop to see what would be left after the detonation."

July 13, 1989, dawned gray and chillier than most summer mornings. There was a sullen feel to the day — the sun could not fight its way through the haze. On this morning An Wang was wheeled from his room in Phillips House, an exclusive wing of Massachusetts General Hospital reserved for the wealthy, to an operating room where Dr. Hermes C. Grillo performed surgery to remove the malignant tumor from Wang's esophagus.

In what the family considered a cruel bit of timing, that very morning the *Wall Street Journal* published a lengthy article about the company. One of the more insightful articles ever published about Wang Laboratories, it was written by William M. Bulkeley, a man Fred Wang liked and respected. "I never felt he had a point of view on an article before he wrote it," Fred said of Bulkeley. "He had an open mind when he started an article."

Fred read the story that morning as he rode downtown to the hospital to await the results of his father's surgery. He and Laurie arrived at 9:00 to begin the long vigil. Paul Guzzi, who was in Doctor Wang's room by the time Fred and Laurie arrived, had already finished the *Journal* piece. Laurie read it while she was sitting in the Doctor's hospital room.

The headline read, "System Errors: Wang, Bogged Down By Debt, Could Face Loss of Independence." One subhead read: "Once a Leader in Computers, It Didn't Match Standards Or Cut Overhead Enough." The second subhead read: "A Father's Rating of Son: 75%."

LOWELL, Mass. — The decline of Wang Laboratories Inc. illustrates what happens to a company that moves too slowly in a fast moving industry.

The now-enfeebled computer giant, bogged down in short-term debt, is a far cry from the company that through the 1970s and much of the 1980s moved adroitly from one successful product to another. In the decade ending in 1983, Wang's growth averaged 40% a year. When the personal-computer revolution hit, Wang, with its huge base in office desktops, "was in a position to own the industry," recalls one Wang veteran who left the company.

But instead of meeting the competition head-on with aggressively priced computers compatible with International Business Machine Corp. equipment, Wang sold high priced, incompatible PCs that appealed only to its existing customers. Meanwhile, its lucrative word-processor business slumped, and its minicomputer business slowed sharply.

Wang isn't the only midrange computer maker in trouble because of the PC onslaught. But it moved even more slowly than its Massachusetts neighbors, Digital Equipment Corp. and Data General Corp., to adjust to the new competition. Wang worsened its problems by keeping employment high and by being slow to follow the industry trend to standardize computer systems and software. It also developed a risky addiction to debt.

And it has paid a heavy price.

Today, the once-stellar company faces a short-term financial crisis and a longer-term decline that, at the least, threaten its independence. For the fiscal third quarter, ended March 31, it reported a $63.7 million loss, and it expects to post further losses in the fourth period and current quarter. Its sales are declining and its customers restive. Its lenders have forced renegotiation of its debts.

"I don't hold out much hope for the company to survive as an independent entity," says Steven Wendler of Gartner Group, a Stamford, Conn., market-research firm.

So a remarkable saga may be unwinding. It's the story of An Wang, a Chinese immigrant who started out in a Boston storefront in 1951 and, with bright ideas and hard work, created an industry and a family fortune. Now the value of the family holdings of Wang stock . . . has dwindled to about $250 million. . . . And today, the 69-year-old Mr. Wang is scheduled to undergo surgery for cancer of the esophagus.

While undergoing chemotherapy, Mr. Wang remained — and still is — the chairman and chief executive. He said in a telephone interview Wednesday that the company has "showed that we are very resilient." He predicts that new products and tighter cost controls will turn it around in the fiscal year just begun.

He also offers a frank appraisal of his eldest son, Frederick A. Wang, who became the president and chief operating officer two and a half years ago. Though acknowledging that the 38-year-old Fred Wang "took the job at a tough time," his father adds: "I would rate him at 75%. I can't rate him super." Nonetheless, the Wang family, which elects up to 75% of the board through its holdings of super-voting Class C stock, is determined to retain control.

The article went on, but it didn't get much more hopeful from the company's perspective.

When the story appeared, there was a collective wince by those close to the family who read the Doctor's quotation about Fred. It seemed incredible — and more than a little cruel — that a father would make such a statement about his son to the *Wall Street Journal*. To believe it, to confess it to close confidants, that was one thing. But to tell the world that he thought Fred's performance had been 75 percent seemed extraordinary.

The timing of the article could not have been worse. The company was in crisis, Doctor Wang was literally fighting for his life, and Fred, who was sitting in his father's hushed hospital room, was faced not only with worrying about the very survival of both his father and his company, but the public humiliation of having been described by his father in less than complimentary terms.

Fred Wang, like his father, is a stoic man, yet he was hurt by the comment. But neither Fred nor his wife say they were surprised by it. "He was a hard grader for Fred," says Laurie. "He was very honest. It's really the way he felt."

When he is asked about it, Fred Wang smiles, shrugs, and says: "That's Dad. His comment to me afterward was I think basically you're doing an okay job, not super." Doctor Wang's assessment only corroborated the convictions of those who believed Fred was in over his head.

An Wang's physicians had told the family that the surgery would take anywhere from three to six hours, unless they found the cancer to have spread too far. In that case, they would be done by about 10:00 A.M. But when that hour passed without word from the OR, there was great relief in the Doctor's room.

"The longer it went, the better we felt," says Fred.

In the middle of the afternoon, they received word that the surgeons were finding the procedure more complex than they had anticipated. But when they were through at about 6:30 that evening — after ten hours of surgery — they said they believed they had gotten all of the cancer cells.

At about 9:30 that night, Fred and Laurie went up to intensive care. An Wang was a shocking sight. He lay motionless, stuck with tubes and various wires connected to eerily lit monitors. A wide length of surgical tape covered his throat where the incision had been made. An oxygen mask was strapped to his badly swollen face.

"I didn't expect him to be sitting up in bed," says Fred, but he also didn't expect to see his father in such a helpless state. To see him in such a condition, says Fred, "was a real shock."

The board meeting on Wednesday, July 26, thirteen days after An Wang's surgery, was crucial for Fred. Though technically Harry Chou, as vice-chairman, would preside at the meeting, there was no question in anyone's mind that with the Doctor in the hospital this was Fred's show. Fred's staff worked hard in advance of the meeting putting together a formal presentation. When they gave Fred the draft, he worked it over extensively until he had rewritten a good deal of it. It was Fred's product.

It was time for Fred to exercise strong leadership, to enunciate clearly that he understood the full dimensions of the crisis, and to outline steps to save the company. The final draft of his presentation having been typed only moments earlier, Fred walked into the board room.

His performance was a disaster.

"He was trying to run the business as if he had time to get things turned around," recalls Louis Cabot. "He didn't have the sense of urgency the rest of us had."

"It was pretty obvious to all of us that Fred wasn't able to weather the storm," says board member Ernest Stockwell. "It was obvious that Fred was not the man to pull this through. Something had to be done or the thing was going down."

The directors were appalled. In the hallways after the meeting, alarmed board members talked quietly among themselves about how bad Fred had been.

"It was obvious he was not in touch," says Peter Brooke. "In my mind, the company was just a step away from bankruptcy, and Fred was business-as-usual. He talked about a management dysfunction. A management dysfunction! The company is falling apart around us and he's talking about a fucking management dysfunction!"

There was absolutely no doubt about what needed to be done: Wang Laboratories needed a new leader.

And unknown to almost anyone at the company — certainly unknown to Fred and his top lieutenants — was the remarkable fact that a search, however preliminary and informal, was already under way to find a successor. On July 18, Edward Grayson, the company's chief legal counsel and a close and trusted adviser to Doctor Wang, had already interviewed a possible successor to Fred.

The meeting between Grayson and Rick Miller was set up by Ken Miller, the investment banker from the Lodestar Group who had been helping to guide Wang through its financial crisis. Since the spring, Ken Miller had been chatting with his friend Rick Miller (they are not related) about Wang and its problems. With the permission of Wang Labs officials, Ken Miller had given Rick some information about the company to look over.

"Ken had mentioned to me in the late spring or early summer that Wang was one of the companies he was working on," recalls Rick Miller. Ken Miller called Rick and said that Ed Grayson was going to be in New York, and Ken wondered whether Rick would be willing to meet with

Grayson. Rick agreed and he and Grayson met at Ken Miller's 59th Street office.

Grayson told Miller that the Doctor's health was a serious issue, that nobody could be sure he would make it, or how long he would live. Grayson said that all confidence in Fred had been lost, that the company desperately needed leadership. Grayson questioned Rick Miller about his background and experience. He asked for Rick's thoughts on Wang Labs.

"It was clear," says Rick Miller, "that we were talking about running the place."

His doctors had said An Wang would be in the hospital for at least two weeks following surgery, but, naturally, he recovered sooner than that. On July 26, after thirteen days, he was up and ready to break out of Mass General.

With Fred and Mrs. Wang in Lowell at a board meeting that day, the plan was for Doctor Wang's driver to pick him up at the hospital. But Laurie thought a member of the family should be there to accompany him home. She arrived at the hospital by about 9 o'clock and found her father-in-law sitting up, dressed in his suit pants and a gray wool sweater-shirt. "He was excited, so happy," but frustrated by the hospital bureaucracy slowing his release. Laurie scurried around getting medicines for him. An hour and a half later, when they finally hit the road, Wang was as close to giddy with excitement as he ever got. Riding along Storrow Drive, following the course of the Charles River westward, he gazed out the tinted windows of his massive black Mercedes, taking in the gorgeous summer morning as the sun showered the river basin, where sailboats slid across the water on a mild breeze. As they rode along, they could see the familiar, and surely, to Wang, comforting, sights of MIT and Harvard across the sparkling water. He asked about his granddaughter. But something stuck in Laurie's mind on the way to Lincoln. Back in the hospital, Laurie had spoken with a social service worker who counseled cancer patients. Dealing with cancer was particularly difficult for people whose diseases were as virulent as Wang's. But the woman told Laurie that her father-in-law was very different indeed from most patients.

"He not only doesn't want support," the woman had said. "He doesn't need it."

Two days after An Wang was released from the hospital, the company announced that it was delaying for a few days the scheduled release of its fourth-quarter earnings. This could not mean good news, and analysts and the investment community girded themselves for bad numbers. A *Computerworld* story that week said analysts worried that Wang's losses could run as high as $200 million for the quarter.

But on July 31, Wang Laboratories announced a truly staggering quarterly decline of $375 million. The *Boston Globe* described it as "an unprecedented loss that raises concern about Wang Labs' viability and could force the family-controlled company to find an outside investor."

The company said in the wake of the announcement that it would suspend quarterly dividends, proceed with another round of layoffs, and shut down a manufacturing facility in Scotland.

On August 1, a *Wall Street Journal* report stated that "one source close to the company's credit problems likened Wang to a Latin American debtor nation. 'The banks are so far into this right now that they couldn't walk away if they wanted to,' he said. He added, 'It's a little late in the game to be renegotiating revolving debt. [Wang] didn't expect things to slow down this quickly, and they clearly won't be negotiating from a position of strength.'"

The quarterly loss bordered on the catastrophic. It was even more ominous taken together with the trend at Wang Labs. During Fred's time at the helm, there had been two years during which the company lost money and two years during which the company made money. But overall during those four years, Wang Labs had suffered a whopping net loss of $351 million.

And, in fact, since the end of the company's heyday, from 1985 through 1989, the company had lost $336 million. Those who took the trouble to check the figures from the late 1970s and early 1980s found an astonishing fact: The losses in 1987 and 1989 were so large they nearly wiped out the massive gains made during *all* of the glory years.

For a seven-year period from 1983 through 1989, Wang Labs did little better than break even. Since 1983, Wang stock, once the hottest on Wall Street, had plummeted from $43 a share to an almost incredible $5.75 a share.

Only a few days after Doctor Wang was discharged from the hospital, Peter Brooke left his downtown office late in the afternoon and drove to Lincoln. An Wang would learn from Peter Brooke what he perhaps already knew: That his dream of a family dynasty at Wang Laboratories would not be realized; that it would, in fact, surely be shattered.

In the weeks leading up to his visit, Brooke had had a number of meetings with other directors, including Louis Cabot, Howard Swearer, and Paul Tsongas. It was clear that the company was in an acute crisis that threatened the very existence of Wang Laboratories. Simultaneously, the company was experiencing a series of problems any one of which in a well-run company would have been judged serious. Wang Labs faced dire cash flow problems, crushing debt, management turmoil, terrible morale, declining product quality, and dwindling credibility in the marketplace.

This once-great corporation was perched on the edge of a precipice, and the slightest wrong move could plunge it into the abyss below.

There was a sense of "just plain fright" among directors, says Brooke. "We had a goddamn disaster on our hands. You knew the guy should never be there. You knew the guy had to go."

Brooke was the obvious choice as emissary. The other possibility was Cabot, but he had already used up some capital with the Doctor by being brutally frank in criticizing Fred. An earlier meeting of the outside directors in the Doctor's office had became unpleasant when Cabot was sharply critical of Fred to his father. And Cabot had dared to broach the subject of selling the company, a suggestion that was guaranteed to anger Doctor Wang.

When he arrived in Lincoln, Brooke found a frail old man in obvious pain who could barely speak. During the operation the surgeons had inadvertently injured the Doctor's vocal cords so that he had lost most of his voice. He was an old man who had presided over a once-glorious company that was now all but in ruins, an old man who may not have been sure whom to trust, whom to turn to in those terrible days. His optimism notwithstanding, he surely knew that he would not live a great deal longer.

Brooke told the Doctor that "the creditors had lost all confidence in Fred." He said that Fred had "lost all credibility, that the bank was supplying the capital for the business and that we had to make a change, that the banks controlled the assets of this business and that for that reason Fred can no longer stay. It was an easier way to put it than to say, 'The kid is incompetent.'"

Doctor Wang thanked Brooke for coming by, and Brooke left, having no inkling what the Doctor would do.

Within days of Brooke's visit, the Doctor also met with his personal family lawyer and trusted adviser, Bill Pechilis, and Pechilis's associate Pete Simons. Pechilis and Simons reminded Doctor Wang that, as CEO of the company, he had a duty under the law to care for the interests of all shareholders, not just the family. They told Doctor Wang that when the leader of a corporation creates a perception that the company is run for the family and not for the shareholders, the company could face substantial liability. Pechilis told Wang that he had to confirm to the investing public that the company was being run in the interest of all the shareholders.

Some of the outside directors were worried about their own liability in the case of a shareholders' suit. They wanted to save the company, and they believed they had done all that they could, short of grabbing the Doctor by the shoulders and shaking him, to convey to him their belief that the company was in grave trouble and needed change. However, they also wanted to protect themselves. To do that, they sought outside counsel. Rather than relying on the company's lawyers, the outside directors — Brooke, Cabot, Tsongas, and Swearer principally — were now represented by Ernest Sargent, a partner in the venerable Boston firm of Ropes & Gray.

Never before had Laurie heard anyone discuss the possibility of Fred leaving the company, but, on Friday, August 4, as Laurie lunched with Fred and Paul Guzzi at the Lanam Club, the subject arose.

No one present remembers who said it, but in the midst of a conversation about bank negotiations and the pressure board members were putting on Fred to do something about the crisis, something was said about Fred leaving. It took a moment for the suggestion to register, but, when it did, Laurie interrupted the conversation.

"Wait a minute, let's back up," she said. "Just so we all understand each other, if it comes to that, if this gets so bad that it means Fred leaving or the company goes down the tubes, then let's be real — the company is our future. Of course Fred will leave."

Fred nodded his agreement. "Yeah," he said perfunctorily.

After lunch, she returned to their North Shore summer estate, while Paul and Fred drove down to Lincoln to meet with the Doctor. Since Wang's release from the hospital, Guzzi, Fred, and Harry Chou had been meeting with him in Lincoln late each afternoon.

Struggling against a virulent cancer, unable to do more than croak words out of his throat, An Wang was forced to choose between his company and his son. It was like having to choose between two children. Fred himself had described the company as his father's "baby. Like Andrea is my baby. The company's his baby."

An Wang chose to fire his son.

He made his decision knowing that it would cause his son great pain and humiliation. "He was very pained by the negative impact that Fred would personally sustain," says a friend of the Doctor's. "He knew he was imposing a sentence on Fred." But he believed he had no choice.

For all the pathos, for all the tragedy of the scene, Fred says it was "very unemotional. There were no tears, no 'this is awful.' It was we have to do something and here are some of the options. It was pretty matter-of-fact."

Whether it was the dispassionate scene Fred and Guzzi describe, or the emotional, wrenching moment others say it was, Fred, in retrospect, says there is no question it was the correct move. "We needed to do something dramatic to buy the company time to regroup," he says. "The company was at a transition point." At the time he and his father met, "It was clear more professional management needed to be brought in. If I were to stay, it would put more pressure on my father. If I leave, it gives him an opportunity to show the outside world he was bringing in professional management.

"My hope was that it would be a dramatic enough event that it would buy time for the company" by lessening pressure from banks, the board, and the press.

"Something dramatic did not mean changing the CFO or the top sales guy," says Fred, "it meant changing the president or the CEO."

On Sunday afternoon, Fred again met with his father to work out the details of how the announcement would be made. They were joined by Laurie, Paul Guzzi, and Harry Chou. Guzzi, Chou, and the Doctor waited in the Doctor's study for Fred and Laurie, who arrived late.

Doctor Wang and Harry sat at the small card table, while the others took their places in black felt easy chairs with stainless-steel arms a few feet away. Everyone was dressed informally, including the Doctor, who was attired in his customary off-work uniform of suit pants and a gray wool sweater-shirt.

When Fred and Laurie arrived, there was a brief conversation about Andrea. It was an odd juxtaposition: A grandfather speaks tenderly about his granddaughter to his son, whom he has just fired.

"It was awful," says Laurie. "Everybody was so uncomfortable. And there was sadness, but a sense of 'Okay, let's do it.'"

Guzzi had drafted an announcement and he passed it around the room for review. Ordinarily, Laurie would be reluctant to speak up at such gatherings, but this was no routine session and when she read the draft press release, she was disturbed. "I read it as Fred's bailing out," she recalls, "as though he was abandoning ship. I said, 'This really makes Fred look like a bum.'"

They worked on the wording to try to give Fred some measure of dignity. When the meeting broke up and Fred and Laurie headed home, it was clear that Fred was resigning as president, but would stay on in the full-time position of vice-chairman. Everyone agreed they would work on the press release the following day.

"I told Fred he would be the brunt of a great deal of criticism," says Paul Guzzi.

On Monday around noon a messenger dropped another draft of the release off at Fred and Laurie's house. This was worse. In this version, Fred was not only resigning as president, he was leaving the company altogether. There was no mention of his being vice-chairman, only a vague reference to his working on special projects. It was "embarrassing, it was so belittling of Fred," says Laurie.

Fred says that he wanted a lesser role with the company. The thought of hanging around and possibly being a bother to his successor appealed to him not at all. He thought a clean break would be best.

Laurie was angry. She was told that a senior executive within the company was pushing hard to get Fred out entirely, arguing that financial analysts would not believe the company was serious about change unless Fred left.

Monday was the Doctor's first day back at work after his surgery. It was on this day that he formally dismissed Fred. The act was made official Monday night during an emergency board meeting in Lincoln. The board members, sitting on folding chairs in An Wang's library, had sandwiches and soda as they voted to accept what they termed Fred's "resignation." They also voted to appoint a search committee of Harry Chou, Peter Brooke, and Louis Cabot to find someone to run the company.

The Doctor issued this statement: "Fred Wang has served the company loyally and conscientiously since he became president nearly three years ago. His resignation is in keeping with his constant devotion to doing what he felt was in the best interest of the company."

Wang said that, at his request, his son would remain a director and carry out special projects for the company.

Fred also issued a statement: "I believe this action is in the best interest of Wang Laboratories at this time. It is a decision that I feel will allow the company to move forward with its restructuring. Employees and customers will be best served by a speedy resolution to the company's current situation."

Fred felt all right after it was over. "I thought I had done something that would buy time for the company and help Dad out."

Guzzi told the *Wall Street Journal* at the time: "The decision was a difficult one, but both Doctor Wang and Fred agreed it was in the best interest of Wang Labs. Ultimately, one person is accountable for the company's recent results, and Fred never shrank from that responsibility."

The market endorsed Fred's dismissal. The news sparked a sharp rise in the price of Wang shares, which climbed one and an eighth to six and seven-eighths.

The press coverage was, predictably, rough. *Boston Globe* columnist Alex Beam wrote:

> Fred Wang had the misfortune to inherit the one job he was not qualified to hold: He was asked to follow in his father's footsteps.
>
> Fred Wang's tortuous, 17-year-long forced march through the executive ranks of his father's firm is finally over. The eldest son of a tradition-conscious Chinese-American family . . . has officially, publicly, failed.

Fred says that even prior to the meeting with his father, he had thought about leaving. "In my mind I had already gone through the option so it wasn't as much of a shock to me as if I hadn't given it some thought already." He had never planned on spending his entire career at Wang Labs. "I had confidence that if I left the company it would not be the end of the world for me," he says. In time, he would describe his departure as having to "move up my schedule of doing something different."

Only a couple of days after his departure, Fred and Laurie drove into Cambridge to the John F. Kennedy School of Government at Harvard University, where they picked up some materials about the school. Fred had an interest in the public sector, and it made sense to at least look into the possibility of going to the Kennedy School if he was serious about public service.

Fred was in no rush to find something. He was certainly under no financial pressure. He had access to tens of millions of dollars in Wang and other stocks, and he would continue to receive his Wang Labs salary of $435,000 — he was paid twice a month in installments of $18,125 each — for four more years. That meant he would be paid about $1.7 million in salary *after* leaving the company.

The story was portrayed as a family tragedy — the *Boston Globe* story reported that "Wang Laboratories Inc. sacrificed a son." That, more than anything, rankled Laurie. "The father and son tragedy wasn't the truth," she says. "Fred had to be the fall guy. There were no other options. That's what's sad. It didn't have an impact on their relationship. It wasn't a family tragedy; it was a business tragedy. Fred and his father's relationship wasn't damaged or strained."

There was proof of that, she says, on the very day that the announcement of Fred's dismissal was published in the newspapers. On that day, An Wang had an appointment with a radiologist at Mass. General Hospital. In September, Wang would begin receiving daily radiation treatments, but prior to that he was being fitted for a mask that would prevent the radiation from penetrating his face and skull. As they had planned, Fred and Laurie accompanied the Doctor that morning. In the hospital lobby, Laurie saw that "people were sitting there reading the newspaper about Fred leaving, and they look up and there's Fred and his father."

Others couldn't believe that view of events. There was no question, they said, but that the relationship between father and son was forever altered.

Fred said he felt no bitterness toward anyone. His only real anger was aimed at the bankers, who he believes caused an escalation of the company's problems beyond all proportion.

"Fred felt he should do what his father wanted him to do and he did it," says Peter Brooke. "It's a great shame for Fred. Fred didn't have the gear and I don't think he had the desire to run a company like that. If you want to run a company like that, you're at work six in the morning and you leave at ten at night. He had a hell of a load put on him and it was unfair."

FIFTEEN

Richard W. Miller

T HE CHOICE of a successor came down to two men. One, John Cunningham, was well known to the Wang people. The other was a man almost entirely unknown to them, a man who had not only never worked at Wang Laboratories, but had never worked in the computer industry. His name was Richard Wesley Miller. Miller was forty-eight years old when he entered the competition for the Wang job. Tall, a couple of inches over six feet, and very thin, but wiry, he was classically handsome, with silver hair, high cheekbones, and a prominent nose. He was unusually articulate, and spoke with precision in a midwestern twang. By far his most arresting physical feature was his intense, steely blue eyes.

A product of Harvard Business School, Miller had excelled at a series of jobs and had proven himself a savvy financial expert. Perhaps most interesting from the perspective of Wang Laboratories, he had earned a reputation as a turnaround expert.

Miller was born in Buffalo, New York, on November 22, 1940. When he was three years old, the Miller family moved to the Buffalo suburb of East Aurora, a Norman Rockwellesque community of 5,500 people. His father, who had been born and raised in Toronto, worked at a variety of jobs, never very successfully. His inclination to drink was his undoing. Miller's mother, the product of an immigrant Italian father and immigrant Irish mother, was a prim, proper woman, active in her church.

Miller went to kindergarten through the twelfth grade in the same school building. Though East Aurora was by no means a wealthy town, most residents held jobs a notch above blue-collar work. Serene and secure, though perhaps too insulated, it was a pleasant place in which to grow up.

Although he was raised in small-town, 1950s America, Rick Miller's was not a Beaver Cleaver background. His was "not a particularly warm household. My mother and father did not get along." Miller saw no alternative but to get used to the problems between his parents and to erect barriers to protect himself. He worked to separate his home life, such as it was, from his friends. He was so successful that some of his closest friends didn't even know what his father did for a living. Even his steady girlfriend in high school found his family life a mystery. "We never went to Rick's house," says one friend, Jean Potter, who was very close to Miller while growing up. "Rick never had anybody come there."

Miller also avoided home life by working. From the time he was twelve years old, he was never without at least one job at any given time. He worked as a paperboy, a house painter, a store clerk, a landscaper. He worked so much and made such good money that in high school he became all but self-sufficient. By his senior year, he had saved enough to buy a car, a 1949 Oldsmobile that may have been eight years old but, to him, was beautiful nonetheless.

In high school, he dated the cute blonde on the cheerleading squad, was well liked, involved in a variety of activities and sports, and nowhere near the top of the list of those considered the most likely to succeed. Although he was not an outstanding student overall, he was solid enough, and he was particularly strong in science and math.

"He was outgoing, but also sarcastic and he had a temper," recalls Jean Potter. "And he was a little bit moody."

Miller liked high school and particularly enjoyed activities such as the school play and sports. He was an average athlete who ran cross-country, made the varsity tennis team, and warmed the bench in football. But he was a star on weekend nights. "He liked to party, and he still likes to party," says Potter.

Miller's friend Paul Weiss, with whom he went to high school and college and who was the best man at his wedding, says Miller was quiet in high school and difficult to get to know. But he liked to let it rip on weekends. "He loved to party," says Weiss. "This was a combination of *Happy Days* and *Animal House*."

With the Soviet launch of Sputnik in 1957, guidance counselors in high schools across America pushed students proficient in math and science toward engineering schools. Miller was steered toward the Case Institute of Technology (now called Case Western Reserve) in Cleveland. Miller's parents played no role in his selection of a college — did not counsel him or travel with him when he went to visit the Case campus. He drove by himself, a boy of seventeen, in the car for which he had paid, down to Cleveland.

During his first week at Case, in the fall of 1958, Miller enjoyed much of the indeed modest amount of success he would achieve during a brief and less than illustrious career there. And that success was not in the classroom. When he arrived on campus, Miller immediately began hosting a daily poker game in his dorm room. He was a skilled player. Miller had gotten bitten by the poker bug when he was only twelve years old. That year, he was one of the winners of a contest among paperboys in the Buffalo area. All of the winners won a trip to Cleveland to see an Indians-Yankees game. After the game, Miller bought a deck of cards and, during the train ride back to Buffalo, he and the other dozen paperboys played poker. Each of the kids had a fistful of money in his pocket for the trip, but by the time the train reached Buffalo, Miller had it all. He cleaned out every kid there, winning himself $100.

During his first week at Case, Miller hit an amazing winning streak and won $800, the equivalent in 1991 of about $4,000. But that first week was the apex of his Case career. After just one semester, he was on academic probation. He performed well enough in his second semester to work his way off probation, but he ended up with only a C average for his first year.

For the first half of his second year, he reverted to his old study habits. Making matters worse, Miller moved into a fraternity house and became social chairman. He was a masterful party organizer whose parties weren't just spontaneous blowouts, but carefully planned thematic adventures. While his reputation as a party organizer soared, Miller's academic standing plunged. He had little motivation and was nagged by doubts about what he wanted to get out of school and why he was at Case in the first place. It seemed pretty clear to him that he didn't want to be an engineer, had little facility for the work, and certainly didn't enjoy it.

He did enjoy the social life, however, at Phi Delta Theta, a jock fraternity. There were other frat houses at Case — populated by what Paul Weiss, Miller's sophomore year roommate, calls "smooth jocks — guys who were very smooth, charming, the type of individual who would never want to embarrass you. And then there were the Phi Delts. This was *the* outrageous fraternity. If the Betas, who were the smooth jocks, would seek to impress by being debonair and refined, the Phi Delts would seek to impress by being more crude."

The planned parties were held Saturday nights, but many other evenings Miller and his pals could be found down the street at the Brick Cottage, a pub where he would while away the hours drinking three-two beer and playing drinking games.

Frank Ilcin, a friend of Miller's from Case, puts it this way: "Rick is a hard driver, a serious person who, no matter what you do, work or play, does it to its fullest." When he competes, his focus on the task at hand is intense and complete. "That stare goes into his eyes and, man, all of a sudden he gets blinders on," says Ilcin. At Case he would compete in anything from poker to drinking games to pitching pennies. "He is one of the world's great competitors," says Case classmate Ron Kananen. "Rick could create a game out of anything."

Years later, after Miller had grown extremely successful in business, Kananen visited the Millers at their Greenwich, Connecticut, home. During the stay, Miller invented a game in which the contestants used broomsticks to bat a beachball around in an effort to knock down a beer bottle stationed under a four-legged chair. He called the game "Flurry," and his attitude, says Kananen, was, "Let's have at it."

But in the academic competition during his second year at Case, Miller did rather poorly. Spending his time on the fraternity's social affairs and at the Brick Cottage and everywhere but at his desk studying, Miller failed his classes and was, once again, placed on academic probation. During the spring semester, he did no better and was forced to leave school. He had flunked out of college. In the spring of 1960, the promising young college man who had gone out to take on the world headed back to East Aurora, humiliated.

But his academic failure at Case told little about Miller. Ilcin describes him as a man with "a brilliant mind" who was entirely out of place at Case. "He was a square peg in a round hole," he says. "He just didn't blend in. He didn't want to become an engineer." At Case, Miller was "pursuing the wrong academic interest," says Weiss. "Engineering was definitely not it for Rick."

After Case, Miller worked a variety of jobs, from laborer doing heavy construction to salesman for a food broker. It was not what Rick Miller wanted to do with his life. He liked East Aurora and had many friends there. In fact, he had returned there even though his parents had moved to Florida a year earlier. He stayed with the families of friends in the town while he worked, but he wanted very badly to go back to school, to go beyond East Aurora into the world.

He started over at the bottom. Finding a college that would admit a student in poor academic standing was next to impossible.

Finally, in the fall of 1961, he enrolled as a part-time student at Western Reserve University in Cleveland, which would soon merge with Case. He was able simply to sign up without meeting entrance requirements, but his courses would not be counted toward a degree. When he signed up, the application asked whether he had ever before been to college. If he answered truthfully, he would be queried about the circumstances and, in all probability, barred from classes. So he lied, rationalizing that the system was unfair and he deserved a second chance.

His intention was to take classes over a couple of years and then appeal to the university authorities to permit him to transfer to Case and get what would amount to retroactive credit for his part-time classes.

While going to school, Miller worked as a teller at the National City Bank of Cleveland, where he earned $75 per week. He found that he liked the work and that he was performing well enough to begin moving up the ladder. By 1963, after two years at the bank, Miller was made assistant branch manager. His responsibilities included supervising tellers, opening new accounts, and taking applications for car loans. He enjoyed the work so much that he took some business courses. He found that he liked them and discovered that, for him, the work was easy. So appealing did he find his new course of study that he took on a full-time load at school. It meant that every Monday through Thursday, after work at the bank, he would go to school from 6:30 until 10:30.

When it was clear that he was performing dean's list–level work, Miller decided it was time to apply for credit for the courses he had taken. He went to the dean and told him the whole story. He confessed to the lie about having never gone to college before, apologized for it, and explained why he had done it. He made the case that his record since returning to school was exemplary, and he asked the dean to give him a second chance and to admit him into a degree program.

The dean was unsympathetic and told Miller he would probably be expelled. "You lied on your application, and that is a character flaw," the dean said. "If it were up to me, I would throw you out."

Fortunately, it was not up to the dean, at least not entirely. His fate would be decided by an appeal panel consisting of three faculty members and two administrators.

Before the vote, Miller visited each of the five committee members and made his case. He told them that he knew he had made a mistake in lying, but he said the alternative had meant being barred from college. No one, he emphasized, had been hurt by his action.

He won the support of all three faculty members and was voted into the university by three to two. He continued his work, and in January 1967 — nine long years after he first entered college — he received his undergraduate degree from Case Western Reserve University. Though it was a long journey, it is something in which Miller takes pride. "I did it myself," he says.

In the meantime, he was doing well at the bank. He was promoted out of the branch to a management training program in the corporate credit department, where the bank's major lending work was done. His job was to conduct credit analyses for senior loan officers, the people who held the prestigious jobs in the bank, a position to which he aspired. During his six years at the bank, Miller had done everything asked of him and done it professionally. He was making a good salary — $8,400 a year — but the young MBAs whom Miller was, in effect, training were being paid twice that.

One day early in the winter of 1968, Miller was called in to the office of the chairman of the board. The chairman said he knew Miller wanted to be a loan officer, but the bank needed him in one of the branches. Miller said he was disappointed to hear that. He wanted to be a loan officer; he was teaching MBAs making much more money than he, and he didn't want to move back to a branch.

In a rather stern voice, the chairman said: "I guess National City Bank is going to have to take a long, hard look at Rick Miller."

Twenty-seven-year-old Rick Miller did not flinch. He said, "I guess I'm going to have to take a long hard look at National City Bank."

With little future at the bank, Miller rushed home and filled out an application to Harvard Business School. He had written away for the application before, and he had been seriously thinking about applying. His meeting with the chairman clinched it.

It is clear that something happened to Miller after he returned to school part-time and while he was working at the bank. Precisely what drove him, what spurred him to work so hard and efficiently, is not entirely clear to him even today. Certainly his parents never urged him on to great heights. He says that he has never had a particular ambition, never felt compelled to get a certain job, take over a particular company.

But he has always, he says, feared failure. And he has always been driven by that fear.

Perhaps more than anything else, he was motivated by his experience in East Aurora after he had been thrown out of Case. He was a young man without an education and with few prospects for a better life. Slogging around in odd jobs, never getting beyond the boundaries of East Aurora — that was failure. And he wanted no part of it.

"Maybe he woke up one day and said, 'I've got to prove to the world I can do something,'" speculates Frank Ilcin. "Something spurred him on to go to Harvard and to excel at Harvard."

If his drive existed earlier in life, it was certainly not visible, at least not to close friends such as Jean Potter and Paul Weiss. But Weiss says that once Miller found business — once he discovered an arena in which he excelled and in which he liked to compete — "it was all systems go."

Though his career at the bank had all but reached a dead end, the bank had given him the opportunity to meet the woman he would marry. While working at the downtown branch, he had met Sharon Betzler, who worked in the same office. She had joined the bank after graduating from Central Michigan University, where she had majored in business. They met in the spring of 1966 and were married the following January.

Miller was placed on the waiting list at Harvard Business School, but it turned out to be an ideal year for him to apply. Harvard was working hard that year to diversify its business school class, and the school made an effort to bring in more women and minorities and to avoid a predominance of students from the Ivy League.

In the spring of 1968, he was notified that he had been admitted. In August the Millers loaded their Volkswagen bug and drove from Cleveland to Cambridge, where they rented a ratty old apartment in a dingy Cambridge building for an amount that stunned them both. But life was grand. Sharon worked at New England Merchants Bank, and Rick had the luxury of going to school full-time. He worked hard and in a disciplined fashion, though he did not kill himself.

It was a time of extraordinary ferment around Harvard Square, which was engulfed in an atmosphere of ongoing crisis. There was anger and turmoil over the war in Vietnam, and over race relations. Students were striking. The midwestern values that were at Miller's core received a severe test.

"So much was going on around here then," he recalls. "Combat in the streets. Whose side are you on? Are the cops wrong? Have the blacks gone too far? It exploded your mind every day. My first reaction was 'This is all crazy.'

"It forced me to rethink everything," he says, growing excited at the recollection of those turbulent times. "It was very healthy for me. If anything, it made me more sensitive to people, gave me more understanding and respect. I came out of it feeling more confident in my own values."

It was during this period that he developed one of his stronger traits as a manager: his ability to listen, to understand precisely what another person is trying to communicate.

The similarities to John Cunningham were striking: Both men had worked from an early age, both liked a good time, both flowered during business school. He did some learning in the classroom, but, more important, he met high-powered people who would remain good friends — including John McArthur, who went on to become dean of Harvard Business School. Miller was also elected president of the school finance club, the largest and most prestigious student organization, which hosted speakers from the world of high finance.

More than anything else, business school gave Miller what it had given John Cunningham: the confidence he needed to climb up in the corporate world. Miller was a superb candidate for a prestigious job at some glamorous U.S. corporation, but of the 350 companies that visited the campus during Miller's last year there, he chose to interview with none. While his classmates flocked to investment banking and consulting, Miller barely considered either. Before taking a job, Miller talked only with companies in trouble. He interviewed with a troubled bank and an ailing insurance company. But the place that captured his attention was the Penn Central Company, the largest transportation company in the world, which was just then teetering on the brink of bankruptcy.

He followed his instinct and went against the grain. "If you see the crowd running one way," he says, "look real, real hard at what they're running away from."

Though he had offers of $35,000 from investment banks in the United States and Canada, Miller accepted the Penn Central job, which paid only $19,000. His classmates, who knew he could make more money on a faster track elsewhere, told him he had taken leave of his senses.

But the decision felt good in his gut. He felt a pull to the company, to railroads, to this dying industrial giant that had helped build America. And more than anything, Rick Miller believed in the great industrial past of the country. Perhaps it was the fact that his maternal grandfather had worked on a railroad all his life; perhaps it was in his blood. Perhaps it was that this company was hurting, an underdog. Miller was so enamored of the great American heartland that when he proposed to his wife he took her up a hill, past a Cleveland junkyard, to a cliff overlooking the Cuyahoga River, looking down on steel mills and their belching smokestacks, at the stamping plants — at *industrial America.*

And it was this same emotional tug that pulled him heart-first to Penn Central. In late May 1970, the Millers loaded their few belongings and their infant daughter Barbara into their Volkswagen bug and headed for Philadelphia. So eager was Miller to roll up his sleeves and get to work that he skipped the Harvard commencement.

On June 1, 1970, Rick Miller started at Penn Central. Twenty days later, Penn Central became the largest company ever to file for bankruptcy.

The Penn Central Railroad had been formed by a merger of the New York Central and the Pennsylvania railroads, two companies that had played key roles in building industrial America. From late in the nineteenth century until the middle of the twentieth, the nation's steel mills, coal mines, and automobile factories were nurtured by these two railroads.

But the growth of both the federal highway system and the U.S. trucking industry cut deeply into the railroads' business, leaving them, in a matter of only a few decades, shadows of their former selves. In the early 1960s, the New York Central and Pennsylvania railroads, which covered much the same territory and had long competed, agreed to merge. So massive was this merger that it wasn't until 1967 that all the approvals were given and the merger became official. Their joining together still created the largest transportation company on earth.

Miller performed an array of projects for a variety of Penn Central executives, including the president. But his most interesting opportunity arose when he was invited to join the management group given control of Penn Central's nonrailroad assets by the bankruptcy judge. Since it included some high-powered people whom he respected — including his friend and adviser from Harvard Business School, John McArthur, Miller eagerly accepted.

The newly formed group, which was given the name of the Pennsylvania Company, was moved to offices in New York, an ornate space formerly occupied by the New York Central Railroad. The Millers moved from Philadelphia to Greenwich, Connecticut. Miller was assigned to work on a Penn Central–owned company called Arvida, a real estate holding company owning one hundred thousand acres of very attractive property, most of it in south Florida. Fifty-eight percent of Arvida was held by Penn Central, while the rest of the shares were publicly traded. Miller began making frequent trips to Florida, and he soon became the Pennsylvania Company's in-house expert on Arvida.

So important did Miller's involvement with Arvida become that the new president of Arvida, Chuck Cobb, who would later be the U.S. ambassador to Iceland, asked Miller to sign on as Arvida's chief financial officer. This was Miller's breakthrough opportunity, and he accepted the offer at once. He was just thirty-one years old, and he was about to become a vice-president and CFO of a public company. He would have managerial responsibility and be number two in the company in compensation. It made having to move, yet again, painless. The Millers had gone from business school to an apartment in Ardmore, a Philadelphia suburb, to a small rented house in Greenwich, and now they headed for Miami.

In Florida, Miller set about the task of hiring new people and building an organization within Arvida. Bob Speicher, whom Miller hired at Arvida, was deeply impressed by Miller's ability. "He is a delightful mix of raw intellectual horsepower with good sense," says Speicher.

At Arvida, Miller honed his discipline. "He has a terrific power to concentrate on the matter at hand and not be distracted," recalls Joan Styers, Miller's administrative assistant at Arvida. "He would not be distracted."

This was part of the somewhat studied Miller persona. "He himself would talk about his steely blue eyes," says Styers. "He would have this effect on people. They would think he's not approachable," although Styers insists he was.

Bob Speicher says that Miller clearly had a sense of humor but seemed reluctant at Arvida to use it. "Sometimes you get the feeling Rick has an impression of what a business person should look like or act like," says Speicher. "He keeps good qualities hidden pursuant to presenting a more businesslike view to the world."

After a year in Miami, Miller moved to Boca Raton, Florida, to take over the Arvida operations there. It was in Boca Raton that Arvida had its choicest real estate and its most serious problems. Boca Raton had just passed an ordinance placing tight restrictions on real estate development — a law that was aimed in no small part at Arvida.

When Miller moved in, Arvida was a dirty word in Boca Raton. It represented the corporate bad guy, a greedy company with no interest other than making a buck out of the community, however much damage its developments might do to the local character.

"Rick's predecessor was in a fight with the city," says Joan Styers. "Rick came into a very troubled environment and set about, in a very orderly fashion, to mend fences."

Miller believed strongly that the best way for Arvida to make money in Boca Raton was by being a good neighbor. He plunged into local community affairs, becoming president of the economic council of Palm Beach County, a kind of chamber of commerce. He took on the task of chairman of the city housing agency. And he reserved much of his time for work on improving the quality of local schools. He played so active a role that the *Miami Herald,* in an editorial, mentioned him by name as a major player working to better local education.

Few in Boca Raton were more surprised by Miller's approach or more impressed with him than Tom Schumaker, the editor of the *Boca Raton News,* part of the respected Knight-Ridder chain of daily newspapers. "When Rick came in, it was refreshing," says Schumaker. "He was not like the typical south Florida developer. He impressed me and the people in our newsroom. He was bright as hell, but what we liked best about Rick Miller was that he was truly a very open individual who had great depth of integrity."

And it helped immensely, says Schumaker, that everything Arvida built — housing, a shopping center, office parks, industrial parks, a beachfront hotel — was high quality. It also helped Arvida's image that when it built housing, the company donated property to the community for schools.

When Miller joined Arvida in 1972, the company was doing less than $40 million in sales with a net income of under $2 million. By the time he left in 1979, sales had jumped to $149 million with net income at $28 million. When Miller started, Arvida was valued at about $70 million. By the time he left, it was worth between $300 and $350 million.

Miller's performance was well noted by senior Penn Central officials in New York, and in 1978 he was asked to become the company's chief financial officer. It was not an easy decision. The family enjoyed life in Florida, and Miller's career there was flourishing. He had even considered the possibility that one day he might get involved in Florida politics, perhaps run for office. But the position of CFO at Penn Central was a big job that paid a great deal of money and would offer Miller terrific opportunities. He took the job, and the family moved back to Greenwich.

Miller's arrival in New York came at a particularly propitious moment. Since Penn Central had previously lost such staggering amounts of money, it was in a position to take huge profits without paying federal income taxes. Using a tax loss carry-forward — tax credits on losses incurred in earlier years — Penn Central bought company after company, and Miller became the point man for Penn Central's aggressive acquisition strategy. The tax loss carry-forward allowed Penn Central to buy a profitable company but avoid paying taxes on that firm's profits. The company snapped up more than two dozen businesses in one year. He would much rather have run a manufacturing operation, but the experience of spending three years making major deals in the big leagues of Wall Street was exhilarating and educational.

Again, the numbers proved that Miller had participated in a significant turnaround. The year before he became the Penn Central CFO, the company did $667 million in sales with a net income of $53 million. Three years later, the company's sales were up to $3.3 billion and net income climbed to $169 million. During that same period, the company's total debt dropped from $2.6 billion to $1.7 billion as the book value of the company's shares nearly quadrupled.

When the Penn Central chairman retired, however, and a new man took over, Miller received a phone call out of the blue from Thornton Bradshaw, the distinguished former chairman of ARCO. Bradshaw, a venerable presence in American business, had just taken over RCA, and he had asked his friend John McArthur whom to get for his management team. Miller's was one of the first names McArthur recommended. Miller, in fact, was one of the first two new people Bradshaw hired. (The other was Grant Tinker at NBC, which RCA owned.)

The idea of working at this grand old American company greatly appealed to Miller. RCA was the inventor of both black-and-white and color television. It created the first television network and many major consumer electronics products. But the company was in some trouble and losing badly in ferocious competition with Japanese electronics firms.

In March 1982, Miller joined RCA as executive vice-president and chief financial officer. He worked hard at the job, leaving his Greenwich home in the pitch dark and arriving at his Manhattan office only minutes after 7:00 A.M. and rarely leaving before 6:30 or 7:00 P.M. It paid off.

"He did a brilliant job at RCA," says Ed Scanlon, formerly a senior vice-president at RCA and now executive vice-president at NBC. The numbers bear Scanlon out. During Miller's years at RCA, earnings climbed from $54 million to $369 million, and net income increased from $7.7 billion to $9.9 billion.

He played so key a role in RCA's turnaround that after three years at the company, Bradshaw asked Miller to take over what was perhaps RCA's toughest line job — chief of a division that included consumer electronics, RCA records, and a variety of other odds and ends, including a picture tube business. Miller would be running $4 billion of RCA's $9 billion business. But it was the piece of business most vulnerable to Japan's relentless attack on the U.S. consumer electronics industry. He took on the job with relish and within months had begun to turn it around.

There was no question in anyone's mind that he was on track to becoming president of RCA.

But Rick Miller would never get the chance to run RCA. In one of the cannier business moves of the age, Jack Welch, chairman of the General Electric Company, persuaded Bradshaw to sell RCA to GE.

When Miller learned of the deal, he was furious. When Bradshaw convened RCA's senior management team to explain the deal, he told them the purchase price, and Miller said disdainfully, "I can get more than that on the phone." He hoped to be able to block the sale, but it was too late. He wondered why, as the *New York Times* put it, "a viable, profitable institution in its own right" had to be sold.

Miller was angry on his own behalf. "I thought I had it all lined up," he says. "I saw it all go down the tubes. I was really disappointed." But he was angry for other managers as well, for the people who he believed had worked hard and played key roles in returning RCA to health. Like every other business executive in the United States, Miller knew of GE's reputation for management excellence, and he believed that very few RCA executives would survive the merger. His plan was to do his best to facilitate the merger of the two companies — he felt an obligation to do that — and then to go out and find another job.

But Miller had yet to be exposed to the considerable charms of Jack Welch. He soon discovered that Welch's reputation as one of the most brilliant and effective executives in the world was not unwarranted. Over a period of months in early 1986, Welch romanced Miller, who was naturally flattered by the attention of such a business giant.

Over dinner and during a series of lunches and telephone conversations, Miller and Welch talked about business in general, Miller's career to date, RCA, and GE. Welch was seeking to learn about RCA, a company Miller knew intimately. But Welch was also trying to learn about Miller and, in the process, trying to sell Miller on himself and GE. Welch, Miller found, had remarkable instincts. He understood how to manage, how to motivate people. He knew when to be tough and when to be laid back. Miller was extremely impressed.

Welch talked to Miller about the electronics business. Both RCA and GE were losing money in their electronics sectors, and Welch wondered whether an American company could make money against the Japanese in that area.

After the two companies merged, there was no job more difficult than managing the combined RCA-GE consumer electronics operations, and Welch paid Miller the ultimate compliment when he asked him to run that operation. Miller would be a senior vice-president of GE. He would have an office down the hall from Welch's, and report directly to Welch.

"I'll help you learn about this company," Welch told Miller. Miller knew that Welch could have chosen a GE manager to run the operation, but chose him instead. That sent a clear message to Miller that the great man had confidence in him. If for no other reason than for the opportunity to report directly to Jack Welch, Miller took the job.

From early 1986 until early 1988, Rick Miller gave everything he had to turning the new business around. In 1985, when Miller took over the combined consumer electronics divisions of RCA and GE, the operation lost $57 million on sales of $3.1 billion. Three years later, the division earned $40 million on sales of $3.3 billion. Even as he dramatically increased income, Miller reduced the work force by a quarter among hourly workers (from 30,000 to 22,200), and by nearly half among salaried employees (from 8,000 to 4,800).

But no sooner had he done so than, incredibly, his operation was again, as it had been at RCA, sold out from under him. Welch walked into Miller's office one day, closed the door, and told Miller he had sold the consumer electronics division to Thomson, the French conglomerate.

Once again, Rick Miller was bitterly disappointed. Any hope he had had of working his way to the top of the company was now shattered. The sale of consumer electronics to the French included the management team. Miller was part of the package. And though Miller hit it off well with Alain Gomez, the chief of Thomson, he turned down Gomez's offer of an attractive and extraordinarily lucrative job with the company. Miller helped smooth the way for Thomson to take over his operation, made sure his management team was taken care of, and then left.

"I felt events were controlling me," he says. "I could have done the Thomson job out of Greenwich, but I felt that to do it right I had to move to Paris. I wanted to step aside and pause and say, 'Wait a minute. What is it I want to do?'"

Miller wanted something over which he had a certain degree of control, something that would allow him to have a normal family life for a while. He joined with several other successful business executives and formed a company called American Industrial Partners.

It was a firm established to invest in and operate manufacturing companies. "The business was established because [the partners] felt that the LBO mania taking place had to come to an end," says Ted Rogers, one of the partners in the firm, "that the basic, fundamental value of creation in manufacturing was being overlooked. People had taken their eye off the basics.

"People who had never seen a manufacturing facility before were making decisions a thousand miles away about the lives and organizations our forefathers had taken generations to establish and nurture. It made Rick mad. It made us all mad."

Though Miller was with American Industrial Partners for only fifteen months, Rogers was impressed with him. "He's a very intelligent, single-minded, extremely energetic man," says Rogers. "Rick is a fellow I liked immediately."

"He is an extremely hard worker," says Rogers. "When we were forming the partnership, there would be long gaps of time. We would make a presentation and wait for a decision. Rick would just about go out of his mind. One day he went home and rearranged everything in the refrigerator."

In August, Miller was scheduled to have lunch with Jack Welch. But he got a phone call that required him to cancel. The call was an invitation to talk with An Wang.

SIXTEEN

"The People at Wang Are Very Lucky"

JACK CONNORS was at his summer home on Cape Cod in August 1989 when the call came. He thought it was some sort of prank when he heard the voice, someone — probably John Cunningham — doing an imitation of the Godfather and claiming to be Doctor Wang. Connors went along with the joke, laughed, and asked who it really was. Doctor Wang said it was he. Connors was taken aback by the croaking voice on the other end of the telephone.

What did Connors think? Wang asked.

About what?

About Cunningham.

What about Cunningham? Connors asked.

Did Connors think his pal would come back to the company?

Oh. Connors didn't know.

Would Connors be willing to speak with Cunningham? To urge him to return to the company?

Of course, said Connors.

Good, said Wang. Maybe that would help. He hoped Cunningham would come back. He really hoped so.

Sometimes it was hard for John Cunningham to believe it. For the truth was that if he chose, he need never work another day for the rest of his life. He had been working for so long — he'd held some kind of job ever since he was eleven years old — that it was strange not having work as an integral part of his life. But his success at CCI put him in a position of complete financial independence. He wanted nothing more than to relax, savor life, and enjoy himself, to spend time with his wife and daughters, to play golf, to travel. He was doing all of those things and loving every moment of it.

On the day Fred's departure from the company was announced, Cunningham was at the wheel of his Range Rover, meandering along the back roads of Maine to Bates College, where his daughter Erin was scheduled for an interview. During the interview, Cunningham relaxed with a book in the office waiting area. His reading was interrupted by a telephone call.

It was his secretary, Jane Wagner, calling to say that Fred was gone and that Ed Devin, head of personnel at Wang, needed to talk with him right away. The moment Jane said Devin had called, Cunningham knew that Doctor Wang wanted to talk with him. The Doctor, he knew, was about to ask him to come back and bail out the company. Cunningham called Devin, and Devin asked whether Cunningham could meet with the Doctor in Lincoln the next day. Cunningham said he'd be there.

Had he been driving his Mercedes, Cunningham could have made some phone calls during the long drive back to Boston that evening, but Erin had prohibited the use of the Mercedes for college visits ("She said they'd think she was a snotty little rich kid," says her father). So as he rode along in his Range Rover, Cunningham had a chance to think about the Doctor, the company, and, oddly enough, about Fred.

Cunningham found himself feeling sympathy for Fred. He couldn't help but shake his head in disbelief at the clumsiness with which the announcement of Fred's departure had been handled. "It was sad," he says. "I didn't understand why the Doctor did it that way. They could have found a smoother way to do it. Fred could have gotten up there at a press conference and said, 'My father and I agreed that we need to find a really strong operating executive.' If the two of them had done it, or Fred had done it, it wouldn't have this aspect of a family tragedy. It would have made the thing a business problem, not this family tragedy."

But Cunningham decided as he drove south on the Maine Turnpike that it was vintage Doctor Wang. "His approach would be to think Fred has to get out of the way," says Cunningham, "so he would say, 'Fred, get out of the way.'"

Cunningham chatted with Erin as they drove along, but he could not help but begin thinking ahead to the next day and his conversation with Doctor Wang. If he were to take the job, to go back and try to save Wang Labs, he would start with the huge advantage of knowing the company, the people, and the markets. He would have to spend no time learning the job. Cunningham also had just come off a turnaround, albeit of a much smaller company. In principle, however, CCI and Wang Labs were rather similar.

The question was not whether he had the ability to turn the company around, but whether it was possible, for *anyone,* to turn it around. Was the company beyond salvaging? Cunningham had kept in touch with many old friends at Wang, but he did not know the details of the company's finances. He didn't know its orders, its technology. He would first have to determine whether he believed the company could be saved, and, if the answer was affirmative, he would then have to face the more difficult question of whether he wanted to interrupt his life to go back and do it.

"Part of me certainly wanted to do it," he says. "Everybody likes to be a hero. But the day-to-day part of me didn't want to do it because I knew what had to be done. And I knew I couldn't do it under the same terms as before, when I was an employee under the thumb of the family. If I was going to do it, I had to do it so that I had independence."

If he was to do it, however, there was no question that it would cost Wang Laboratories a great deal of money. "John was just off the CCI deal, riding high," says his friend Jack Connors. "To John, each deal had to be bigger than the deal before."

When they settled into the Doctor's study on Wednesday, August 9, An Wang pulled out several sheets of paper on which he had made some notes. The notes, Cunningham was startled to see, listed the pros and cons of bankruptcy. As they talked, Cunningham was further surprised to see that Wang seemed all but sold on the idea. He saw bankruptcy as a way to save the business. The bank negotiations were going poorly, the Doctor said, and if he filed for Chapter Eleven, the company could keep and control its assets while he would have time to restructure before paying back creditors. He said he knew he would have trouble convincing the board to go along, but he believed that it was the best thing for the company.

They had been talking for no more than five minutes when Doctor Wang said that he wanted Cunningham to come back to the company as president and chief operating officer. He said he wanted an answer by Saturday.

"I said I was uncomfortable moving very quickly," says Cunningham. Cunningham was gun shy because at CCI he had moved too quickly and found himself in a situation far worse than he expected. Before he made any decisions, Cunningham said he wanted to review the business. The Doctor agreed to open the company's operations to Cunningham's inspection for what amounted to an exercise in due diligence.

Before he left, Cunningham couldn't help but ask what Fred thought about the idea of Cunningham's coming back to run the company.

"Fred thinks it's the stupidest thing I could do," the Doctor told Cunningham.

Harry Chou joined them for the final few minutes of the meeting. As Cunningham was leaving, Chou pulled him aside. "Your friend is in real trouble," Chou told Cunningham. "You have to help him."

"Harry, I know he's in trouble," Cunningham replied, "but this is a business deal. I'll help him if I can. I hope I can."

Cunningham immediately rounded up his CCI team of Harold Koplow, Dave Moros, and Dick Krieger, who had been the CCI chief financial officer. Koplow got on a plane in L.A. Wednesday, arrived in Boston Thursday, and went directly to Cunningham's house, where Moros and Krieger had already gathered.

By Saturday morning, they had met with the Wang management team and collected enough information to make an assessment. They huddled together in Cunningham's office on Route 128 in Waltham, and drafted a letter to Doctor Wang.

On Sunday, August 13, Cunningham drove to Lincoln to tell the Doctor what he and his team had found. He handed a four-page letter to Wang and gave a copy to Harry Chou, who was also present. Then Cunningham walked them through the contents of the letter.

The situation, Cunningham told the Doctor, was critical. The only encouraging news was that Koplow and Moros had been impressed with the products the R&D group had produced. Koplow, who was a difficult man to please, had pronounced them "as good or better than the rest of the industry."

But beyond that bit of encouragement, there was little to cheer about. Cunningham told the Doctor he was not at all sure that Wang Laboratories could survive. The company's finances, he said, were in much worse condition than he had anticipated. It was clear, Cunningham said, that the company would fall short of its sales forecasts for the first nine months of the calendar year, and it appeared quite probable the company would default on a bank loan.

Cunningham raised the issue of whether it was in his personal interest to take the job. He discussed his desire to spend time with his family, to avoid stressful business situations. He worried that his reputation would be damaged if the turnaround did not succeed. And he did not relish what he knew would be a very unpleasant task. At CCI, Cunningham had cut 30 percent of the employees, but they had been people he never knew. Wang was filled with old friends who would see his return as their salvation when, in truth, he knew he would have to lay off thousands of people.

Wang listened carefully to the presentation, but never more carefully than when Cunningham raised the issue of control. He stated candidly his fear that the Doctor would frustrate him by not yielding the level of control Cunningham would need. At CCI, he had run the show entirely, and he had grown comfortable with that method of operation.

Cunningham's letter was full of ambivalence. Though it was clear the prospect attracted him in some ways, it was also clear that he would go back to the company with reluctance. He also felt the chances of success were better with him than if the company hired anyone else.

Friends say the financial package Cunningham outlined made it clear that he didn't really want the job. The proposal called for Cunningham to be president and chief operating officer of the company with full power to hire, fire, and reassign employees. Under the initial terms proposed — which were a result of Cunningham's meetings with his lawyers at Hale & Dorr in Boston — Cunningham, Koplow, Krieger, and Moros would, as a group, receive a three-year contract to run Wang Labs. They would be paid an annual management fee of $5 million with two years' worth — $10 million cash — payable up front. The group would receive options for five million shares of stock, about 3 percent of the outstanding shares — then worth about $35 million — at a below-market price of about $25 million.

In all, their up-front package would be worth $20 million. The proposal required that, in the event the company was sold, Cunningham's group would receive a fee of $25 million.

The up-front part of the compensation was important to Cunningham. His outside attorneys and he worried that the company might slip into bankruptcy, and he knew that bankruptcy courts had nullified some executive compensation packages when companies went into Chapter Eleven. As insurance against that, he wanted a large chunk of money up front, money the courts, should the company go down, could never touch.

It was a staggering amount of money, but, in Cunningham's view, "it was not a big number given the scope of the problem."

But there was another, crucial reason that Cunningham put such a huge compensation package on the table: He believed it would effectively give him control of the company. Cunningham knew that the most difficult issue of all for Doctor Wang was control, but Cunningham was determined not to go back to the company with the same relationship he'd had before with the Doctor. Cunningham believed that given the compensation package he had outlined, the Wang board would have been forced to back Cunningham in any dispute with Doctor Wang since Cunningham's decision to leave the company would cost Wang Labs such an enormous amount of cash and negative publicity. With $15 million at stake, Cunningham believes he would have had great leverage with the board. "If there was a conflict with me and the Doctor, the board would have pushed him out," says Cunningham. "I didn't want that, but the structuring of that deal was my protection. If there was any conflict between me and him, I'd win in a board confrontation. Within five days I'd be CEO and he'd be out of the picture."

During their meeting, Cunningham raised the issue of control, and he didn't like Wang's response. He didn't believe the Doctor was ready to yield the reins. Cunningham wanted control because he believed that the Doctor's interference would prevent a successful rescue of the company.

Cunningham wanted control for another reason: He cared deeply about how he was viewed by the world.

The compensation package Cunningham outlined meant that if he were to walk away from Wang, he would do so with $15 million in his pocket. "I didn't want to get pushed out the door after three or four months," he says. "If I did, the outside world would have said, 'Cunningham is a real jerk for doing that deal.' If I was going to leave, I was going to walk with some cash.

"I'd spent eighteen years at Wang, and it had been a good deal for me and a great deal for Wang, and I wasn't going back unless it was reversed. I wasn't going to do it unless when terms of the deal came out that would be viewed as a good deal for Wang and a *great* deal for me."

At the conclusion of the meeting in Lincoln, Cunningham told the Doctor and Harry to think about his proposal. Then he left and drove one town farther west to Concord and the home of Peter Brooke. Brooke pulled a bottle of Stoli out of the freezer and made a couple of martinis. Cunningham walked Brooke through the letter as he had Doctor Wang.

Brooke didn't like it.

Brooke told Cunningham he thought both the under-market stock and the $25 million fee in the event the company was sold were problems.

"There's probably not enough in it for me to do it if those two things are not there," Cunningham said.

Brooke said they were going to be serious obstacles to a deal.

"That may very well be a show-stopper," Cunningham replied.

The following day, Grayson called with what amounted to the official company response to the proposal: "It's too rich."

The Doctor's reaction was similar to Brooke's. He liked neither the under-market stock nor the fee. Grayson said the company was talking to another candidate for the presidency who wasn't asking for under-market stock or a fee in the event of a sale.

Cunningham told Grayson: "If you can get somebody else who can fix it and doesn't need those two things, then go hire him."

But Cunningham didn't like that idea, really. Although he had begun the process only slightly more interested than indifferent, the truth was that his appetite had been whetted. By the time Grayson called, Cunningham says he was "getting a little bit interested."

Cunningham's proposal *was* rich, but he truly believed it was reasonable. Hadn't he made $18 million for fixing CCI, a company barely a tenth Wang's size? Weren't the presidents of other major computer companies getting a half percent or, in some cases, several percentage points of the stock? Cunningham was asking for 1.5 percent of the Wang shares.

But the Wang people had been put off by the proposal — by numbers they found incredible. Senior company officials, including the Doctor, thought Cunningham guilty of naked greed.

The next day, August 16, Cunningham dispatched a memorandum to the Doctor, Grayson, Brooke, and Cabot defending his original letter. He sought to justify his proposal so that, as he wrote, "if nothing else, history will not show me to have been unreasonable, ridiculous, or unrealistic."

He explained that the $5 million in annual fees that he was proposing his team be paid was double what the compensation package would be for the four major players involved — himself, Krieger, Koplow, and Moros. And he argued that his request to purchase options at $4.25 a share — well under the current share price of $6.90 — made sense because he predicted (accurately) that the share price would drop to $4.25.

He argued that if the company were turned around and sold, that it would likely be at a price that would gain about $2.5 billion in value for shareholders and $700 million in value for the family. Under those circumstances, Cunningham argued, a $25 million fee for his group was reasonable.

Cunningham's written justification swayed no one. Neither the Doctor nor the board members were comfortable with the size of the numbers Cunningham was tossing around. With the rejection of his proposal, however, Cunningham's interest was renewed — his ambivalence diminished. Perhaps it was that he simply didn't like being turned down, but, suddenly, he wanted rather badly to return to Wang Laboratories.

While Cunningham's memo was being read by the Doctor, Rick Miller was talking with Lodestar's Ken Miller about ways to raise the capital that Wang desperately needed. Ken Miller called Rick to ask if he would help introduce Wang officials to people from GE Credit. Rick did that, provided advice on how to approach the GE people, and set up a conference call for the following day, Tuesday, August 15, between Wang and GE Credit.

On the day of that phone call, An Wang reached his limit with the banks. He had had enough. They had been asking for more and more and more and would not stop. It seemed to Wang that they wanted his flesh and blood.

The Doctor decided to engage in a bit of brinksmanship. He instructed his financial people to stop all payments to banks for both principal and interest on loans. The company would pay nothing. If the banks then wanted to shove Wang Labs into bankruptcy, they could do so. But it would mean they would never recover all of their money. The Doctor was all but daring them to push him off a cliff.

"We're not going to give any more," Wang told Fred. "If the banks want to be known for forcing the company into bankruptcy because they are inept at doing what's right, then so be it."

It was a gutsy, dramatic, and desperate step by a company on the verge of collapse, but it was the only move that might jar the banks into stopping their merciless hounding of the company. When Wang refused to meet its principal and interest payments, all negotiations between the two parties over a new credit line collapsed. For the first time in months, the company had a measure of leverage. It simply would not give the banks another dollar until a new credit agreement was worked out.

It was at this moment that Rick Miller drove up from his home in Greenwich to meet with An Wang. On Wednesday morning, August 16, Miller walked into the Doctor's cavernous office and found a sick old man who was discolored and weak, who was in obvious pain, who could only whisper. But when they met, Miller felt that they communicated well immediately. That was far from true of most people upon first meeting

Wang, but Miller — like Cunningham — was a particularly good listener, and he arrived in Lowell that day with an instinctive feel for the company's problems. He had also taken the trouble before chatting with the Doctor to study the company's history and to read Doctor Wang's autobiography. Nothing that Rick Miller heard during the meeting surprised him. He learned that the company's morale was poor, that there was a lack of discipline and the worst internal politics he had ever seen.

The most pressing concern Rick Miller had was identical to Cunningham's major concern: control. Doctor Wang had never before allowed anyone to run his company, and the question was whether he was sufficiently desperate now to let go of the reins.

Both Cunningham and Miller believed that to have a shot at saving the company, they would need control. The Doctor would have to yield what had been, through the years, more important to him than anything else.

While Cunningham had been under the clear impression that Wang was not ready to yield control to him, Miller came away convinced Wang *was* ready. "I had a very good feeling after that meeting," says Miller. "He was ready to let someone run it."

Doctor Wang obviously felt good about Miller, too, for he decided on the spot that he wanted him to meet the directors as well as several members of the company's senior management team. Miller had a good session with Peter Brooke. He talked with Louis Cabot, who considered the matter so urgent that he placed a phone call to Nantucket where his friend Jack Welch was playing golf and asked that Welch be called in from the course to talk about Miller.

That night, headed for a dinner meeting with board members Paul Tsongas and Howard Swearer, Miller felt that things were happening very quickly. Yet, for all the urgency and the gravity of the situation, Miller felt comfortable with the company's problems. He had moved into adversity before — as bad as the Wang situation was, could anything match starting a job twenty-one days before Penn Central went bankrupt? He had seen disarray and he had proven he could work effectively within it. He felt quite confident.

Miller arrived a few minutes early, which allowed him to place a call to his wife at their summer home on Martha's Vineyard. She took the news of the fast-moving events in stride. She'd been through rapid changes before, too.

The three men met at the Sheraton Tara Hotel in Braintree, just south of Boston. They were joined by Ed Grayson. Tsongas, who drove up from his summer home on Cape Cod, had been growing a beard while on vacation and was dressed in grubby old clothes that indicated the haste of his trip. During dinner, the directors asked about Miller's background, his family, and the relevance of his experience to Wang Labs — he had, after all, never worked in the computer industry.

Dinner went well.

Afterward, Miller headed south toward Woods Hole to catch a late ferry to the Vineyard. As he drove through the night after one of the most dizzying days of his life, Rick Miller realized that in just seven hours he had met and talked with five directors of Wang Laboratories.

Things were happening very fast indeed.

Rick Miller spent much of Thursday on the phone with Ken Miller and Wang officials discussing negotiations with the banks. On Friday, the company hired a helicopter to fly Miller to Long Island, where he met in the Hamptons with Tom Neff, a headhunter who had been retained by Wang to help find a new president. Searches for heads of multibillion-dollar companies generally take time. But the crisis dictated that this search be very short, and company officials wanted to hear Neff tell them that Miller was as good or better than anyone else they were going to find. The two men met for an hour and a half, then Miller was shuttled back to Lowell.

Whether Rick Miller was to become president of Wang Labs wasn't yet clear, but what was clear was that company officials valued his advice. On Friday, after returning home from Long Island, Miller was back on the phone with Wang officials discussing a crucial meeting with bankers scheduled for Saturday afternoon in Boston. Saturday morning the Wang team planned a strategy session, to which Miller was invited, to prepare for the afternoon meeting. He drove up from the Cape early Saturday morning and found himself in a huge conference room at the downtown offices of Bingham, Dana and Gould, law firm for the Bank of Boston. There, he was surrounded by a crowd of perhaps thirty people, including company officials and lawyers, both from the Wang Labs law firm and from Skadden, Arps. There were also accountants from Ernst and Young and investment bankers from Salomon Brothers and Lodestar.

Thirty bright, highly paid professionals were gathered together, and what became clear to Rick Miller with frightening speed was that there wasn't a hint of leadership in the room. It was, Miller realized, utter chaos. Miller was not about to be shy or political. When he was asked his opinion, he could have played it safe and agreed with the approach advocated by Grayson and other Wang officials. He knew his comments would offend them, but he wasn't about to hide his views to prevent a few ruffled feathers. He said they ought to use the one word that terrifies bankers in that situation — bankruptcy. "When you're negotiating with bankers and they've got you, the one thing they don't want to hear is bankruptcy," says Miller. "Bankruptcy means they lose control."

He told them they also should insist on borrowing more money to set aside as restructuring reserves. But Grayson said they had already cleaned up the company. Miller didn't believe it for a second. "I felt it was right on the edge," says Miller. "This company almost lost control of its own destiny. It was so vulnerable. It was like a ship tottering. If some other big thing goes wrong, it could have wound up reeling so badly, it would have been unsalvageable."

But they did not take his advice. In fact, Grayson and the others seemed offended by what he had said. Since Miller was not formally aligned with the company, it was inappropriate for him to attend the afternoon meeting with the bankers, so he headed back to Martha's Vineyard. The next day, both Ken Miller and Grayson called to report that they were moving toward an agreement with the banks. But Rick Miller did not believe it would be an agreement that would allow the company the flexibility it needed. Any agreement, however, was better than no agreement, which would mean paralysis.

On Monday the logjam was broken. The company and the banks struck a deal to restructure $575 million in debts. As part of that agreement, Wang Labs resumed debt payments that it had suspended a week earlier. The deal was not a great one for the company, but it was a breakthrough of sorts that relieved, for the first time in many months, at least some of the acute financial pressure on the company. Wang Labs could now go about the task of trying to turn itself around without having to spend day after day negotiating a new financial lease on life.

Over the weekend, Rick Miller was asked to return to Lowell on Monday to meet with the Doctor. The two men talked about Rick's meetings with board members and about the weekend session with bankers. Though the Doctor said nothing formally, it was clear he wanted Miller to take over as the company's new president. Miller raised the issue of chain of command and told the Doctor that a stipulation of his employment would be that the only boss he would ever have during his time at Wang Labs would be the Doctor. There was no need to spell out that Miller wanted to make sure that, in the event of the Doctor's retirement or death, he wouldn't be reporting to someone else — a member of the Wang family. An Wang accepted that condition.

Miller made one other request that seemed to surprise the Doctor. He asked for a meeting with Fred. He had been hearing that Fred would be a real problem and Miller knew that Fred, as a member of the board and former president and COO, could make Miller's life difficult if he chose to do so.

The meeting was set for that afternoon at the Lanam Club in North Andover. Miller was pleased by Fred's tone and attitude. It was immediately clear to Miller that "Fred wasn't going to be an enemy."

Miller did not want to be indelicate, but this was, after all, his professional life he was about to commit to Wang Labs. So he asked Fred what Fred's plans were in the event of his father's death. For if Fred's intention was to come back and run the company, Miller would almost certainly have to walk away from the deal.

But Fred made it clear that "he wanted to pursue something outside the business. He talked about the need for change, about freedom."

Fred asked Rick how he planned to approach the company's problems, how he thought he would work with the Doctor. In Fred's mind, there was no question who would be in charge and he told Miller that. "It's Dad's company," Fred said.

But Rick Miller believed that Fred was wrong; he believed the Doctor would permit him to run the company and would not plague him with incessant second-guessing.

That night, Miller joined Ed Grayson, Ed Devin, Wang's head of personnel, and Tom Neff, the headhunter, for dinner at the Marriott in Burlington, a Boston suburb along the Route 128 belt. They discussed Miller's employment package. The financial deal was straightforward: Miller was guaranteed minimum cash compensation of $1 million per year for at least three years. He would also receive options on 2 million shares of Wang stock at market value.

The formal announcement was made on Wednesday, August 23, sixteen days after Fred's departure. A prepared statement from the Doctor read: "I have great confidence in the ability of Rick Miller to assume total control of the operations of Wang Laboratories."

Analysts reacted positively to the news. "The people at Wang are very lucky," said Mark Hassenberg, an analyst at the New York investment firm of Donaldson Lufkin & Jenrette, who watched Miller at both General Electric and RCA. "He is a fixer, a doctor. He will bring discipline to a company that has lacked discipline for some time."

Miller was in New York at the time the announcement was made. He talked to reporters from the *Wall Street Journal,* the *New York Times,* and several other newspapers before returning home to Greenwich, packing, and driving to Lowell at about eight o'clock. It was after 11:00 P.M. when he pulled up to the Appleton Inn near the company's headquarters, where a reservation had been made for him. Looking rather bedraggled in shorts, Top-Siders, and a T-shirt, Miller went inside and said that he had a reservation in the name of Miller. The desk clerk was taken aback. Not the new president of Wang? she asked. He admitted he was. She quickly scurried into a back room and promptly returned with the hotel's manager, who had been waiting since six o'clock with personal greetings to the most important new man in the city of Lowell.

The day before the announcement, John Cunningham knew the company was talking with Miller, but he had no idea that the deal with Miller was done. Cunningham still believed he had a good shot at getting the job, and it was clear that his ambivalence had disappeared. That day, after the deal was done with Miller but before it had been announced, Cunningham met with Grayson and offered a new proposal, drastically scaled down from his earlier one. Cunningham also suggested the possibility of not running the company but of coming in and doing some consulting for the new COO. He offered to go out into the field and rally the troops, to stroke the customers. But it was too late.

Even after it was announced that Miller had won the job, Cunningham did not give up. On Monday, August 28, Miller's third day on the job, Cunningham had yet another proposal to involve himself in the company. He suggested to Peter Brooke and Louis Cabot that he come in on a consulting basis as a staff assistant to Miller. There was a note of urgency to Cunningham's request. It was clear that he now had a burning desire to get back into the fray, to be part of the action. At one point, the notion of going back in as anything less than president with complete control had been unthinkable. Now he was actually proposing that he sign on part-time as a member of the new president's staff. In that slot he could help with customers and with the sales and field forces, he argued.

Cunningham and Miller met for lunch and Cunningham said, "Hire me as a consultant."

Miller was inclined to do so. Miller said he had broached the possibility with the Doctor, who had said it was fine with him. But a few hours later, the Doctor sent Guzzi to tell Miller that if Miller decided to use John it would cause a problem within the family, but he made it clear it was still Miller's decision.

"I told Miller, 'Hey, forget it. You're trying to build a relationship with the guy,'" says Cunningham.

"I really felt I could help," he adds. "It was foolish not to use me, absolutely foolish."

Once again, John Cunningham would sever relations with Wang on a less-than-pleasant note. He billed the company for the work that he, Koplow, Moros, and Krieger had done. Their assessment and written analysis of where the company stood and where it should go was worth a great deal, Cunningham felt. Already people at the company were using his work as a game plan. He attached a price tag of $40,000. The Doctor was livid and, at first, refused to pay anything. After painful haggling, the company paid half that and John Cunningham, once again, left Wang Labs behind.

When it was all over, Fred said that there was absolutely no possibility that Cunningham would have been hired by the Doctor. And Peter Brooke says bringing Cunningham back would have been difficult for the old man. "Wang would have really had to swallow to bring John back," says Brooke. "I don't know if he could have done it. I just don't know."

Brooke says it worked out for the best. Cunningham "might have been a quick fix" to the company's problems, says Brooke, but "there wasn't the feeling that he was the long-term solution to Wang's problem. We needed a guy grounded more deeply in workouts. I didn't think he was serious. Miller moved his family, laid everything right on the line, not through a consulting company" as Cunningham had proposed. "If times got tougher, John would have gone back to the golf course and I wouldn't have blamed him."

SEVENTEEN

The New Wang

ON THE MORNING of August 24, 1989, Rick Miller waited in the hallway for the 6:30 opening of the dining room at the Appleton Inn, where he had spent the night. Even before he started work on his first day at Wang Laboratories, Miller knew, at least in the broadest sense, what needed to be done. He had to cut costs drastically, and that meant layoffs — big layoffs — in a company where employees were already reeling from slashes in personnel. He had to sell a staggering $600 million worth of assets — and do it during a recessionary economy — to pay off the bank debt. And he had to do these things without jeopardizing the company's ability to do its day-to-day business. Finally, before he could figure out a way to grow the company's revenues and get it back to profitability, he had to convince customers, analysts, the press — the world — that Wang Laboratories was not going to fall away into the great abyss. It was a daunting, perhaps impossible, task.

As he sat over his breakfast that morning, only moments before he walked across the street to start his new job, Rick Miller heard two men at a nearby table discussing the company he was about to take over. The two were talking about "this new guy Miller."

The new president and chief operating officer of Wang Laboratories heard one of the men say to the other: "I wouldn't take that job for anything in the world."

From the moment he started work — seventeen days after Fred's dismissal — Rick Miller received from An Wang something the founder had never before relinquished — control of the company. The man who had built this once-great enterprise, who had always jealously guarded his power, saw Miller as a kind of savior. Wang Laboratories Inc. would live or die under the leadership of Richard Miller.

Speaking in the company auditorium to several hundred middle managers that day, Miller said that his first task was to stabilize the company financially, and to do that he needed to reduce the onerous short-term bank debt. He said he wanted radical change in the way the company operated, that he wanted it centered on the customer. "Our customers like our technology," he said, "but they say we're impossible to do business with. We frustrate our customers. We fall down with regard to execution. We're going to start listening to our customers like never before."

They'd heard it all in the past, said one woman in the audience who challenged him during the question-and-answer session. "What makes you different?" she asked. "How are you going to do it?"

"With a baseball bat," he shot back, as he stalked over to where the woman sat. Miller's tall, thin, angular figure loomed above her. His intense, penetrating gaze sometimes gave him an almost menacing air. He asked, "Don't you think I can?"

From the beginning, some of the top executives didn't much like him. He was a hard-ass, they complained, a tough guy who sometimes bullied them. Bill Taupier, a former Lowell city manager who had worked many real estate deals on behalf of the company, met Miller only once, but his impression was that Miller was "made of steel from his toes to his head to his heart. He's a corporate guy, which will be good for Wang."

Miller says he had no choice but to be tough. "You can't take a couple of years to nurture and mold the place. This is urgent stuff."

A story got around that Miller called a meeting of the more than fifty vice-presidents of Wang Laboratories and, when they arrived in a room containing only thirty seats, someone said, "Rick, there aren't enough chairs." To which Miller was said to have darkly replied: "Yes, there are."

Although the story wasn't true, it immediately became part of the Miller lore.

Wang had a reputation as a fat company top-heavy with management, where layers of bureaucrats lived charmed lives. One manager had been transferred nine times in five years because no one wanted to fire him. There was deep resentment on the part of lower-level workers — or, as Miller called them, "individual contributors" — who had labored long and hard and had seen their company tumble. Miller needed these workers' support. There would be no turnaround without them, he knew. He immediately sensed the depth of the workers' anger toward the company's upper management. The workers held the company's executives responsible for the terrible demise. "When I got here there was such hate and bitterness from the employees," says Miller. "They really wanted me to fire everybody at the top of this company."

During his first few weeks on the job, he struck a few symbolic blows for the little guy. "I wanted them to feel that I was their man," he says. "I needed them on my side." On his first day, he toured a manufacturing facility, where he spent some time talking with workers. He let it be known that he intended to sell the $14 million Gulfstream jet. He shut down the executive dining room, where managers ate free, and he made a practice of eating in the company cafeteria and sitting with a different group of workers each day. He also abolished reserved parking for management, a move that was not greeted warmly by executives, who could barely see the distant reaches of the vast Wang parking lots from their tower windows. Not only would managers lose reserved spots near the building, but the fourteen most senior people in the company would lose access to the fourteen indoor parking spaces in the basement of the building.

When he informed senior executives of this move, one man actually complained. "I'm going to ruin my shoes," the fellow said. "I wear $300 shoes."

Miller did not hide his disdain. He glared at the man and asked derisively: "Why do you wear such cheap shoes?"

Among the company's upper ranks, he found a startling lack of teamwork. Even worse, during private sessions he had with the top executives early on, nearly everyone denigrated at least one other member of the management team. He found some good, talented people who worked hard, but there was little effort made at working together. "The culture was paternalistic, reverent," he says. There was also "a general lack of discipline."

Motivating employees and resuscitating their shattered morale amid the devastation of layoffs was not easy. But Miller pushed good news hard and held out hope for a bright future. He told his employees in mid-October that the company had found a credit source that would give them the breathing room of $175 million in working capital. He told them that a company with Wang's installed base worldwide — with major corporations around the world having made huge investments in Wang machinery — wasn't going to blow away overnight. He said that although he expected the company to lose money for the first three quarters of the fiscal year, he predicted a profit for the final quarter.

He had already met with some two hundred customers, he said, and he found them loyal to Wang products. But as Miller found out in the weeks that followed, though customers liked Wang products and felt a loyalty to the company, they also often found Wang a frustrating company with which to do business. The survey Miller had commissioned from consultant Ira Magaziner, with whom Miller had previously worked at GE, found that customers were often put off by Wang's bureaucracy, disorganization, and slow-footedness.

Miller found the archetype of Wang's problems only a few hundred yards from the towers in the company's main U.S. manufacturing plant. It was astounding how utterly chaotic Wang had been able to make the basic steps in the manufacturing process. The fundamentals — placing an order, assembling a product, shipping the product, and sending out a bill for it — had become ensnared in a tangle of bureaucracy that was choking the company. It was so bad that it sometimes took two full weeks for an order even to arrive at the factory. The plant itself could be a kind of manufacturing black hole into which orders would occasionally disappear.

"The factory used to receive eight hundred phone calls a *day* from the field," says Miller, "from our own people and from customers saying, 'Where's my order?' Do you know what gets said to the eight hundredth person, who calls at 4:30 in the afternoon?"

The system — or lack thereof — was a vestige of Wang's go-go years, when the company's products were so hot that customers happily tolerated lengthy delays and chaos. In the new, more competitive industry, delays were unacceptable.

The irony was that Wang Labs sold computer systems capable of solving such problems. Miller moved to use that equipment, to computerize the operation so that the instant a salesperson entered the order on computer, it was received in the factory. Within hours, the factory computers would have determined when the machinery could be produced and a delivery date would be dispatched to the customer. At any given point in the process, any order could be tracked live via the computer. In a matter of months, the new system all but eliminated the avalanche of distracting phone calls into the plant and increased orders delivered on time from 77 percent to 92 percent.

*   *   *

During the fall and early winter, Miller moved simultaneously on four fronts: He began selling off assets to raise cash to pay off the bank loans; he slashed expenses, principally by laying off thousands of employees; he radically reorganized the company to center its activities on customers; and he instituted a training program to teach every Wang employee — from the top of the organization to the bottom — about quality.

His most pressing concern in the early days was the crushing bank debt of $575 million. Knowing that the company could go nowhere until it was financially stable, Miller moved swiftly to pay down that debt. He aggressively set about selling everything that was not essential to the company's core business. On the block went the corporate jet; the Wang Country Club, which had been bought for the exclusive use of employees; the expensive Brussels headquarters building; and the huge leasing companies that Wang owned and through which it leased equipment to customers. Since the world knew how financially desperate Wang was, it was clear that the company would get beaten up on price, but Miller had no choice. He needed an immense amount of cash fast.

By January, he had sold more than $200 million worth of assets including the Wang manufacturing plant in Scotland, the Wang Credit Corp., for $139 million, and a 30 percent interest in a Wang Taiwan manufacturing facility for $90 million.

As that work continued, Miller was forced to face up to the wrenching task of laying off people. To stabilize the company financially, he needed not only to reduce the bank debt but to cut ongoing expenses by the staggering figure of $500 million annually. There was no way to achieve the kinds of savings needed without massive layoffs.

Wang Labs was no stranger to layoffs. In just a single year, from June 1988 to June 1989, the number of employees worldwide had fallen from 31,516 to 28,300. Miller had to let 1,500 more go in September, almost 900 in October, 500 in November, and more than 2,000 in December. By the end of 1989, he had reduced the employee count to 22,928. In just over a year and a half, Wang Labs had laid off nearly 10,000 employees — almost a third of its worldwide work force.

On the day that he cut 2,000 people just three weeks before Christmas in 1989, a senior manager advised him not to go down to the cafeteria for lunch, where he had been eating nearly every day since he had arrived. The situation was too volatile. Who knew what an enraged, overwrought employee might say, or do. But Miller had to go downstairs, get in line, and look these people in the eye. He had to take the stares filled with resentment. He had to get employees to believe that his interest was not in cutting jobs, but in saving 19,000 jobs. If he hid upstairs, how would they ever trust him?

Once, in 1986, the company had employed 13,400 people in Lowell alone. Now, at the end of 1989, that number was down to 8,000. The reductions hurt not only Wang employees, but they were painful for the many businesses in Lowell that fed off of Wang and that had thrived along with Wang during better times. There was an air of unease in the city as well as in the towers. Employees who had survived the massacre walked through hallways once jammed with busy people. Now, the corridors were silent. Row upon row of offices and cubicles were empty, eerily hushed, like a cemetery.

An Wang returned to work at the towers soon after Labor Day. He would go to his office in the morning for a few hours until he tired and then he would return home. Most days he took a nap, but was then back up, working in his office at home. Though his health had improved some, he had lost so much weight that his suits hung off him as if he were wearing the clothes of a beefier big brother.

Throughout September and October, Miller met privately with Doctor Wang nearly every day. During that time they never had a serious disagreement. The Doctor permitted Miller to do whatever he wanted. Any accomplishment, no matter how small, would bring a beaming An Wang into Miller's office, arm outstretched, to shake Miller's hand in congratulations.

Around the middle or end of October, Wang's physical condition improved and he became a bit more active at work. He was particularly interested in getting the company's PC business revved up. He believed the company had an excellent machine and the potential to win more of the PC market. The Doctor began holding informal meetings with a variety of people from throughout the company to discuss various parts of the PC business. After a few weeks of this, it was clear to Miller that Wang was creating a phantom organization for his PC work outside of the structure Miller was imposing on the company. It was all perfectly well intentioned, of course, but it was also disruptive and counterproductive.

Company veterans watched this development with great interest. It was precisely the way the Doctor had always operated, and they were curious to see Miller's reaction. It placed Rick Miller in an uncomfortable position. He wanted the Doctor to back off and to permit the people he had rounded up to do their jobs.

When the Doctor's activities grew into daily meetings involving fifteen or so people, Miller felt he had to do something. "If he had been 100 percent healthy and strong, I probably would have been in his office right away," says Miller. "I was trying to let him make a contribution. But I couldn't let that effort confuse the organization and dilute the focus and discipline I was trying to put in place."

Miller went to the Doctor's office one day and sat down with him alone. "Doctor Wang, we're confusing our people," he said.

Wang appeared puzzled.

Miller explained that Wang was confusing people who reported to Miller about what their priorities should be. The Doctor said that the company had never got its PC business going properly and he said he had to provide the leadership to do that. Miller said he didn't think it would work the way the Doctor was approaching it. But Wang insisted that it would be fine.

"It's okay, it's okay," the Doctor kept repeating. "I'm going to get PC business going."

Miller looked directly at him and said: "Doctor Wang, we're not talking about the PC business right now. We're talking about how we're going to run this company."

Miller's words stopped Wang cold. He sat up and looked Miller in the eye.

Miller paused before continuing. "I came here to do a job," he said. "I believe that we have a good chance to turn the company around, but we can't do it with two heads to the company. There has to be one. And right now we're going in a direction that's going to hurt our objectives. I can't tell you that there's a right way and a wrong way to run a business. I have my ideas and you have yours. But I do know that decisiveness and clear direction is absolutely essential at a time like this. What we are talking about is running Wang Laboratories. If you want me to continue to run it, you've got to let me run it."

The Doctor, who had listened carefully, was quiet for a moment. He asked, "Do we need to go from 100 percent to zero percent in one step?"

"Of course not," Miller replied.

"What do you propose?" An Wang asked.

Miller relaxed. "Why don't we come back tomorrow morning and we'll have a further talk about this, and I'll make a proposal as to how we go forward."

The next day Miller made his proposal.

"See what you think of this," he said to the Doctor. "We will have an ad hoc PC committee to develop a plan, not to implement a plan. To develop a strategy for how we take the next steps in the PC business. You will be the team leader. When you have the plan, if you're comfortable, I'd like you to tell me about it and we will decide together on implementation. That means in the meantime not draining the organization's energies."

"I like that," the Doctor said. "Whatever you want."

The management team was informed and peace reigned. But it was clear who had won the confrontation. Miller had emerged with a precious commodity — control.

Changing the way the company did business meant reorienting all operations toward the customer and instilling within the company culture an insistence on quality. Operation Customer was Miller's way of describing the radical changes he was making at Wang Laboratories. In addition to massive layoffs, the program included a redistribution and reorganization of the company's workload to the surviving employees. It was billed by Miller as "a revolution — a radical and fundamental reordering of the way in which" the company conducted business and a means of dismantling the suffocating bureaucracy.

Ironically, central to the Operation Customer reorganization were several notions that Fred Wang had pushed as president — particularly the delegation of authority out from the central headquarters. Miller told his employees that he wanted to give "responsibility and authority to those directly designing, building, selling, and servicing products and to have these individuals accountable for results."

He wanted products delivered on time. He wanted the customers' needs, as determined by the customer, "to shape and drive our priorities."

For years there had been complaints about the quality of Wang Labs service and manufacturing. While the products were often brilliantly designed, they were not always well serviced or manufactured. John Cunningham had targeted the quality problem, or tried to, through the White Paper Task Force, but superior quality had never been part of the Wang culture. The company could get away with that when the industry hadn't been so competitive, but that was no longer the case.

There had been scores of stories about Wang service failures through the years, but none scarier than the instance in 1988 when the failure of the Wang VS 5000 — and the subsequent inability of Wang service people to get it going — forced the cancellation of a meeting of the board of directors at one of the largest corporations in the United States. Miller sought to make sure that nothing like that ever happened again.

At GE, Miller had seen a quality training program work remarkably well, and he introduced that process to Wang. It required several hours of training per week for up to fifteen weeks for every Wang Labs employee worldwide. "Quality is everything," he told employees at the time. "It must become the foundation for our corporate culture."

"We're not talking about improving quality in the production line," he said. "We're talking about an overall mentality, about the way we think about ourselves, the way we conduct our business, about our values, about the way we talk with each other, the way we listen to each other, the way we communicate with customers and represent the company."

Through the holidays Doctor Wang seemed slightly better. He could work for only two or three hours at a time before he tired, and his voice was a raspy whisper, but he seemed to have some of his color back. In January, An and Lorraine Wang headed for California for a vacation. Before leaving, the Doctor offered a small but revealing hint about how much control he had ceded to Miller. Rather than simply flying west on the company jet, as was his custom, Wang asked Miller's permission to use the plane, which was on the block but not yet sold. Of course, Miller told him.

As he had grown older, the New England winters had begun to bother Wang, and he had enjoyed occasional escapes to his home in Hawaii, but, once there, he had felt too far removed from his company. He donated the place to Harvard and bought another vacation home in Hillsborough, an affluent San Francisco suburb, where Harry Chou also had a home and where Wang felt more in touch with Lowell. Though it was a magnificent place, the Wangs spent only about a week or two there each year. They avoided San Francisco and instead gathered with Chinese friends at the informal Chinese restaurants in Hillsborough and Belmont.

Their trip in January was planned as a two-week vacation, but after only about a week the cancer, reappearing in Wang's throat, swelled and further constricted his esophagus. It was so bad this time that he had trouble swallowing even saliva. The doctors in Boston suggested the trip be cut short so they could examine him. As it turned out, they were able to open up his throat with a relatively minor procedure that made him more comfortable.

But through February his condition worsened, and on March 6 he was readmitted to the hospital. The cancer had spread, devastating his entire body. Ordinarily so self-sufficient, An Wang was now essentially helpless. For his family and his close colleagues, it was painful to see him in this terrible condition. It was not long before he was so weak that he was unable to walk. His voice was gone — killed by the combination of the cancer and a tracheotomy.

This did not mean, however, that he was too weak to worry about his beloved company, or even too sick to conduct business. In fact, as he lay in the hospital in steadily worsening condition, An Wang conducted an interview with an executive the company was attempting to recruit. The man was escorted by Paul Guzzi to Mass General, where Doctor Wang lay in his bed, scribbled a few questions, and listened as the man responded.

Just a couple of months before his father went back into the hospital, Fred had begun graduate work toward a master's degree in public administration at the John F. Kennedy School of Government at Harvard. The school was ten minutes away from the Mass General Hospital, just down and across the Charles River.

"When he was in the hospital, I spent lots of time in there with him," says Fred. "We enjoyed each other's company. I'd go in there at 9:00 A.M. until class at 10:00 or 11:00. Laurie would be there from 11:00 to 1:00, and I'd come back and be there until 5:00 or 6:00. My mother would come in until 8:00 or 10:00."

Fred would tell the Doctor what was going on in the news, and his father would write notes about a variety of topics, mostly business. Fred says his father's notes emphasized "the importance of asset sales, of supporting Rick. He really thought Rick was a good man."

When Courtney was in town from Dallas, he, too, would visit his father. And Juliette regularly came by to keep the Doctor company.

An Wang was not a man who had ever lost sleep worrying. He had weathered an extraordinary array of hardships — the war and devastation in China, the loss of half his family, the emigration to a new world with a strange culture and a language he never quite mastered. He had survived business turbulence and near catastrophe. He had survived the terrible pain of firing his own son, of living to see not the realization but the shattering of his dream.

But his time had come to an end. He set about the business of tying up loose ends.

One such loose end was his unexpressed affection for his children. In a terrible irony, by trying to run his company primarily for the benefit of his family, Wang had harmed both the company and the family. And although his family's interests came first at Wang Laboratories, he had never been a man who sought to excel as a father. Through the years there had been many missed Little League games, weekends when other boarding-school students saw their father but the Wang children did not. When Fred was growing up, he recalls, his father was "working most of the time."

For his offspring, An Wang's work produced a fortune. The Doctor established two trusts, one for his children, a second for his grandchildren. The first trust, established in the mid-1950s, eventually grew to contain a substantial amount of Wang stock. At one point, that trust alone had been worth more than $500 million.

But for all the money, the Wang children had encountered some difficult times in life. Fred, of course, suffered the humiliation of being fired by his father and being blamed publicly for the company's decline. Courtney still harbored ambitions to run the company, consistent with his father's original dream. But now the notion seemed preposterous. Courtney was a thirty-three-year-old branch manager in the Dallas office, and hardly a major player in the company. Of course, the family could, through its control of the board of directors, place Courtney in charge. But that would require unanimity on the part of the family — and it was not at all clear that Fred would support moving his brother up. Such a move would also mean the loss of Rick Miller, for Miller's contract stipulated that, other than Doctor Wang, he would never be subordinate to any individual at Wang Labs. Besides, the board and the family were quite happy with the progress Miller had made with the company.

And Wang's youngest child, Juliette, had had some difficulties that had caused her parents a good deal of pain. When she was barely into her twenties, she phoned her parents one night to say that she had eloped and was getting married. That she was marrying someone who was not Chinese crushed Lorraine Wang. That she was doing so without even a traditional wedding was even more distressing.

While her parents and brothers had been strong students, Juliette had struggled with school. She excelled during her years at Boston University at ice hockey, and played on the women's varsity. She liked hockey enough, in fact, that she and her husband, Mark Coombs, made a move to purchase the Boston Bruins. Reports at the time were that she would pay $25 million for the club, but the deal never went through.

Far more troublesome was a financial problem into which Juliette and her husband blundered. In the winter of 1984, they received a cold-call telephone solicitation from a stockbroker and soon thereafter opened an account with the broker at the firm of Dean Witter, according to press reports. They started the account with $13.5 million worth of Wang Labs stock. Within a couple of years, the couple had lost $2 million and sued Dean Witter, charging that the brokers had engaged in highly speculative ventures without their knowledge. Juliette's husband, who had worked closely with the Dean Witter broker, was found dead of carbon monoxide poisoning in a car in August 1988.

For Juliette, at least, and perhaps for Fred and Courtney, as well, there was a feeling that An Wang had withheld himself from his children. His life story was a remarkable one yet he had not shared much of it with his children. Fred learned about his father's experiences in China only as An Wang sat and shared some of his past with a ghostwriter. He never told his children that he had been married once before he met their mother. He made no real effort to pass along Chinese culture or traditions to his children. And, sadly, Juliette says, "he never really communicated to us that he loved us."

In the final days of his life, however, he tried to convey his feelings. "He wrote in big letters 'I love you' and underlined it a bunch of times and put exclamation points after it," says Juliette. "And he would hold it up and show us."

He was immensely strong, but he was, after all, only human. Surely he was frightened, though he did not show it.

In the final days, his doctors said it would be all right for him to go home, but that seemed somewhat impractical, and he felt more comfortable in the hospital, where the doctors were nearby. Although Wang chose to remain in the hospital, Fred says he gave his doctors explicit instructions not to take any heroic measures. "He didn't want to be stuck to a machine," says Fred.

Near the end, Juliette read him Dylan Thomas's poem "Do Not Go Gentle into That Good Night." She said that it was "one of the few things he really enjoyed" during his last days, this poem that urged him to "Rage, rage against the dying of the light."

But his rage was insufficient. The predawn hours of Saturday, March 24, were cold and wet with sleet. At 5:41 A.M., while it was still dark, An Wang lay in his room at Phillips House in the Massachusetts General Hospital, where he died, alone.

He was lavishly praised in death, as he had been in life. Major news organizations throughout the world ran long obituaries in which he was variously described as the shy, bow-tied entrepreneur who held forty patents and twenty-three honorary degrees; one of America's wealthiest men, who had given away tens of millions of dollars to charities; and a recipient of the Presidential Medal of Liberty. Many of the stories briefly recapped his life: born the son of a schoolteacher in Shanghai, earned his Ph.D. at Harvard, worked at the Harvard Computation Laboratory and contributed to the invention of magnetic core memory, started his own company, invented one of the first electronic calculators, pioneered a word processing system that rocketed Wang into the ranks of the world's most successful computer companies, a man who started with nothing and built Wang Laboratories into a worldwide empire with more than thirty thousand employees and revenues in excess of $3 billion.

The wake, held at the MacRae–Tunnicliffe Funeral Home in Concord, Massachusetts, only minutes from the Wang home, attracted thousands of people. Employees and former employees lined up, two and three abreast, waiting to file slowly through the modest funeral parlor, to shake hands with family members, and perhaps to kneel and say a prayer over the Doctor's body, which lay in an open casket.

Peter McElroy was typical of the mourners. He had worked at the company for a decade, had prospered in the best of times, and, like some ten thousand others, had been let go during the decline. There was a deep emotional attachment between these people and the company. "The company got into our blood," observed McElroy. "People can't get Wang out of their system. It was not just a job; it was not just another company. It was a way of life."

The memorial service was set for Tuesday, March 27, at Memorial Church in Harvard Yard. Bundled in winter coats, the men and women walked solemnly through Harvard Yard and into the magnificent church.

Just as the service was getting under way, with the company's most senior people in attendance, rank-and-file employees began gathering outside the towers in Lowell. As the company's in-house newspaper would later report, that morning, two customer service representatives, Gail Taylor and Patrick Wisler, had invited people to join them for a moment of silence outside during lunch hour. It started with Taylor and Wisler, small groups, and then larger groups and whole clusters and waves of people until, finally, there were hundreds and hundreds of employees, many weeping openly. They stood, hands joined together, and formed a human chain so large that it encircled the towers. At 1:00 P.M., they bowed their heads in silent tribute to An Wang.

At that moment, according to the *Wang Times,* although it was 4:00 A.M. there, the massive sign atop the Wang Australia headquarters in Sydney, overlooking the opera house, went dark. In Rydalmere, Australia, at the top of a flagpole so massive there was room within it for a staircase, the 1,800-square-foot Wang flag was lowered to half staff. In Hong Kong, a eulogy for Doctor Wang was offered and a group of mourners stood and bowed their heads. At the Lanam Club in Andover, where the Doctor had so often eaten lunch, the management placed a reserved sign and a photograph of the Doctor on his usual table.

At the memorial service, once the organ music that filled the church had subsided, the minister introduced four speakers: Juliette, Courtney, and Fred Wang, and Michael S. Dukakis, then governor of Massachusetts.

Juliette Wang spoke first, and read John Donne's "Death Be Not Proud." She finished with a Stephen Spender poem, which, she said, "has a lot to do with what he's done with his life."

Courtney Wang, a slight man with slicked-back hair, was introduced next. "I'm not sure if any of us are ever really prepared for the loss of a true friend," he said. "For me, this was not only a true friend, but a very dear father — I think, to the world, a great man. Virtually all of us here today are here because we knew my dad for either social or professional reasons. But whatever those reasons are, all of us who have been part of his life have been changed by it. Many of us have benefited from it. I know for myself I've been an extremely fortunate beneficiary of being an integral part of his life. One thing I think all of us have in common today is that we're all very fortunate, very thankful, and very grateful for having been part of his life."

The formal eulogy was given by Governor Dukakis, who said, in part: "Each of us has his heroes, and Dr. Wang was one of mine. More than a friend, more than a colleague, he was the personification of the American dream. Not merely a success by anyone's standard, but a man whose genius and generosity made it possible for others to reach their dreams."

And, finally, Fred Wang rose to speak.

That morning, at his magnificent stucco mansion in Needham, a suburb outside Boston, Fred Wang had gone to a small alcove off the living room. It was far from the kitchen and den, from his family, far from the bustle and noise of the household. The living room was hushed. It was a large, formal room, but the beautiful chintz covering the sofas and chairs and the large stone fireplace gave it a cozy, Old World feel. Fred sat down at a round table of inlaid wood in an exquisite Chinese design. Beyond the window was a vast expanse of manicured lawns within a tall fence that walled the property off from the road.

He began to write. After a while Laurie came in to help. He thought, of course, that it was important to reach back and celebrate what his father had done with his life. But he thought also that his father had always looked forward and that it was important now for Fred to do the same.

"My family and I would like to thank all of you for coming and joining with us today and showing your respect to our dad," said Fred. "Although he himself was not one for pomp and circumstance, I'm sure he would appreciate this sharing in the celebration of his life. Over the past few [weeks] the family was able to spend quite a bit of time with him while he was in the hospital. While we were keeping company with him, he would jot us little notes. And some of them include his thoughts and ideas on success. And I know he would want to share those with all of you today. First, he said, 'Don't dwell on the past, but look to the future.' I'm sure that for you employees here he intends for you to continue the turnaround and bring the company to the greatness that it has the full potential to be.

"Second, he always depended on education. His father, my grandfather, was a teacher, and he grew up in this educational atmosphere. In 1946, when he arrived here in America, he was one of a group of people who were to start up the new business leadership of China. But instead of applying to a number of business establishments to get a year or so of experience, he applied to graduate school — here, in fact. And he has since continued to donate to the educational and cultural institutions where he had a chance to spend his time.

"Third, he told me, 'Always be humble. Acknowledge your weaknesses and learn from them. Don't only listen to yes-men, but heed the critics.' Finally, he wrote, 'I always tried to do my very best. Sum this up by saying the world does not need us, but we need the world. If you practice these keys, then you will be great and worthy.' We love you, Dad, and we'll miss you greatly."

It was a touching scene, especially so for those few Wang executives and former executives with a genuine fondness for Fred, who wondered whether Fred hadn't misread his father's message a bit, whether the message that Fred had thought intended for the company — "Don't dwell on the past, but look to the future" — was actually an intensely personal message for his oldest son.

The memorial service ended with a powerful bit of symbolism when Lorraine Wang was escorted from the church not by a member of her family or a close friend, but by Rick Miller. Two days later, the board of directors of Wang Laboratories met and voted Miller to replace An Wang as the company's chairman of the board and chief executive officer. Other men in the history of the company had been president — John Cunningham and Fred Wang — but no one except the Doctor had ever been chairman and CEO.

After the Doctor's death the family attempted to douse speculation that the company might be sold by announcing that they had every intention of maintaining control over Wang Labs. As though to punctuate that, Courtney Wang was appointed to the board of directors, joining his mother and brother and returning to three the number of Wang family members on the board.

He wanted very badly to be remembered. It was not for nothing that An Wang gave his company his name. There was a reason why he paid to have Boston's leading center for the performing arts named for him; a reason the new Mass General Hospital wing was called the Wang Ambulatory Care Center; a reason the school he founded was the Wang Institute. Certainly he was a generous man. But he was also a man who longed to be remembered.

In the final days of his life, how he would be remembered was very much on An Wang's mind. When Rick Miller received the final communication from the Doctor, Miller learned just how passionately Wang cared about not being forgotten in death.

The two sheets of paper arrived on Rick Miller's desk wrapped tightly in white surgical tape. One sheet was blank, evidently meant as a shield to prying eyes. The other contained the note.

"Dr. Edwin Maynard" — one of his physicians — "please give to Paul Guzzi." Below that Wang had written, "Paul Guzzi — please give this sealed to Rick Miller."

Miller picked up the package and began unraveling the sticky lengths of tape. He supposed it contained some final instructions and he was sure they would be along the lines the Doctor had already described to him, and, indeed, that was the case.

The note was written with blue, ballpoint pen on white lined paper.

Rick: You are my God send to take over WLI at the most critical time and you almost finished the first phase of financing part and take a long step on the expense restructure and sales revenue side.

Keep up the good work WLI need you and Wang Family Need you

I mentioned to you that I wonder if you you can finish my work and build WLI like Ford, DuPont who can paint their immigrant's name on one of the major industrial company in USA. With out Stock Structure Junk Bond or Not you might do it.

Thank you,

Signed An Wang

In a conversation that the Doctor and Miller had had weeks earlier — their last face-to-face encounter — An Wang had talked about his hopes for the future of his company. He had asked Miller to try to preserve the Wang name; to save the company if he could, to keep it independent if at all possible. But in the event he could not do that, the Doctor asked that he do his very best to let the name live.

"Whatever you do, try and preserve name," he said to Miller. "I want it remembered as company founded by immigrant."

As they spoke, An Wang became choked with emotion. And he cried.

And though the name remained on the company, An Wang was, in one way, forgotten all too quickly. For a year after his death — a year after he had been laid to rest — the plot of earth covering his body remained without a headstone.

By September 1990, Richard Miller had worked Wang Laboratories out of debt. He sold Wang's international leasing subsidiary for $215 million. InteCom, a Texas maker of telephone switching systems that the Doctor had purchased in 1986 for $229 million worth of cash and stock, brought a paltry $26 million.

Immediate good news came on the heels of the company's new financial stability. Wang Laboratories reported a net profit of $2.6 million for the quarter ending September 30, 1990, and the company won the largest contract it had ever been awarded — an $800 million deal to supply Wang computer equipment worldwide to the United States Department of State.

The progress brought kudos from Peter Brooke for Miller. "He's a rather remarkable guy," says Brooke. "He tells it like it is. He's a calm guy. He gives people confidence. He's a very good listener who is very sure of himself."

In October 1990, analyst John Adams observed that "Rick Miller and his team have done an outstanding job of bringing Wang back into contention."

And the Gartner Group, Inc., a respected Stamford, Connecticut–based company that analyzes trends in the computer industry for large corporate clients, issued a special report on Wang on November 28, 1990. Its title was "Prospects Brighten at Wang Labs." The report praised the company for "an impressive combination of organizational change, financial restructuring, and focused business strategy."

But when the worldwide recession hit, simultaneous with the outbreak of war in the Persian Gulf, in the winter of 1991, it was clear that Wang Laboratories was in trouble. And Miller knew it.

Anyone looking objectively at the company saw a grim picture. Wang Labs had lost money in two out of the past six years. While the industry had been growing by upwards of 20 percent through the late 1980s, Wang was shrinking. When the recession struck, the sectors on which Wang relied most heavily were hardest hit, including banks, insurance companies, law firms, and governments. It was clear that Wang was unlikely to survive on its own. If the erosion in revenues continued, the company would eventually collapse.

In 1991, Wang was still a proprietary minicomputer company in a world where open standards was the trend and where minicomputers were fast becoming dinosaurs (George Colony of Forrester Research in Cambridge referred to minis as "flapping Terodactyls").

Not long after the Doctor died, Miller began quietly considering various options, including merging with another company, seeking a minority investor, selling parts of the company, or forming a strategic alliance of some sort.

Miller wanted to move Wang away from manufacturing and selling hardware toward selling software and advising customers on total computing solutions to their business problems.

Like many others in the computer industry, Miller saw that the future depended not on Wang's success at building and selling boxes, but on the company's ability to offer software, consulting, and systems integration services — that is, making a customer's technology work to improve the customer's business. It was clear by the early 1990s that many companies were getting nowhere near the productivity gains their computers were capable of achieving. They didn't need new computers so much as they needed help in making their computers work more productively.

Miller talked with the heads of a variety of companies in the United States and abroad. Most discussions didn't get past an initial conversation. Often the talking was done by phone. He was searching, calmly and very privately, for the right fit.

"I didn't want to look like we were panicking or putting the company on the auction block," says Miller. "We were looking for capital. But we were also looking for someone with strong credentials and good products." If Wang were to ally itself with another company, it had to be an outfit with strong products, since Wang hadn't had a hot new offering in years other than imaging. Also, Wang was losing customers not only because it didn't have new products, but because customers were afraid Wang wouldn't be around much longer. With so many other strong computer companies to choose from, why should anyone take the risk of buying from a company that might not exist in a year or two?

The more Miller thought about what the company needed, the more he thought about IBM. Big Blue had many of the best-selling products in the world. It was a company in whom customers had enormous confidence. And there wasn't any fear that IBM might go under — it would always be around.

During the second week of April 1991, Rick Miller called IBM chairman John Akers and asked for a meeting. The following week, on April 17, Miller flew on a commercial commuter plane to White Plains, then drove to Armonk, New York, where he had lunch with Akers at IBM.

The discussion was general. Miller outlined the situation his company was in. They talked about industry trends. The two men hit it off. Miller found Akers to be warm, smart, and easy to communicate with. Miller found himself very comfortable with Akers. "We understood each other right away," says Miller. "He understood exactly what I was trying to do."

Miller left Armonk after a couple of hours feeling he had established a rapport with Akers. A few days later, Akers called Miller to chat some more. Additional phone calls ensued. They exchanged letters.

By early May, the two men agreed that they had something serious to talk about. To determine whether a relationship would make sense, each man formed a team of executives and the two groups met for formal discussions. At Wang Laboratories, the senior management team worked feverishly for six weeks, struggling with negotiations.

A deal was struck. IBM would invest an immediate $25 million in cash in Wang Laboratories and would make an additional $75 million available. In return, Wang would sell its customers IBM equipment. Though it was not explicitly part of the agreement, there was also a possibility that

Wang would make its potentially valuable imaging technology available to IBM.

The most immediate advantage to IBM was that it would now have the worldwide Wang sales force selling its products. Over the longer term, IBM would gain by having Wang office software systems run on IBM computers.

For Wang, the immediate benefit was IBM's cash, but a far more important advantage was the IBM name. There had long been fear among Wang customers and potential customers that a company in Wang's precarious financial position might one day sink. Its customers would then be abandoned. But customers knew IBM wasn't going to just disappear, and Wang's alliance with IBM gave Wang renewed credibility.

When the deal was announced, it met with far from universal approval. John Cunningham, for one, thought it was a dreadful mistake. And George Colony, the Forrester Research president, though he thought very highly of Miller, considered the IBM arrangement a blunder. It was wonderful for IBM, Colony said, because it gave Big Blue an additional distribution and sales network for their products. But for Wang, it insured their eventually giving up the manufacture of hardware and would surely lead, Colony believed, to the death of the Wang VS, the company's most enduring source of revenue. Months after the IBM deal was done Colony believed that it would eventually lead to Wang's becoming about a $700 million company that does little more than resell IBM boxes.

Miller, of course, has a radically different view. He believes the deal will save Wang Labs. It will give product-starved Wang salespeople some of the most popular computer products in the world to sell. And will save Wang the huge expense of designing and manufacturing their own minicomputers.

The hardware business had been Wang's mainstay through the years. Now, the company, in addition to selling its own boxes, would sell IBM hardware. But those IBM boxes will be used to power systems with Wang software that Wang engineers design and implement.

Miller likens the arrangement to what Boeing does in the airline industry. Though Boeing is the industry leader, it doesn't even make airplane engines — it buys them from GE or Rolls-Royce or Pratt and Whitney. Then it puts everything else together and makes the airplane work. Think of an airplane not as a piece of machinery, says Miller, but as a system. Boeing creates some of the hardware and buys some. But what the company is best at is putting the various pieces together and making the system work. Miller says the basic computer is like an airplane engine. Wang doesn't have to build the boxes to be successful in the computer business. It just has to convince customers that it can make an office system work.

"We know the customers," says Miller. "We understand their business."

Whether the deal will eventually mean the salvation of Wang Laboratories will not be determined for years. But in the Wang-IBM affiliation, there is rich irony. IBM was the company that enraged An Wang during the early 1950s, when the company bought his core memory patent. Though he emerged from that deal with $400,000 — a fortune at the time — he was left embittered by the way in which he was treated by IBM. Through the years, Wang competed fiercely with IBM, particularly in the word processing market. Who would have thought this company for which An Wang had so little respect and which, in his greatest delusion, he planned one day to overtake, might now be the salvation of Wang Laboratories?

EIGHTEEN

The Tragedy of the Doctor

I T IS SHORTLY BEFORE CHRISTMAS. John Cunningham swings off Route 128 and accelerates north along Route 3 toward Lowell on the route he followed back when he was president of Wang Laboratories. But on this cold, sunny day, Cunningham pilots his new $100,000 Mercedes 500SL past Lowell, on to Route 495, where he heads deeper into his Wang past. The forbidding gray Wang towers come and go without a comment from Cunningham. He continues along 495 for ten or fifteen more minutes before another Wang facility becomes visible. Like the Lowell operation, it is hard by the interstate, but unlike the towers this series of buildings is long and only a couple of stories high at its tallest. As he pulls into the parking lot, Cunningham points out the string of perhaps a dozen thick high-power lines that bisect this eighty-five-acre property. He explains that Doctor Wang bought this land because it was cheaper than a more attractive setting without the lines.

No longer is it Wang Labs' property, however. It was sold to a real estate development company as part of the drive to raise money through the sale of assets. Wang Labs rents space from the new owner.

Inside a small yellow-brick building, Cunningham greets Joe Klementovich, a technician who rose through the ranks to plant manager at Wang years ago. Klementovich, who has long since departed Wang, has started his own small company, and he leases space in the original Wang building from the new owners.

As they stroll through the old buildings reminiscing about friends who worked in the now dusty, abandoned offices, Cunningham shakes his head at the vastness of the empty space. He and Klementovich stroll from one end of the facility to the other, a hike they begin in the original building and that takes them through seven additions in all — each of either cheap yellow brick or cheaper yellow cinderblock — ending in a cavernous high-bay warehouse. The original building and the seven additions cover three-quarters of a million square feet. It may not look like much anymore, says Cunningham, with its cheap, worn carpeting, false dropped ceilings, and room after room of empty space, but not too many years ago it vibrated with life. Wang Labs' move to Tewksbury came in 1964 and coincided precisely with the rise of the company on the popularity of its calculators. The place was much too large for the tiny company Wang was in 1964, but from almost the moment the company moved in the space was overcrowded.

At the height of Wang's success the excitement here was palpable. First there were only a few dozen people, then there were hundreds, then, by the mid-1970s, more than six thousand people worked at the Tewksbury facility. The place sweated and heaved with life. Pointing to the loading docks at the warehouse, Cunningham recalls that during the busy periods — and it was nearly always busy — trailer trucks would have to line up, waiting their turn to back into one of the more than eighteen docks and load up with the products for which Wang customers were clamoring. But as he stands and gazes out at the loading bays, there are no trucks. Not a single bay is occupied. Joe Klementovich says it is a rare sight indeed when a truck backs up to the building.

Standing in a paneled office once occupied by An Wang, Cunningham recalls precisely where the Doctor's desk, workbench, couch, and blackboard were. He even remembers the cabinet in which Wang kept his Chivas.

Cunningham wanders through the old offices, through the original classroom where salespeople were taught, past the company's first cafeteria, through R&D, manufacturing, marketing and sales, accounting, and into the warehouses. His tour just about complete, Cunningham starts back to the original building, but, en route, he finds himself in a large, low-ceilinged storage area in Building Six, where there are thousands and thousands of unused square feet. But Cunningham notices a pile of some sort over in a half-darkened corner, and he walks over for a closer look. The light is poor, but there is enough to see that he has stumbled upon an island of packages, returned orders, and products bundled and ready for shipping. He looks it over, an archaeologist examining the remains of a long-forgotten civilization. Some of the products are in large boxes, others are padded and tightly encased in plastic shrink-wrap. He spots the base plate for the 700 series calculator. There are workstations for the VS minicomputer. There's a Wangwriter, Wang PCs, an early word processing workstation. There are peripherals for the 2200 computer, and more, products or pieces of products that represent the golden age of Wang Laboratories. They are here in a dusty, darkened corner of an all but empty building. Cunningham walks slowly around the pile, identifying each product. He circles the island once and stops. He pauses for a moment and is silent. Then, quietly, as though out of respect for the dead, he moves on.

Rick Miller struggled mightily to save the company. By late 1991, it appeared that his work might enable Wang Labs to find a niche in the marketplace and survive as a much smaller enterprise, though that was by no means certain. What was clear was that Wang would never regain its earlier glory.

So far had the company fallen that even as it began to get back on track, many former Wang executives talked about it in the past tense — as if it no longer existed. In a way, it didn't. The Wang Labs of an earlier incarnation had disappeared. Under Miller, it was a radically different company that had gone from revenues of nearly $3 billion a year and 32,000 employees to revenues of $1.5 billion with only 14,500 employees. Some who knew the company well predicted it was headed for a day when there would be fewer than 10,000 employees and no more than $1 billion in revenues. Even in its own advertising in 1990, the company referred to itself as "the new Wang."

Inevitably, those who knew the company and who cared about it looked to assign blame for its fall. The small cadre of Wang executives and former executives as well as industry analysts who know or have known Wang Laboratories well, who have followed its course through the years, who know the players and the industry, offer various explanations for the demise.

It was the wild West corporate culture, in which management systems were lax or nonexistent.

It was the sudden shift in the industry, a jarring ratcheting up of the level of competition.

It was the inexperience of the management team.

It was the board of directors' inability or unwillingness to fight the Doctor vigorously enough when it was clear he was making errors.

It was R&D's failure to produce another home-run product.

It was the banks' fault — they put the screws to the company at a crucial time.

And surely there is veracity to all of these theories. Ultimately, however, the truth was that real blame lay with two men named Wang.

The management problem was a serious one. It was a problem born of the speed and size of the company's growth, in which many of the conventions of business were tossed aside. There were no business plans and few controls.

"There was no discipline, no middle management, and top-level management was poor," says George Colony. "They struck oil with word processing and money poured out of the ground. When the money stopped pumping, there was no foundation to go on to the next product. There was always the mentality that they wanted to hit the home run."

The undisciplined Wang culture was blamed by some on Cunningham and his swashbuckling style.

"Their thought was: Why do we need good management?" says Colony. "We're growing 50 percent a year."

The company was so obsessed with growth during the glory years that until well into the 1980s no one took the time to step back and ask whether the management structure made sense for the company Wang had become. When, finally, in the fall of 1983 John Cunningham formed the White Paper Task Force to take a long look at the company, the Doctor and Fred ignored the report's findings and recommendations. The focus at Wang was on one question: How do we grow? Energy spent on planning was deemed a waste.

It was a management problem, but it was also an industry problem. Like every other minicomputer manufacturer, Wang Labs was hurt by the environment in which it was forced to compete during the late 1980s. Competition became keener than it had ever been, and the industry was stuck with an oversupply of products. At the same time there came the move to standardize, which seriously threatened Wang's profitable proprietary systems. It was a very different environment from the one in which Wang Labs had earlier flourished.

Growth in the computer industry slowed dramatically as the 1980s progressed. Up until 1985, the industry's annual rate of growth was in the neighborhood of 20 percent, but by 1989 it had dropped to just 5 percent.

Worst of all, demand shifted away from the kind of products Wang made. Customers moved toward PCs and workstations and away from minicomputers and mainframes. This fundamental change hit minicomputer makers the hardest, companies such as Wang, Digital, Data General, and Prime. Makers of PCs and workstations, companies such as Apple, Compaq, and Sun Microsystems, rode a new wave in the world of computing. By the late 1980s, desktop machines had become so powerful that when linked with a central server — a version of a minicomputer — they could supplant minicomputers and even in some cases mainframes.

"A bunch of PCs tied together by a network and linked to a data-filled electronic library called a file server can take over whole corporate departments and small businesses," noted a February 1990 article in *Fortune*. "This setup — $3000 for each PC plus $25,000 for the file server and the network — does the job previously handled by larger minicomputers that cost from $100,000 to $500,000."

The proof of the problem was in the numbers. From 1984 to 1990 the share of industry sales going to minicomputers declined from 34 percent to 27 percent.

Wang's decline also resulted, to a certain extent, from a banking problem. The banks exerted more pressure on the company than was necessary. And far more than was healthy for Wang Laboratories. Peter Brooke, who had the unique perspective of having been at Bank of Boston and having served for many years on the Wang Labs board of directors, harshly criticized the banks. Brooke went so far as to write an article for the *Boston Globe* in which he wrote that Wang, during the good times, "was pursued by bankers who basked in the image of the company's success." But when times got tough, Brooke wrote, "the once-friendly banks not only turned their backs on the company, but . . . imperiled its existence."

There is little doubt that all of these obstacles could have been overcome by management that was strong, experienced, and visionary — all qualities that eluded Fred Wang.

Fred wants badly to avoid going down in history as the major cause of the company's demise. "I don't want the reputation of having brought down," he says, pausing and choosing his words carefully, of having "made a profitable company unprofitable. It's clearly not a Fred Wang problem."

But by almost any definition, Fred was unsuited for the job in which his father had placed him. He lacked experience, had not been tested by fire, was not a leader. His most costly mistakes involved trying to force the three development team leaders — Koplow, Siegel, and Kolk — to work together rather than letting them work independently as they always had.

He made a mistake in warring with John Cunningham. Jack Connors, the Wang Labs advertising man who is personally close to Cunningham, likes Fred, considers him a "gentle, thoughtful person." But he says that "Fred made one mistake. He saw John as an ox to be gored rather than a cow to be milked. He never saw that John was a way to increase his fortune."

Fred made another mistake in not insisting upon his own management team. He appointed Gene Bullis to the position of chief financial officer and says in retrospect that Bullis didn't do the job. There were huge gaps in expertise with Fred, his father, and Harry Chou running the company. None of the three had any great marketing skill; none was a financial expert.

"Fred needed a much stronger team than we were able to give him," says Paul Guzzi. The weakness of that team — and of Fred as a leader — was most painfully obvious during the financial crisis of 1989, when Peter Brooke said that Fred was in "never-never land."

Fred blames Bullis for not making him aware of the company's growing dependence on the banks during 1989, but Fred's complaint about Bullis only reveals his own shortcoming. An experienced executive wouldn't have needed someone else to point out to him the seriousness of the company's dependency on the banks. An aggressive leader who was on top of the company would have been acutely aware of the gravity of the situation. Fred says that when the company lost access to the commercial paper market in April 1989, it was not a very big deal. Yet others with vastly more experience than Fred say it was crucial.

Cunningham says that the indications of trouble were obvious from the very beginning of 1989 and even earlier. "They were like an inexperienced train crew that ran through the warning signs — the economy, order trends, debt, costs," says Cunningham. "They didn't know. The whole team didn't know, didn't have the experience to know. Fred's not a bad guy. He just didn't know."

Perhaps Fred's most serious mistake was taking the job of president in the first place. Fred knew his father better than anyone, and he knew that his father would not permit him to run the company the way he wanted. Although Fred held the title of president, he could do only what pleased his father. When Fred wanted to make changes in the senior management team, he was blocked by his father. He never had full control. He was always second-guessed. Perhaps Fred would have failed even if his father had turned the company completely over to him. Fred's critics say it didn't matter. They say that if Fred had had full control he would have failed anyway, only faster.

When those close to him suggested one move or another — that he bring in a star financial person from the outside, for example, which he wanted to do — Fred would say: "You know Dad won't let me do that."

Fred had his father's optimism and his father's sense of invincibility, but he lacked his father's genius. There was an evangelical expect-a-miracle attitude at Wang, a sincere, yet terribly naïve belief that everything would work out just fine.

"Fred got carried away with the infallibility of the Wang story," says Peter Brooke.

If Fred Wang had been Fred Jones, would he ever have been made president of Wang Laboratories?

The question is put to Brooke, who responds with a look that suggests the notion utterly preposterous.

"'Course not," he replies in a clipped tone. "'Course not."

Fred was the perfect fall guy. In the end, however, the tumble he took obscured reality. In the end, no price was too high to pay if it meant protecting the deity of An Wang, even if the price was the sacrifice of his own son. The way in which Fred was dismissed not only did not minimize blame on Fred, it maximized it.

In the aftermath of Fred's departure, Paul Guzzi warned him that he would be inundated with requests for interviews from the news media, but Guzzi advised that he turn them all down. Guzzi, whose loyalty to An Wang was always fierce and sometimes blind, suggested a strategy of a "dignified silence." This approach insured that Fred would take all the blame. For he would now have no way to defend himself.

Guzzi told the *Wall Street Journal* at the time: "Ultimately, one person is accountable for the company's recent results, and Fred never shrank from that responsibility." This extraordinary statement by a top-level official told the world that it was the company position that it was Fred's fault. If, however, "one person is accountable for the company's recent results," why was that person not the company's chairman and chief executive officer?

The same *Wall Street Journal* article in which Guzzi was quoted stated that "analysts applauded the change at Wang, though some said the father had to bear much of the burden of the company's problems. 'In a way,' said Judith Hurwitz, a consultant with Patricia Seybold's Office Computing Group in Boston, 'Fred is the sacrificial lamb here.'"

John Thibault put it more bluntly. "Fred," he said, "took a bullet for his father."

The slug did not kill him, but it did badly wound him.

Fred has sought to get beyond the trauma. He has been very much removed from the company since he left in August 1989, and in a sense, he has put the company behind him. At least he has put it behind him as much as that is possible for a man whose name is Wang, for a man who sits on the board of directors, who is former president, and whose father founded the company. He has evinced little interest in the company since he left. He has, in fact, missed many board meetings, and he did not show up at the 1990 annual meeting. He chatted with Rick Miller occasionally, but they talked only in a very general sense about the direction of the company.

He does not regret not having hung on to some position there — either doing special projects or holding some other senior-management title. He does not believe he would have been much help to Miller.

There is an edge of sadness in his voice when he says, "I don't really know the company anymore."

In a way, however, leaving Wang Labs was liberating for Fred. "It freed Fred up to look at his own life and at what he wanted to do," says Paul Guzzi. "It freed Fred to become his own person and not live in the enormous shadow of his father."

Shortly before graduating from Harvard's Kennedy School of Government in January 1991, Fred sent out feelers to the new Republican state administration in Massachusetts. Fred's résumé stated that he wanted "to assume a responsible position in state government involving business–government–consumer relations, education, or the environment."

Perhaps it was because he was a Democrat, perhaps because he lacked government experience. Perhaps it was because he had been tarnished at the company. But there was no position for Fred Wang in the new administration. The company had fallen from a great height and so too had Fred. On paper, his résumé is immensely impressive: Wang Laboratories president and chief operating officer, executive vice-president and treasurer, executive vice-president–chief development officer, and on and on. Back in the late 1970s and early '80s Fred's contemporaries at the company had greatly envied him. Ted Leonsis recalls that he and the other ambitious young men seeking to rise through the Wang ranks would say that they wished they were Fred Wang. But in the winter of 1991, Leonsis, who had long since left the company to start his own successful public relations firm in Florida, was in Boston talking with another Wang alumnus. They recalled the old days, and they talked about what had happened to Fred. Both agreed that they were very glad indeed that they were not Fred Wang.

The saddest part of the Wang story is that it was An Wang who was responsible for the damage done to his beloved company and to his son. Doctor Wang did not make a great many mistakes, but the ones he made were serious and carried long-term ramifications.

He permitted, and perhaps even encouraged, the creation of an aura of invincibility around himself that fostered a dangerous and ultimately destructive overreliance on him. He was not one of the guys, not another executive. He was not "Andy," as he had been known around the Harvard Computation Lab. He was more even than Doctor Wang. He was "*the* Doctor." He was a man raised above other men.

"The old man wished things to happen and they happened and he thought over time it was his divine right," says John Cunningham.

The mythic An Wang was a humble man, but "he didn't run the business as a humble man," says Peter Brooke. "He knew what he wanted to do and what he wanted to do was right. There was precious little criticism he would accept."

John Cunningham described him as a "humble egomaniac."

His presence within the company was so large, and the faith in him so great, that Gene Bullis goes so far as to say that the meltdown of 1989 would never have happened if Wang had not fallen ill. "The Doctor was the spiritual leader of the place," says Bullis. "He energized all of us." Senior executives deluded themselves with the irrational belief that somehow, the Doctor would pull them through. "There was always a sense that we have problems but we can deal with them," says Paul Guzzi. "The Doctor was always there!"

But the Doctor would not pull them through the crisis of 1989. He had had so many successes for so long that it seemed reasonable to expect him to produce some magic yet again. The cancer was a harsh reminder that An Wang was human. By then it was too late. The aura around Wang served as a kind of buffer, keeping out unwanted distractions but also excluding the kind of criticism and dissent that it is crucial for the chief executive to hear.

Doctor Wang insulated himself, says Peter Brooke. His pride, his ego, exerted themselves. "When you don't look around, when you don't take outside advice and bring in people with new ideas, then your pride is so omnipresent that it cuts you off from reality and your view of the world begins to decline," says Brooke. "If you really think you're some world-beater, that's the beginning of the end. You've got to wake up every day and make bloody sure you're being critiqued."

Even after he had begun to lose touch with the fast-breaking new realities of the marketplace, even after the environment in which the company had to operate had drastically changed, An Wang continued to insist upon complete, obsessive control.

Bob Kolk wonders whether he was hurt at the company because he once challenged Fred. He recalls that he and Fred had a disagreement over a particular product idea. "He wanted to do some crazy thing with a terminal," recalls Kolk. "I told him it won't work, that it would put us all out of business. I told him, 'It's my company, too.'" Kolk wondered whether the Wangs would forever resent a person who challenged them so frankly. "In good management," he says, "an open discussion of issues is critical to success."

John Thibault openly disagreed with the Doctor one day. "I went in there one time and told him something was wrong," says Thibault. "He said, 'This is my company. My name is on company. We'll do it my way.'"

For many years the Doctor's vision was great, but there came a time in the 1980s when it failed. He first faltered over the issue of personal computers. It was not that he was entirely blind to the potential of these machines. Quite the reverse was true. It had been Wang Labs that first made computing power — in the form of the Wang Word Processing System — available to the masses. Had he taken the word processing machine to the next generation, the history of Wang might have been very different. "If he had continued on that path, he would have arrived at the PC or workstations," says Frank Trantanella, an engineer who worked at Wang before starting his own firm. "He would have gotten there five years at least ahead of IBM."

However, when An Wang finally did take the next step — after IBM — he failed to see that IBM was to become the standard for PCs. It was the Doctor who insisted that the Wang PC not be compatible with IBM. And it was the Doctor who was the driving force behind the purchase of InteCom, on which Wang lost about $170 million. Furthermore, the Doctor was blind to the obvious good sense of the White Paper Task Force.

Wang's biggest mistake was placing his son in crucial positions within the company — first as chief of research and development and later as president.

"His ambition to have the kid take over was his undoing," says Jack Connors. "It was an unfair thing to do to the kid."

Long before placing his son in charge of the company, An Wang assured outside members of the board of directors that he would run the company as CEO and that he would bring Fred along gradually.

"The Doctor believed he [An Wang] could overcome most if not all the problems," says Paul Guzzi. "The Doctor would always be there. He honestly felt Fred would and could learn and that the Doctor would be there to backstop."

Had the Doctor listened to the pleas of the outside directors during the lunches held at the Union Club, if only he had agreed to bring in an experienced industry star to manage the day-to-day operations of his company, it is quite likely the outcome of this story would have been very different.

"The company needed an operations officer," says consultant George Rich. "Fred was definitely not that man. The great weakness of Doctor Wang was being a proud father."

"When a family business is established and stable in a stable environment, as IBM was when Tom Watson turned it over to Tom Jr., you can turn it over to your kid," says John Cunningham. "You can put anybody in at the top. But you can't do that in an unestablished business in a difficult environment."

It is impossible to determine how many private decisions An Wang made that placed the interests of his family ahead of the interests of the company's shareholders. But there is no doubt that two critical decisions involving his son — placing Fred in charge of research and development and later making Fred president of the company — placed the interests of the Wang family ahead of the interests of the 30,000-plus employees and ahead of the millions of men and women whose pension funds and savings were invested in the company.

Louis Cabot was in a unique position to observe An Wang. Cabot had been the heir to his family's fortune and the man in charge of Cabot Corporation. In the interest of his family and the company's shareholders, Cabot drove family members out of the company and then, after turning the reins over to professional managers, he too left. But he saw something very different in Wang. With the Doctor, "the family comes ahead of everything else," says Cabot. "What really mattered to him was family control of the business."

Fred described it well when he said that to his father, the company was "his baby — like Andrea's my baby, the company is his baby."

Wang sometimes used the company as his private fiefdom. He permitted both of his sons to work in vaguely described jobs where they did little real work. Fred says his year as an "ombudsman" for his father wasn't very productive. And Courtney offers unintended insight into the special status he enjoyed as a family member: "In my first year I was really kind of assigned to the New England office in Burlington. I'm not sure I really reported to anybody."

Would other employees have said they were "kind of" assigned to one office or another? Or that they weren't sure they even reported to anyone?

Through the years, Wang ignored anyone who suggested to him that he turn the company over to anyone but his son. Back in the early 1970s, long before the Union Club lunches where Brooke, Cabot, and other board members tried to persuade the Doctor that he should bring in outside management, Gerry Jones suggested that Wang send Fred off to get some experience elsewhere.

"I was honest with Wang," recalls Jones, who was vice-president and in charge of international operations until the mid-1970s. "I thought Fred should go work for somebody else for a while. Otherwise he would just be known as the owner's son. He would have no credentials. I was stepping on quicksand." It was not long before Wang got rid of Jones.

"Control by the family was one of the great weaknesses," says Peter Brooke. "After a while it insulated him."

After having known Wang for forty years as the family's private attorney, Bill Pechilis declared that "with the Doctor, the company and the family were synonymous."

But as the head of a publicly traded corporation, Wang had a responsibility to his shareholders above all else. It was not a responsibility that he always honored.

An Wang had "a blind spot with his family and he let it go on too long," says Harold Koplow. When, ultimately, Wang decided he had to fire his son to honor his commitment to the shareholders, says Koplow, "it was too late."

*   *   *

In a classical tragedy, a great man, a heroic character, finds himself confronted with disaster, death, or both as a result of choices that he has made.

At the end of his life, An Wang saw that the great empire he had built was crumbling. He watched his company, under his son's presidency, face dire cash flow problems, crushing debt, management turmoil, terrible morale, declining product quality, dwindling credibility in the marketplace. He knew that his company had come within a razor's edge of bankruptcy.

Perhaps he even realized that *his* choices had led to his company's demise. Permitting his son — a man who plainly was not up to the task — to take key roles in the corporation was by far Wang's worst sin. Ultimately, he was guilty of hubris. He believed he could solve any problem, that even if he made a mistake he would recognize it quickly enough to rectify it. It was not some mysterious outside force that drove the company and the family to their terrible fate. The man who must finally take responsibility for what went wrong with the company — for the damage to so many lives, including that of his own son — is An Wang.

In the end, the tragedy of Wang Laboratories is the tragedy of the Doctor.

Acknowledgments

THE IDEA for this book was hatched in August 1989, shortly after Fred Wang was dismissed from his job. Since that day many people have helped me understand the Wang story.

Thanks to Jack Connors, Frank Gens, Anne Finucane, Hap Ellis, John Sasso, Ted Oatis, Dick Connaughton, Bernard M. Gordon, George Colony, Charles A. Coolidge, Jr., Frank Trantanella, John Ellis, Curtis Wilkie, Peter Dromeshauser, Wally Elliott, Sam Gagliano, Dale Jelley, J. Carl Masi, Karen Smith Palmer, Ron Smith, Peter McElroy, Werner Gossells, Jake Jacobson, Ed Lesnick, Gerry Jones, Philip Hankins, Ted Goodlander, Ted Leonsis, Laurence Gosnell, Joop Spanjaard, John Adams, Bob Plachta, Beth Riley, Bob Doretti, Professor H. C. Lin, Joe Davis, Dr. Kenneth Sih, Stanley Hsu, John Thibault, Tony Christy, George Rich, Stamen Zlatev, John Raffo, Frank Kinsey, Chuan Chu, Gene Bullis, Bill Pechilis, Ande Zellman, John Cullinane, Eugene Linden, Ian Diery, Deborah Miller, Ellen Cunningham, Sybil Ashe, Frank Chen, Laurie O'Connor, Copey Coppedge, Paul Guzzi, Moira James, Mark MacLennan, Ken Miller, Alice Ma, David Cheng, Joe Davis, Jane Wagner, Jean Mulvaney, Kathleen Heggenbart, Robin Ellis, Charles Stein, Courtney Wang, and Juliette Wang Coombs.

I want to acknowledge a debt of gratitude as well to John Marttila, Dan Payne, Tim Gens, Tom Vallely, Tom Kiley, Robert F. Drinan, S.J., Jim Ewing, Tom Kearney, Ken Zwicker, and Herbert Gutterson.

I am grateful to the three Wang Labs development team leaders, Bob

Kolk, Harold Koplow, and Bob Siegel, as well as to Dave Moros who was particularly patient in explaining the development of the Wang Word Processing System.

Many friends at the *Boston Globe* have helped in one way or another. Lisa Driscoll of the *Globe* library has as sharp a research eye as there is. The only good part of encountering computer trouble was that Sean Mullin, the *Globe*'s techno-wizard, not only solved all my problems (with help from Ken Whitney), but he did it with consistent good cheer. Thanks to Jack Driscoll for giving me the time off I needed as well as to Ben Bradlee for giving me a place to land when I returned.

Flip Brophy, my agent at the Sterling Lord Literistic, helped make the book a reality.

Portions of this book were written at Hewitt Hill Farm in North Pomfret, Vermont. To my friends there, Blair and Gordon MacInnes and Victoria Vallely, I am grateful.

For reading the manuscript in various stages and offering suggestions I want to thank Bob Ano, Gordon MacInnes, and Dayton Duncan. My good friend and colleague Bob Turner read the manuscript and offered many helpful suggestions.

My editor at Little, Brown, Jennifer Josephy, did what only the best editors do — she made this a better book.

Key members of the company board of directors helped illuminate the story. I am grateful to Louis Cabot, Howard Swearer, Paul Tsongas, the late Martin Kirkpatrick, and Ernest Stockwell. I owe a particular debt to Peter A. Brooke.

Ge Yao Chu, who worked at the company, served on its board, and went to high school and college with An Wang, provided important information and many insights.

Finally, thanks to my family: to my son, Charlie, and my daughter, Elizabeth, for being so wonderfully patient; to Agnes Hagerty for providing the stability we all need; to my brothers, Mike, Tom, Patrick, John, and Tim, for inspiring me.

I am particularly grateful to my wife, Annie, for her strength throughout what was not always an easy process, and for her wise counsel.

I owe by far the greatest debt to the only three men other than An Wang who have held the title of president of Wang Laboratories. Fred Wang gave generously of his time and talked at length about topics that must surely have been painful. Rick Miller took time from his efforts to rescue the company to help me understand what had gone wrong and how he was trying to set it right. And John Cunningham, who knew Wang Labs more intimately than anyone except the Doctor, guided me through the history of the company and, more important, helped me to understand An Wang. To all three men, I am deeply grateful.

Index